Praise for *Mindful Money*

"*Mindful Money* isn't just another personal finance book full of graphs and charts: it's a frank talk about how money fits into the bigger goal of a satisfying life. This book makes you ask yourself, 'How much money do I really need to be happy?' Once you've decided where you're going, Jonathan DeYoe will help you get there."

— Jennifer Lee, author of *The Right-Brain Business Plan*

"The Beatles sang 'money can't buy me love.' Nor can money buy you happiness. In *Mindful Money*, Jonathan K. DeYoe pierces common money illusions and focuses readers on the elements that underpin true happiness."

— Tadas Viskanta, founder and editor of *Abnormal Returns* and author of *Abnormal Returns: Winning Strategies from the Frontlines of the Investment Blogosphere*

"In a world where total net wealth has reached record levels and yet contentment and joy remain way too subdued, many people are trying to unscramble the riddle of how to pursue wealth while achieving true happiness. *Mindful Money* offers a commonsense and inspirational framework that serves as a road map to happiness and offers a thoughtful reassessment of how money is just a tool, not the destination, of life's greatest purpose. Just as important as financial planning is to wealth, having a plan to achieve happiness is equally essential to unlocking the most that life has to offer. Jonathan DeYoe delivers a structure rooted in a values-based financial plan that delivers a path toward something more than money: it plows a route to the harmony of wealth, purpose, meaning, and happiness."

— Burt White, managing director and chief investment officer of LPL Financial

"DeYoe's *Mindful Money* teaches you to put wealth-building ideas into action. Well beyond a money handbook, it manages to interweave the pillars of money, investing, and wealth together with a path to happiness. If you read one money book this year, let it be *Mindful Money*."

— Barbara A. Friedberg, MBA, MS, expert investor, educator, website publisher, and author of *Invest and Beat the Pros*

"If there were a smarter and better way to manage your money and your life, you'd want to know right away. So open this book and start reading."

— Bob Seawright, chief investment officer of Madison Avenue Securities and blogger, *Above the Market*

Mindful MONEY

Mindful MONEY

SIMPLE PRACTICES *for* REACHING YOUR FINANCIAL GOALS *and* INCREASING YOUR HAPPINESS DIVIDEND

JONATHAN K. DEYOE, CPWA

Foreword by ALICE WALKER

New World Library
Novato, California

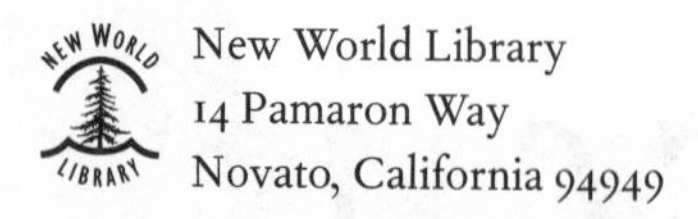
New World Library
14 Pamaron Way
Novato, California 94949

The material in this book is intended for educational purposes only. No expressed or implied guarantee of the effects of the use of the strategies discussed can be given nor liability taken. Any securities mentioned are for illustration purposes only and should not be taken as a buy or sell recommendation. You cannot invest directly in an index. Past performance is never a guarantee of future results. All investing involves risk, including possible loss of principal. The techniques and strategies described may not be suitable for your situation. Please consult a financial or tax professional when appropriate.

Text design by Megan Colman

Library of Congress Cataloging-in-Publication Data is available.

First printing, February 2017
ISBN 978-1-60868-436-6
Ebook ISBN 978-1-60868-437-3
Printed in Canada on 100% postconsumer-waste recycled paper

New World Library is proud to be a Gold Certified Environmentally Responsible Publisher. Publisher certification awarded by Green Press Initiative. www.greenpressinitiative.org

10 9 8 7 6 5 4 3 2 1

For Eli & Annie

It is our choices, Harry, that show what we truly are, far more than our abilities.

— ALBUS DUMBLEDORE, in *Harry Potter and the Chamber of Secrets* by J. K. ROWLING

CONTENTS

Section Two: Finding Your Happiness

Section Three: Making a Plan

FOREWORD

Counting My Eggs

I had my first paying job when I was seven. My two older brothers and I were hired to pick daffodils by the wife of the man who owned the land our parents worked. In this part of middle Georgia there are thousands of gigantic pecan trees, and it was under such trees that the three of us set to work. There were deep-yellow and pale-yellow daffodils (which our boss, in a strong Southern accent, referred to as "jon'quils") almost as far as the eye could see. To a child it seemed a fairyland, and I set to picking daffodils with delight. We were paid a nickel a bunch (our boss lady sold them in town for a quarter a bunch, which we didn't know and didn't care about), and I proved to be a speedy and efficient picker. I might have earned as much as half a dollar each day.

This went into a piggy bank that was shaped like an actual pig. My hardworking parents instilled in all their children, early on, that saving was to be a habit that would mean we could afford to buy presents for ourselves as well as for others at Christmas.

A few years later, when I wanted desperately to learn to play the piano, my mother decided to let me have all the eggs laid by our chickens. I sold these to a market in town and was able to pay the fifty cents per lesson my teacher required. In winter, though, the hens laid less, and eventually I had to give this up. Not until fifty years later would I circle back to this dream, hire a piano teacher, and learn to play six songs, among them James Weldon Johnson's "Lift Ev'ry Voice and Sing" (commonly known as "The Negro National Anthem") and Beethoven's "Ode to Joy."

Having learned these six songs, I promptly forgot how to play the piano; which is one of those mysterious happenings in life that makes you wonder. I don't even recall the names of the four other tunes I learned! But what I gained from the experience of paying fifty cents per lesson by selling eggs until the eggs ran out was that I needed to develop a sense of planning and some knowledge of the means and reliability of production.

One of my father's biggest dreams was to own a car. When my older brothers grew skilled enough to keep one running, my father bought one. It was not the little red sports car of his dreams, but it was roomy and rugged, and he could get almost all of his large family inside it. In this car the two of us, when I was thirteen or so, rode off to his lodge meetings, where I was designated secretary and took notes, or "minutes," as they were called. We also rode into town to visit the bank. If the family had accumulated even ten dollars above the month's expenses, into the passbook of the Farmers & Merchants Bank it went.

The egg experiment taught me something that puts me at odds with the endless growth idea of classic capitalism and made me a budding socialist. I could see that the number of eggs required to fund my musical expansion was finite. I could also see that the eggs my passion for music was taking from my protein deficient family would in the end undermine the health and stability of all of us.

Babysitting, waiting tables, and working as a "salad girl" at a local 4-H retreat for white youth all meant I could, by the time I was a junior in high school, take care of all my clothing, hair, health, and dental needs. This was fortunate because, after raising eight children, my parents were exhausted and struggling with their own health.

Many years after I, the youngest, had left home, it was a joy to learn that my mother, who had always stayed home after getting everyone else dressed and ready to leave the house, learned to drive a car and at some point found her way to the ocean, which she had never seen. Not even bothering to take off her stockings, she plunged in, as if she could swim. There is a wonderful photograph of her beaming and sopping wet, as if she'd just met her own mother. (And of course she had!)

How clever it was of my father to take me with him to his boring (to me) lodge meetings, where I was to take down information that had zero meaning to me. I see it now as preparation for the writing life that has been mine since I was in my teens. And how positively resolute it was of him to take me with him to make deposits in the Farmers & Merchants Bank, the only unsegregated establishment in the county and the only place white people seemed almost happy to see him.

I somehow developed, with the guidance of my parents and the love of my community, a sense that I could learn the mechanics of life: find work, do it well, enjoy it as much as possible, and use my earnings to support the yearnings that sprang, apparently, from my soul. Right up to my forties I made a monthly list of every purchase and every anticipated expense, and measured it against what income I might expect to receive. I had a profound sense of my indebtedness to both my parents on the day that I knew I could singlehandedly pay all my daughter's expenses as she went off to Yale.

Being mindful about money is a habit that has stayed with me to this day.

When you finally have enough money to invest in something other than a house, books, music, education in general, a car, clothing, furniture, good causes, and so on, what do you do? The piggy bank was a good idea when one was seven, but now there are inflation and other horrors to worry about.

The student in me wants to know how grown-up money mindfulness works, in a system that I don't pretend to agree with or understand. *Mindful Money*, a book grounded in a belief system that is deeply compatible with my own spirit, teaches the lessons I have been waiting for.

— Alice Walker, Pulitzer–Prize winning author of
The Color Purple and *Hard Times Require Furious Dancing*

INTRODUCTION

This book offers practices and techniques that will teach you how to become truly wealthy by mindfully focusing your efforts on the only financial goal that really counts: happiness.

Money is not happiness. Money is a *tool* we can use to enhance the conditions that support happiness. Since sustaining a happy and fulfilling life in the twenty-first century requires a lot more cash than many folks have on hand, money often buys us more anxiety than satisfaction.

The good news is that growing our money doesn't have to be as complicated or stressful as we are led to believe. A few simple practices can help us achieve financial equilibrium far more effectively than the shiny new investment strategies, exchange-traded funds (ETFs), and mutual funds Wall Street rolls out every year. Once we accept that our own behavior is the single most important determinant of long-term success, we can coexist peacefully with the daily uncertainties of the stock market. By following what Buddhists call "the middle path," we will find our way to financial sanity and earn what I call our happiness dividend — the joy and satisfaction that come from a life well lived.

Maintaining this sane perspective can prove difficult because we are often wildly confused about money. Much of what we know about money we absorbed in childhood from parents and members of our extended social circle, who themselves may have been wildly confused about money. What we often learn from others is not financial wisdom, but emotions and attitudes. Fears and cravings. Unhealthy attachments.

Pema Chödrön, an acclaimed Buddhist scholar and teacher, uses the Tibetan word *shenpa* to describe the emotion-laden attachments that hook our attention and lead us to behave in unconscious and unproductive ways. For many of us, money is the ultimate shenpa, causing us to do some very stupid things. This shenpa makes us vulnerable to impulsive financial decisions and to terrible investment advice.

There's plenty of the latter around.

Warring "experts" are constantly bombarding us with fear-laced advice about how to manage our money. Who gets our ear? Who should we believe? Whose advice should we follow? Most of us have little basis for sorting the few precious grains of wheat from all the chaff.

When we lack money knowledge, shenpa runs the show. We end up gravitating to one extreme or another. Either we avoid money like a communicable disease or we become hyperfocused on getting more, which never seems to be enough. While ignoring money is a recipe for disaster, since it leaves our future to the whims of fate, focusing too much on money is a recipe for misery. It drives us to grind away at jobs we hate and micromanage our financial lives, leaping from one investment strategy to another at the slightest dip of the stock market.

Walking the middle path with money requires taming our emotional attachments and choosing to make mindful financial decisions. We must learn to keep quiet faith in those decisions and detach ourselves from the nonstop daily chatter on the airwaves. This middle path frees us from worrying about money every minute because we possess a financial view that stretches for years.

The two biggest demons we meet on the middle path are our own ignorance and fear. Mindfulness practices help us overcome our demons by teaching us to look at things as they really *are*, stripped of our mental and emotional illusions. Mindfulness teaches us to remain serene, present, and nonreactive in the face of our fear. These are the fundamental skills we need to develop to pursue a successful journey toward financial stability.

How can we develop a serene relationship with money in such a nonserene world? We must first get our heads straight about what money is and what it is *not* by untangling our ideas about money from our ideas about happiness. True happiness never comes from money. Happiness comes from intangibles like rich human relationships, a sense of purpose, and a feeling of optimism.

Nonetheless, money does support conditions and experiences that can enhance our happiness, such as taking a family trip, helping a friend in need, retiring in a place we love, or having the free time to finally write our novel. Money's sole purpose is to help us sustain who we are and what we truly value. It is a tool that can get us where we want to go, not an end goal in itself.

Once we understand that money is a tool, how do we get it to work for us? By putting in plenty of hard work of our own. This challenging task does not include an exhaustive search for the "best" money system or guru. Instead, we must turn our gaze inward and focus on our own behavior and thinking around money.

We hold far more power over our personal fortunes than we realize. We gain this power by following a few simple practices that increase both our happiness and our financial well-being. These practices have remained unchanged for generations. Follow them diligently, and we'll find ourselves well on the way to financial health. Take shortcuts, and all the clever financial tricks in the world won't get us back on track.

The practices aren't complicated. All the elements of mindful money management can be reduced to just four deliberate steps:

1. Cast aside our illusions about what money can and can't do for us.
2. Become luminously conscious of what really makes us happy.

3. Make a simple money plan to support our vision of happiness.
4. Stick calmly and nonreactively to our plan.

As Porky Pig says, "Th-th-th-that's all, folks!"

Mindful Money is divided into three sections that guide you through the first three steps: "Unmasking the Illusions," "Finding Your Happiness," and "Making a Plan." Every chapter offers simple Mindful Money Practices designed to transform your relationship with money. Ranging from reflective writing and daily mindfulness practices to nuts-and-bolts accounting, these practices will prepare you to complete the Financial Action Plan template in the appendix.

The third section, "Making a Plan," establishes the real connection between money and happiness by helping you launch your dreams into action. You'll learn timeless, uncomplicated steps for achieving financial stability and growing your money. These steps can be taken no matter what the economic weather may be and no matter how loudly the pundits are screaming.

My hope is that this book helps you develop resilience, healthy practices, and confidence around money. We all have a quiet, alert place within ourselves where we can ride out the panic, the doubt, and the shenpa-driven impulses that arise when it comes to money. If we just sit mindfully, we'll find that place.

I know because I did. When I started my career in financial services over twenty years ago, I was also pursuing a master's degree in Buddhist studies. One of the first challenges I grappled with was how to reconcile planning for my own financial future with the concept of living in the present moment. After years of sitting with this question, here is the beautiful answer I discovered: My financial plan does far more than pave the way for a happier future. My plan greatly adds to my optimism, self-esteem, and sense of purpose *in the here and now*. Planning for tomorrow brings hope and joy to the present moment, which is a true happiness dividend.

SECTION ONE

Unmasking the Illusions

CHAPTER 1

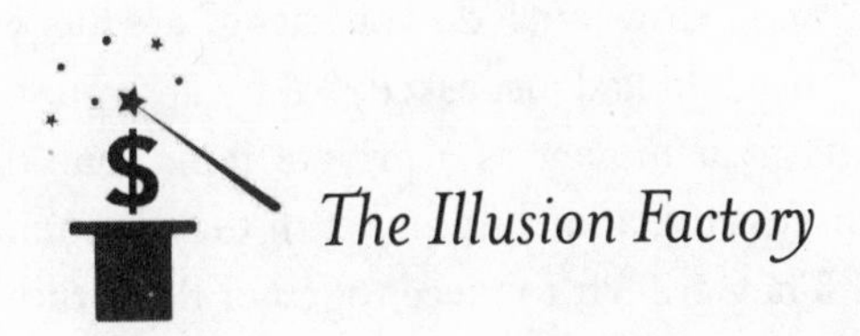

The Illusion Factory

What's money? A man is a success if he gets up in the morning and goes to bed at night and in between does what he wants to do.

— Bob Dylan

We live in a world of illusion, and these illusions keep us from our happiness — especially around money.

Money drives our world. We organize our whole lives around it: earning it, worrying about it, spending it. Yet many of us are taught next to nothing about it. The whole point of Buddhism, and all forms of mindfulness, is to deal with *what is*, to look reality straight in the eye. To sit with it, breathe it in, hold its hand. To "wipe the dust from the mirror," as the Buddhist saying goes. When it comes to money, most of us rarely, if ever, deal openly with *what is*. We spend our entire lives chasing fantasies or running from our fears. Money is the eight-million-pound gorilla sitting in the middle of the town square. We bow to it, serve it, fear it, beg for its blessings, but we don't discuss it. We behave as if money is our god, and we avert our eyes in deference.

In elementary school, we learn a thing or two about *currency*. We're taught how to make change from a five and how to figure sales tax and tips. In middle school or high school, perhaps we take a home economics course that shows us how to balance a checkbook and manage an online bank account. Lesson complete. Whew.

We don't learn the simplest truths about money itself — such as its nature and how it grows. In fact, many people are actively discouraged from learning. We are taught that money is private. It's rude to bring it up. Casual questions from a child, like "How much did that cost?" and "How much do you earn?" are met with admonishments, as if the child had just asked, "Why are you so fat?"

Most adults treat money as a private topic, one they are uncomfortable discussing, and children learn that discomfort, not the reasons for it. They are left to piece together the "truth" for themselves. They shuffle past the giant gorilla every day and create their own mythology about it. These myths are based largely on emotion rather than knowledge.

It doesn't have to be that way. I was extremely fortunate as a child. My economics education started early. Conversation at my family's dinner table was different from that at my friends' tables. We talked about finances. We talked about taxes and investments. We talked openly about how much money my dad and mom made. It wasn't a lot! We talked about how much *this* pair of sneakers cost versus *that* pair of sneakers, and the relative merits of each. We understood limitations and trade-offs. My parents walked me through their tax returns when I was nine. I bought my first stock that year, too. I was exposed to the simple *what is* of money, not the fears and secrecy. It's no accident that today I find money fascinating and fun.

Many people are not so lucky. They absorb only illusions about money put forth by three main sources: family members, culture and media, and Wall Street.

Family Illusions

All of us grow up absorbing our parents' relationship with and feelings about money. Most of this learning is observational, not formal. Perhaps we learn, for example, to be afraid of talking about money because money makes people fight. Or that money causes anxiety. Or that earning a lot of money is a game we must try to win. We learn these beliefs before we know we're learning. That's what makes them so difficult to untangle later on.

When we *are* formally taught about money within our families, these lessons are usually colored by beliefs inherited from our grandparents or great-grandparents.

Many of these beliefs about money are rooted in simple pleasure and pain, in attraction and aversion. The Buddha observed that life is suffering. That is, life inevitably confronts us with pain and discomfort. When it does, we often react reflexively to try to remove the causes of pain and increase the sources of pleasure. Neither of these solutions are lasting, however, and so our efforts end up generating more pain in the long run. Out of this endless cycle, suffering is born.

Human beings are even more motivated to avoid pain than to pursue pleasure. This means most of the so-called truths we live by and pass on to *our* children are based on pain avoidance. Pain avoidance is a very primitive, reflexive way of living. It does not look at the big picture or the long term.

For example, when it comes to money, many people inherit a fear or distrust of "the stock market." Where does this fear come from?

It may come from the Great Depression. It may come from the late-1990s dot-com collapse. It may come from the Great Recession of 2008. Yes, the stock market is volatile and frequently experiences losses, occasionally huge losses. But as the Buddha also observed, the nature of life is impermanence, which is why another thing we can reliably say about the stock market is that over time it grows. The stock market bounced back from each of those historic crashes, and in fact, it has recovered from thirteen major dunks of 20 percent or more since the end of World War II. The market will continue to grow as long as there are people in the world who seek to improve their lives. *That's* the investable thesis, in my opinion. Everything else is just smoke and mirrors.

When we buy into illusions like "stocks are too risky," we may succeed in avoiding the heartache of short-term loss, but we will invest our money in a way that cannot possibly keep up with the rising cost of living. The real danger isn't losing money in the stock market. The real danger is outliving our money because we failed to grow it sufficiently to keep pace with inflation.

This is just one example of how harmful money illusions passed on to us in our families can create negative outcomes.

Cultural and Media-Driven Illusions

Our culture's all-time favorite illusion is that consumption leads to happiness. This illusion has always had its devotees, but today's omnipresent media grinds the message into us so relentlessly that many of us never think to question it. We are conditioned, from cradle to grave, to consume.

I remember my son discovering catalogs when he was only six. One day he said, "Dad, let's sit down and read this together."

I said, "There are no good stories in there."

"No, but I want to show you what I *want*," he said.

So it begins.

A certain level of material comfort makes life pleasant and relieves anxiety, but once we've achieved that basic level, more stuff doesn't make us happier. Nonetheless, one very healthy growth industry in America today is self-storage facilities. We own so much stuff we can't fit it in our houses.

Nicer stuff doesn't make us happier, either. Upgrading our car's grille emblem to a pricier one gives us maybe a fifteen-minute buzz of pleasure. After that burst, our happiness resets to its default level. A thousand-dollar watch might be one or two seconds per year more accurate than a seventy-nine-dollar watch. How much value do those two seconds add to our life?

Even if we're cynical about the claims of advertising, we can easily fall prey to the illusion that the popular media is a reliable source of truth and information. It isn't. Sometimes the financial media genuinely tries to inform us, but it is *always* trying to capture our attention and keep it captive. It does so on behalf of its advertisers, who are always selling something. At the same time, the media is also always selling something else: itself. And besides sex, the most reliable way to get the public's attention is fear. Most media stories about economic matters are intended to scare us — note the tense background music and flashing graphics to keep us clicking the mouse to learn more.

The one-hour Flash Crash of 2010 is a good example. On May 6, 2010, the stock market experienced a nearly thousand-point drop. One blue-chip stock, Procter & Gamble, went from sixty to forty dollars in thirty seconds. Why? A once-popular theory was that some trader with a "fat finger" accidentally pushed the wrong button, but this has been discredited. Instead, the reason for the mayhem is now considered to be a young guy deliberately manipulating market vulnerabilities out of a bedroom in his parent's house in London. But when it happened, no one knew what was causing the drop, and the media picked up the story and ran with it. People panicked because the media covered it the same way it covers everything in finance: like it was the end of the world. The markets are in freefall right now? Panic! Y2K? Panic! Brexit? Panic! The Federal Reserve may hike interest rates? Panic!

Bad news = good copy, but the media's pursuit of ratings gains can unfortunately drive short-term market movements. Anyone with a teaspoon of common sense knows that *nothing* can make an established company like Procter & Gamble lose a third of its value in half a minute. There was obviously a mistake. The stock market *had* to bounce back, and in this case, it recovered almost entirely by the end of that same day. But that's not the tack the media took. Dire tones were employed. Average people who owned pretty much any blue-chip stock wanted out after hearing the latest, breaking news. Those who actually *did* get out regretted it an hour later.

The market responds to our faith in its resilience. Fear undermines that faith, so by selling fear the media retards recovery. As for me, I take the simple route. I reject daily freneticism. I trust that even big issues will resolve themselves in good time. I choose to believe that the market will improve. I don't know how or when it will happen, but when I'm doing long-term income planning, that's all I need to know. Thus far in history, panicking out of the market has never worked. Not once.

The media doesn't only sell fear. It also sells excitement and trendiness. That is how stocks can skyrocket to crazy-high levels virtually overnight. As Warren Buffett famously said at a recent shareholders meeting, "The market is a psychotic drunk." The media, it seems, is its drinking buddy.

I came into the financial management business almost twenty years ago, and I can't remember a single time when the media's hyperbolic approach has helped the everyday investor.

Fear shuts down our higher thought processes and puts the primitive "lizard brain" in charge. The lizard brain is all about survival and attacking immediate threats. It does not possess long-term perspective or use thoughtful analysis.

When the media sells us fear, we don't have to buy it.

Wall Street Illusions

When we do buy in, Wall Street proceeds to take that fear and run with it to the bank by selling us investment products designed to salve our fears. Even when the economic news is bullishly enthusiastic, fear still does the selling: the fear of missing out on a hot market trend. Wall Street spins out newfangled mutual funds and complicated exchange-traded funds every year, not because these edgy new investment products are truly beneficial, but because it knows we're too afraid not to buy them.

In 2000, at the peak of the market, there were more growth-oriented mutual funds than ever in history. In 2009, after the big market meltdown, we saw the rise of so-called tactical allocation funds. These funds helped allay the fears of investors who were afraid of going down with the stock market ship if it tanked again. Interestingly enough, these new funds have underperformed more traditionally managed funds since they began proliferating. That doesn't mean they're bad products, but they were sold at a time when people were predisposed to buy them because marketers pandered to their fears.

The same thing happens when the market is hot. People are encouraged to buy out of emotion. This is how bubbles are created. In 1999, Wall Street urged people to flock to dot-com stocks. Then the bubble burst. Over the last few years, fixed-income products have become the rage. A few years ago, it was real estate. Another time it was oil.

Wall Street plays us something like this: The market falls. The client is afraid. Wall Street sells the client products that won't fall anymore. But they won't go up, either. Then the market goes up. The client, whose products won't go up, is upset about missing out. So Wall Street offers products that *will* go up, but the client doesn't buy those products until *after* the market has already gone up. By that time, the market goes down again, the client becomes afraid, and the cycle continues until the client is broke. Wall Street gets paid on every transaction, so its incentive is to keep the client buying something and to keep the money moving. The public suffers on both ends, and as an added bonus, they pay Wall Street to create the next product to sell. Loss for the average investor is turned into opportunity for Wall Street.

The point is not whether any particular financial product is good or bad. It's that the client doesn't usually know what he or she wants or needs. Wall Street is aware of this and relies on *emotion* to entice clients into choosing products. Wall Street knows that people are hardwired to run away from pain and run toward pleasure. On that basis, new products are focus-grouped to determine, "Will this sell today?" rather than, "Is this good for our investors' long-term portfolios?"

All the tailored suits, the sophisticated financial jargon, and the oil paintings of hunting dogs conspire to create the illusion that staid and responsible money managers are *taking care of* their clients. But in many cases people are being *taken advantage of*.

Of course, Wall Street professionals aren't inherently evil. Many are sincere and well-meaning. Few intend to cheat customers, but when a client walks in the door looking for "safety" or "higher returns," they will sell the client what he or she wants without necessarily knowing what that person needs. They are salespeople in the business of selling financial products, just like car manufacturers or restaurateurs sell their products. People, in turn, have to be wise and thoughtful shoppers. We need to develop a simple financial plan and stick to it, rather than gobbling up every new product that Wall Street creates to satisfy shifting public appetites.

To understand money's true role, we need to empty our cups of all the nonsense and misinformation we've been fed in our lives. Before we can approach money sanely and mindfully, we must break free from the illusions that have hypnotized us since childhood.

Mindful Money Practice

Each chapter in this book ends with a Mindful Money Practice. Many of these are writing exercises that ask you to put pen to paper and express your thoughts, desires, feelings, and goals in writing. Although we live in a digital age, I highly encourage setting aside your laptop or iPad and taking an old-school, hands-on approach to the writing exercises. Plucking ephemeral ideas from your head and making them concrete on the page is a powerful first step toward turning your intentions into action. Only you need to be able to read these exercises, so don't worry if your penmanship is appalling.

The first part of this exercise is the easiest of the lot: Choose something to write on and something to write with. Be creative or practical. Use a spiral notebook, three-ring binder, hardbound journal, or yellow pad for documenting each Mindful Money Practice in the book, and choose a writing implement that sings to you. I myself am a sucker for fountain pens, but a no. 2 pencil is more than adequate. Every time you open this book, have your pen and notebook within reach, so that you are ready for the exercises and can jot down any thoughts for future contemplation.

The second part of the exercise is harder: use the first page of your notebook to tell your family's financial story.

- What facts and fictions were you taught about money growing up?
- What good and bad habits did you learn?
- What feelings and fears did you absorb?
- What successes and failures did you witness?
- What childhood financial lessons and illusions have you carried into your adulthood?

This story doesn't need to be long, but it should describe the financial truths you live by today.

CHAPTER 2

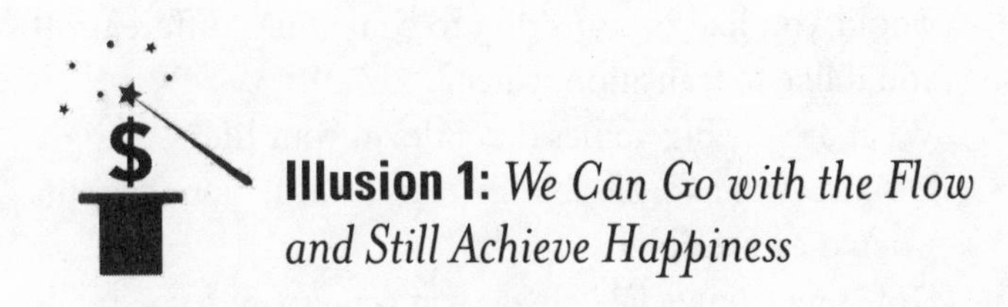

Illusion 1: *We Can Go with the Flow and Still Achieve Happiness*

Money is only a tool. It will take you wherever you wish, but it will not replace you as the driver.

— Ayn Rand

The reason our illusions are so powerful is that we don't consciously recognize them as illusions. We don't even know we've taken them onboard. Adults who are relentlessly conscientious about which refrigerator or phone plan to buy can still somehow adopt passive, magical beliefs about money and how money relates to their major life goals.

One of the most prevalent and harmful illusions is silent but deadly. We unwittingly allow popular culture to define happiness and our financial goals *for* us. I call this the "gateway" illusion because, like a "gateway drug," it opens the door to so many others. If we don't know, clearly and distinctly, what we want for ourselves, others will be more than happy to tell us and *sell* us on their visions for our lives.

If we planned to build our dream house or write a book, few of us would borrow someone else's ideas and hope that the project turned out as we wished. But when it comes to our biggest life decisions, we often passively "go with the flow" of society's default choices. Many of my clients have a difficult time answering the most basic questions about their personal goals during their first financial planning interview. I ask them questions like these:

- When would you like to retire?
- How do you want to live in retirement?
- Do you want to work at one career your whole life or would you like to transition to something different? If you'd like to transition, when?
- What are the big values that inform your life?
- Do you want to be able to take care of your parents when they are elderly?
- How much financial help do you want to give your children?
- What kind of legacy do you want to create and leave behind?

The truth is that happiness is specific, not generic. If we want specific things out of life, we must actively choose them, plan for them, and allocate personal and financial resources toward them. Things don't just "happen." They must be intentionally worked toward.

Living by Default

The biggest financial error many of us commit is failing to carefully consider the money choices we make. We go with society's flow, instead of following our own path. The one question we should ask ourselves before every financial decision is: Does this align with who *I* am today and where *I* want to go in life tomorrow?

When we live by default, we don't put our day-to-day financial choices in the context of a personal vision for a whole, happy life. Instead, we look outside ourselves for cues about what will make us happy. Since popular culture tells us to spend, we spend. When *today's* self wants a vacation or a BMW, we give that self what it wants, without considering the impact on our *future* self. What we don't realize is that when we buy things we don't really need or want, we are trading away a piece of our future happiness, which we start creating today.

There's nothing wrong with nice things. But the only things that bring *lasting* value are those that are congruent with who we really are and what we really want. A boat may be absolutely integral to one person's happiness, but for others it might be just an impulse buy or a status symbol.

The practice of examining and questioning our motivations is at the heart of Buddhist thought. The focus of Buddhism is on *awakening* by peeling back layers of untruth in order to realize the truth. We must awaken to what truly nourishes and fulfills us, instead of reflexively buying into the "consumption = happiness" message the media sells us 24/7.

Most people have limited resources. But whatever our resources, we need to invest them in the things that are critical to *our* dreams and values, not someone else's bottom line.

To do that, we first have to identify our values and who we want to be. If we don't decide these things, life will decide for us. If we mindlessly go with society's flow by default, we give up choosing, and we won't achieve the life of our dreams. The current will carry us along from cradle to grave, taking us where *it* wants to go.

Living by Design

To live by design, rather than by default, means making conscious decisions about who we want to be and how we want to live. It means deciding what we value and making concrete financial and life choices in support of those values.

For example, in my case, I want to be a good father. To me, this entails things like giving my kids a good education, spending meaningful time with them, and teaching them the value of committed effort. These goals have practical consequences, like needing to save money for their college education. These choices require trade-offs.

I choose not to drive a luxury car so I can save money in a college fund instead. Since I want to be home in the evenings with my kids, I choose not to work a job with crazy-long hours and a killer commute. I'm willing to disappoint a few people in order to make this happen and to catch some grief from friends and colleagues from time to time. I choose to do meaningful activities with my kids, like grow a vegetable garden. That means buying a home with a good-size yard and spending time gardening. All these choices involve specific commitments of time, money, and attention. Of course, being a good father can be defined in countless other ways, but given my definition, these are the things I need to do. This means I can't participate in many of the default things society pulls me toward.

The Easy Path Gets Harder Over Time

When we live by default, it's usually because we think it's easier to go with the flow. It lets us off the hook from doing the conscious work of choosing our values and life goals. It allows us to walk a well-paved and socially approved path.

But a curious thing happens over the course of a lifetime. Living by default seems easy at first, but it becomes harder as time goes on. When we are not crystal clear about what we want and value, we unconsciously give in to the messages that bombard us every day. For modern Americans, that means buy, buy, buy. We become dedicated consumers, and this mind-set takes over our lives and maxes out our credit cards. We work hard so we can buy more and more of the things we're told will make us happy. As these things fail to bring us lasting joy, we move on to the *next* thing.

For example, as a teenager, I remember becoming obsessed with buying a Canon camera to take on a trip I'd planned. After seeing numerous ads that touted the wonders of the Canon, I was sold. I bought this camera, even though I had never taken a picture in my life, and it cost close to six hundred dollars. Then, on the trip, I shot several rolls of film, and every photo was overexposed because I hadn't learned to use the camera properly, since photography wasn't *really* my thing. I had gone with a flow that definitely wasn't mine, and I never, ever took another shot with that camera. Ever since, for thirty years, it has been sitting on my closet shelf. I keep it there as a reminder. That six hundred dollars, compounded at 8 percent interest, would be over six thousand dollars today.

When we live by default, life begins to feel like an exhausting grind. We end up *pushing* ourselves through an endless stream of workdays in order to support the ever-growing collection of stuff we think we want. As the decades go by, the stuff brings fewer rewards, and the pushing feels harder and more exhausting.

When we live by design, on the other hand, we are selective and purposeful about our investments of time and money, and we choose only those things that align with our deep values and desires. We don't have to push ourselves through such a life. We feel *pulled*. A life of design gives us all the energy in the world. Each time we act in support of a goal that we *really* value, our self-esteem goes up. Each time we achieve a step toward our *real* dream, we get an infusion of positive reinforcement. Each time we invest in a thing or experience that makes *us* uniquely happy, we become more of who we really are. Friction disappears. Enthusiasm replaces stress. Life works.

Mindful Money Practice

Sometimes we give in to the illusion that we can get the *perks* of a designed life while going with society's flow by default. This is self-delusion. If we want to live a life in which we realize our authentic dreams and values, we must consciously identify those dreams and values. And we must make mindful and concrete money choices that support them.

Take a moment right now to identify an unused "six-hundred-dollar camera" in your life. Describe that "camera" in your notebook. What enticed you to buy it? Why do you regret the purchase? What do you wish you'd done with the money instead?

Next, move that "camera" to the front shelf of your mental closet. For the next month, every time you open your wallet to buy anything other than groceries, ask yourself: Is this another "six-hundred-dollar camera"? Am I defaulting to society's flow, or is this part of my design?

CHAPTER 3

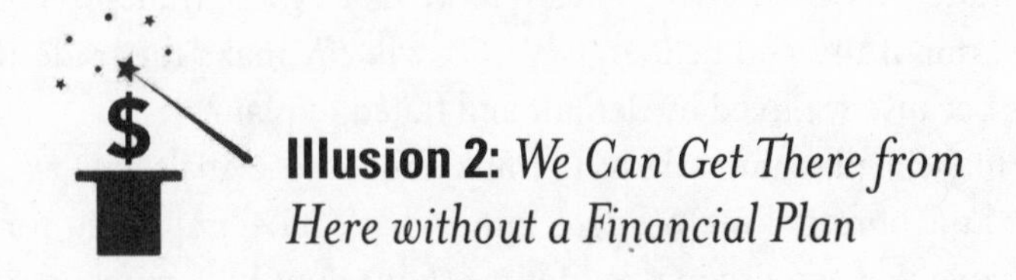

Illusion 2: *We Can Get There from Here without a Financial Plan*

> I didn't get there by wishing for it or hoping for it, but by working for it.
>
> — Estée Lauder

Sometimes people operate under the illusion that they'll arrive at a happy financial future without any planning. They somehow think they can go anywhere they want in life, and they don't consider the trade-offs or costs of particular destinations. However, we'd never take a vacation without planning where we're going, what we want to see, how we're going to get there, how long it will take, and how much it will cost. Why wouldn't we map out our life journey with the same detail? Financial planning is the tool for doing that, and it's essential for success.

At its most basic, a financial plan is a series of commitments we make to ourselves:

- We commit that the amount of money flowing *into* our coffers will be more than the amount flowing *out* — and that this trend will continue over time.
- We commit that we'll weigh and measure the long-term impact of any significant financial expenditures before we open our wallets.

- We commit that surplus money beyond our daily lifestyle needs will go toward things we truly want and not toward things we can easily live without.

Along the road of life, each of these commitments will require us to forgo short-term gratification at times and to make hard choices between equally compelling destinations. When it comes to money, such trade-offs are unavoidable. Will *we* make these trade-offs ourselves, mindfully and deliberately? Or will *life* make the trade-offs for us because we lived by default and failed to plan?

Financial planning asks us to think about those goals with an eye toward the bottom line. We determine what's most important for us to achieve and acquire in this lifetime, figure out how much money will be required to make those things happen, and devise strategies to generate that money. There's nothing mysterious or complicated about the process. In fact, many folks often do a bit of basic financial planning for small purchases like a vacation or a new refrigerator.

For some reason, people often avoid planning for the big things, such as paying for an infant daughter's college education, changing careers, or enjoying a long and fulfilling retirement. Instead of mindfully taking steps to realize these goals, people blindly trust that the dollars will be there when they need them. Without a solid plan, they won't.

However, before making a financial plan — which is the focus of section 3 in this book — you'll need to assess your situation. There are three important things you must consider to ensure you are headed in the right direction:

1. You need to be honest about *Here*, or where you are now.
2. You need to be clear about *There*, or where you want to be.
3. You need to consider the *Route*, which involves making trade-offs, or paying the costs, required to get from Here to There.

Each of us needs to know these coordinates before we begin any financial journey. If we don't know where we're coming from (which I term our "Here"), where we're going (our "There"), and how we're planning to get there (the "Route," which involves those pesky trade-offs), we may find ourselves hopelessly lost.

Being Honest about Here

Mindfulness asks us to be keenly aware of where we are right now, and where we are is always Here and nowhere else. As such, the first step to making a mindful money plan is an unflinching assessment of where Here is for us. We may not be thrilled about where that is, but acceptance is a profound thing. In fact, accepting things as they truly are, rather than the illusion of how we wish them to be, is considered the very key to what Buddhists call enlightenment. Enlightenment is a tall order, but to make a plan that will get us anywhere, we must understand ourselves and our starting point.

Acceptance is simple for animals, plants, and mountains, but we humans have a notoriously hard time with it. We reject, deny, or ignore conditions we deem undesirable. We twist and distort the uncomfortable facts of our lives into a form that fits our fragile mental framework. When things don't go the way we hope or expect, we resist reality. We don't dwell in *what is*, we dwell on *how we wish things were*. Nowhere is this truer than in the realm of money.

People often feel bad about some aspect of their financial circumstances, which makes it difficult to enjoy a healthy relationship with money. We want more of it, and we can feel shame if we don't have enough. If we are not where we want to be financially, we may blame ourselves. If we have lost money by behaving stupidly, that loss may be so painful we don't want to look at it. No matter where we are on the financial scale, we tend to compare ourselves to those who have more and so feel incomplete. We focus so much on where we *should* be that we can't see where we *are*.

Shame gets us nowhere. But if we want to get to a better place financially, we must be honest about where we are right now. We must look at our costs, our earnings, and our debt. Our saving and spending patterns. Our taxes, investments, and credit card statements. Our 401K and Social Security accounts. Then we must ask ourselves a tough question: Where will we be in five, ten, or twenty-five years if we continue to follow the path we've been taking thus far? Many times, the answer will be nowhere near to achieving our dreams.

What needs to change? How do we need to behave differently?

First and foremost, we must let go of the *shoulds*. They aren't a factor in this equation. We also need to stop comparing ourselves financially to others. It doesn't matter how many people have more or less than we do. Comparing our investment accounts to stock market benchmarks like the S&P 500 doesn't matter, either. What *does* matter is how much money we personally have today as compared to how much money we'll need to get us where we want to be in the future.

Being Clear about There

After accepting our Here, our next daunting task is to clearly and specifically define There, or our destination.

When we only have vague ideas about where we're going, it's easy to be vague about the Route we'll take and what trade-offs will be necessary. Further, if everything Here seems to be working okay, we may harbor the illusion that everything There will work out okay, too, and without much effort. Perhaps it will, but we may not be happy with where we land.

Defining There requires asking ourselves searching questions about the kind of future we want. What career do we desire? Do we want to have a family? If so, what opportunities do we hope to provide our children? What sort of lifestyle do we want? What income level do we need in order to make that happen? How do we envision our retirement? What legacy will we leave when we're gone?

Defining There also means considering our needs in the present. What experiences do we want to be having right now? What passions do we want to be pursuing? Do we want to turn those passions into a career or keep them separate? What are the main values we want to live by?

Being specific about our aspirations, especially in the context of money, takes us out of the realm of illusion. It helps us recognize that everything we truly want in life requires resources, attention, and effort. All of these things are finite. When we calculate what we want in terms of the costs in time and money, it quickly becomes clear that we cannot afford everything. We must prioritize. We need to ask ourselves: What are the things we absolutely *require* in order to live a happy life? Most of those things won't be *things*.

Though we can't have everything our hearts desire, we probably *can* have the essentials. To do so, we will probably have to pass up a few nonessentials, like that Jet Ski, maybe.

The bald truth is that achieving our essential must-haves in the here and now *and* enjoying a half-decent retirement in the future will cost substantial money. Earning that money will require dedicated, proactive planning and attention, not coasting by on the illusion that we can have it all without knowing how we're going to pay for it.

Planning the Route and Calculating the Trade-Offs

How do we get from Here to There? By planning the Route and calculating the trade-offs, then reprioritizing our goals as necessary.

Most of the time we have more than one goal in life. That's natural. Yet too often, our goals may be so incompatible that they couldn't possibly coexist in the real world. To avoid choosing, we often noodle around and leave our goals vague and half-formed in our heads. We want to buy a vacation home next year, leave the rat race when we're fifty-five, *and* enjoy our current lifestyle until we're a hundred. Or we want to live a quiet life in the country, master the violin, *and* run a successful urban restaurant on the side. Or we hope to retire to Costa Rica *and* maintain close ties with our friends and grandkids who live in New York. In this last example, it's easy to see that geography will directly undermine the goal to remain close to family, and something will have to give.

Our goals need to be congruent and complementary if we hope to reach them in this lifetime. What is most important to us? Living in a tropical paradise may not be worth missing our granddaughter's first day of kindergarten, but working until we're sixty so we can buy that cabin in Tahoe might be something we're willing to consider. Once we've figured out our absolute must-haves, we need to make sure our secondary goals support those primary ones, and we must forgo putting our time, money, and energy into endeavors that don't serve those goals.

We also need to address the inherent conflict between now and later. We can't have everything we want in the present *and* everything we want in the future. Nor does our happiness *require* that we do so. As we establish our priorities for the future, such as helping our kids pay for college or going back to school to earn our own PhD, we will need to pass up many things we might want in the present. In other words, we must make trade-offs *now* to achieve what we want *then*.

Our *today* self can't have every new gadget if we want our *tomorrow* self to afford a comfortable retirement. But most of us *can* have the experiences and objects that really, really matter to us, *if* that's the only stuff we splurge on. Every time we open our wallet, we should ask ourselves whether those dollars will bring us closer to or further from what truly makes us happy. Otherwise, we'll end up spending our money on immediate *nonessentials* at the expense of future *essentials*. I can't stress enough the importance of this point.

There's no way to get rich quick, but we feel much richer when we mindfully choose to spend money on our *particular form of wealth* and trim the excess indulgences. If music is in our blood, perhaps we can buy a top-of-the-line sound system, but we give up the premium movie channels. If great food is our thing, perhaps we can dine at an amazing restaurant once or twice a month, but we skip the impulsive bookstore purchases. If we have the travel bug, perhaps we can save our pennies for an annual vacation by only having and maintaining one car. Of course, vacations and fancy feasts are discretionary purchases that we can decide to forgo altogether. Retirement, on the other hand, *isn't* optional. It's a financial reality that may conflict with key goals like paying for our children's college education, requiring us to carefully weigh and measure what trade-offs we're willing to make.

When we make such thoughtful trade-offs, any envy or jealousy of others tends to lessen or disappear. When we are making choices to achieve the things we care about, it doesn't matter if our sister-in-law went to Paris last spring. When we are doing what is most essential to our own happiness, we don't get caught up in social comparisons, which trade our personal satisfaction for someone else's opinion. When we spend our money only on the things that have personal value to us, and we let everything else go, our Route from Here to There becomes much more direct.

When We Can't Get There from Here

After you've carefully considered your current circumstances, your priorities, and the trade-offs you're willing to make in order to achieve your goals, you may come to the hard realization that you are not going to have the resources to achieve all of your must-haves. In that case, the only options are to downgrade your expectations or to increase your resources by creating a larger income stream. This can involve often-challenging measures, such as the following:

- getting an advanced degree in your field
- starting your own business
- growing a business you already have
- accepting more risk in your investments
- changing your career
- taking a second or third job
- working longer

Each of these options involves further trade-offs and challenges. What is the time frame for completing that degree? How will you study while working full-time? Will you need to take out student loans? Where will the money come from to repay them? When we don't plan adequately, the logistical challenges can mount and thwart our goals.

If we have reached this sobering point in our financial lives having done very little conscious planning, beyond getting up and going to work in the morning, it's time to change. Whether we're happy or unhappy with our circumstances, here we are, and the only way to get to a more satisfying tomorrow is to plan for it. It's an illusion to think we can continue going with the same flow and reach a happier future. No matter how daunting Here is, you can still reach a more meaningful There if you create a financial road map, a Route. After all, a plan is simply the opportunity to set and achieve meaningful goals, which is what gives life structure and purpose. Drifting along year after year, hoping for the best, may feel like an easier way to live in the moment, but that also has a cost. It's the down payment on a life without direction.

The ultimate goal of all money management and financial planning is to create an income stream that we can't outlive. That means growing our money at a pace that generates the income we need now, *and* that keeps up with inflation, *and* that builds a steady surplus for tomorrow. When we do this right — and many don't — we have more money on the day we die than at any previous point in our lives. The odds of this happening without a financial plan are about the same as the odds of authoring the Great American Novel without actually sitting down to write it.

Mindful Money Practice

Find ten minutes to make a fast but fearless accounting of where you are now, where you want to go, and what you may need to give up to get there. I call this exercise "Setting an Itinerary" because the focus is on destinations rather than a specific route. Coming exercises will help you determine *how* you're going to reach your goals. For now, just consider *where* you'd like to go and identify detours you may or may not have the time, energy, or money to make.

First, divide a page in your notebook into three columns labeled "Here," "There," and "Trade-offs." Starting with the "Here" column, list every important aspect of your current financial picture that comes to mind.

Next, in the "There" column, list any and all short- or long-term goals that come to mind. Be as specific as possible. For example, instead of listing a vague goal like "retirement," write a more detailed description, like "Retire by age sixty-eight, move to the coast of Maine, and take up landscape painting."

Finally, review the first two columns and consider what trade-offs might be necessary to make those top priorities a reality, then list these in the "Trade-offs" column.

When you're done, bookmark this Itinerary. We will turn to it again later, and it's a useful reference as you develop a more mindful relationship with money.

CHAPTER 4

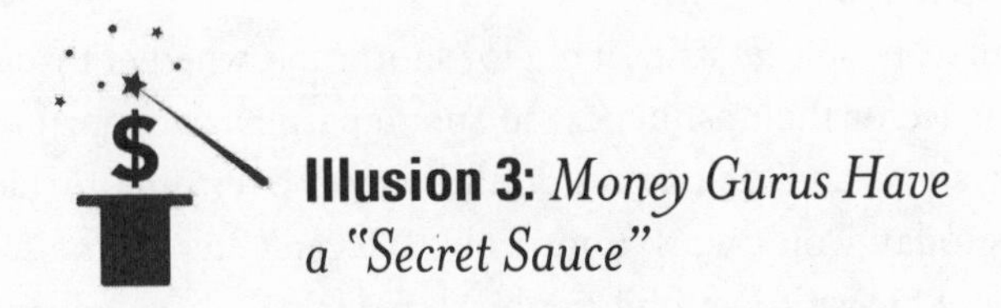

Illusion 3: *Money Gurus Have a "Secret Sauce"*

> We've long felt that the only value of stock forecasters is to make fortune tellers look good.
>
> — Warren Buffett

The world of money and investments can seem so complicated that some people don't even try to understand it. Instead, they seek out and defer to the wisdom of financial wizards, gurus, prognosticators, and geniuses. Like Dorothy looking for the great and powerful wizard who can help her get back to Kansas, people may wander from one end of Oz (aka: the internet) to the other searching for experts to give them an answer that's already at their feet.

The world of finance includes plenty of bright folks, but one thing I know for sure is that there are no financial wizards or gurus who can consistently and repeatedly outperform all the other wizards and gurus. That's an illusion that sells advertising and drives mouse clicks. In my twenty years as a financial adviser, I've seen countless financial stars rise and fall. I've watched myriad trends come and go and endless theories fizzle. There are too many variables and unknowns for anyone to *predictably* and *reliably* outperform others in the investing game.

Yet we still hope our investment managers will do the impossible for us. Even as money managers issue the standard disclaimer that "past performance is no guarantee of future success," we choose to believe the opposite — that there are people smarter than us who can reliably deliver riches in record time. That belief is why scam artists like Bernie Madoff are able to rob investors of millions upon millions of dollars.

Of course, people *do* strike it big for short runs, whether through random chance or their astuteness to spot a particular opportunity, but their systems and techniques don't hold up over time. A tactic that works today won't work tomorrow. We can't step in the same river twice. This isn't just philosophical musing. Impermanence is a fact. The conditions of life *are* constantly changing. The world is being reborn every moment. On this, both monks and physicists agree.

This means we have to be very careful about who we listen to and what advice we follow. Practicing mindful money habits will serve us much better in the long run than some stranger who knows nothing about us or our goals. We must shed the illusion that any money guru can take us to the promised land of consistent, market-beating returns. Chasing the Next Big Thing will only get us hopelessly lost.

The Need to Believe

Why are we so predisposed to defer to experts in any field? In part, it's a healthy sense of humility. We realize that some people have trained long and hard enough to know much more about certain subjects than we do. But often, we don't want to accept the responsibility of making healthy decisions for ourselves. Either way, abdicating our personal power to the experts can become a dangerous crutch.

A good example of this is medicine. The human body is extraordinarily complex; understanding it takes more effort than the average person wants to put in. So we choose to trust our doctors, and modern medicine in general, and this trust is often well deserved. But we still have to make informed choices in order to take care of ourselves. If we overrely on doctors, and underrely on ourselves, we may ignore basic healthy practices — like eating right, getting regular exercise, and avoiding harmful substances — and count on doctors to fix our own mistakes with a magic pill or procedure.

A similar thing happens in finance. We can follow many simple practices that will keep us in excellent financial health, such as earning more than we spend. Yet if we disregard these common-sense measures, perhaps running up our credit card balances by buying unneeded luxuries, we may easily find ourselves in over our heads. At that point, we look for an expert with some special trick for instantly creating untold wealth.

Some financial wizards are only too happy to encourage our bad habits. They constantly tell us to stop whatever we're doing and do what *they're* doing. "Everyone should buy this group of stocks today." "Now everyone should buy *that* group." Few seem to be selling a long-term, healthy approach to money these days.

Fortunately, we *all* have six senses, or *ayatana*, as they are called in some Buddhist traditions. We have the standard five senses we recognize in the West, and Buddhism adds *mano-ayatana*, which translates loosely as "mind" or "ideas." All human experiences derive from these six *ayatana*, and a financial guru's six senses are not more finely tuned than anyone else's. The pundits on the morning talk shows share the same human frailties and foibles we all possess. These experts have more financial training than most folks, but they possess no secret for successfully gaming the system over the long term. Using the six senses we all share, we can follow the simple, logical money principles that maintain our everyday health and which will serve us much better in the long run than switching from one money guru to the next.

One of these principles is patience. The Buddhist practitioner knows it may take lifetimes to reach enlightenment. Perhaps we can wait a few years to reach financial success.

The Luck Factor

I love and admire my dad tremendously. He taught me almost everything I know about how to manage money and life. But even a smart guy like my dad had a tendency to get wound up about the latest cutting-edge financial theories. He was always following some new pundit, and periodically he'd become convinced that he had hit upon a great new angle for getting rich. When I was in high school, for example, he got overexcited about his small-cap mutual portfolios because some guy with a radio show and a systematic approach to investing fired him up. Three years later those investments had all collapsed back to what they were long before he bought them.

None of the "hot," guru-driven schemes my dad tried for quick wealth-building ever panned out. Not one. My mom is lucky he was practical enough not to *rely* solely on those ideas. What *did* work for my parents, in the long run, were simple, healthy financial practices like saving money, dollar-cost averaging, making intelligent tradeoffs, avoiding debt, and being disciplined with spending.

When it comes to money strategies, everyone gets lucky and unlucky sometimes. When we remove the luck factor, no one consistently and predictably emerges as a guru. That's the true *what is*.

A lot of recent research has focused on the role of luck versus skill when it comes to investment success, and it appears that the former is a far greater factor in finance than most of us would like to believe. If we look at a thousand financial "experts" with a hundred different techniques over a fixed time period, a few of them will be wildly successful, a few will fail spectacularly, and the vast majority are going to end up somewhere in the middle. The bell curve reigns. The problem is, we like to focus on the outliers.

We try to emulate the moves of the mega-successful and avoid the moves of the flops. But both the successes and the failures can be explained more by chance than by any other factor. It boils down to this: Out of any group, during any particular period, someone has to do well and someone has to do poorly. It's the law of averages. Mindfulness requires that we recognize the limits of our own mental abilities. These same limits apply to everyone. What's impossible for us to know is impossible for others to know as well.

Plenty of studies have confirmed the randomness factor. If we take eight hundred managers in a particular investment category, such as large domestic companies, look at the top 25 percent in performance for a given three-year period, and *then* look at the *next* three-year period, we'll see two completely different pictures. Three years later, among the initial two hundred top-performing managers, perhaps fifty will still be in the top 25 percent, fifty will end up in the second 25 percent, fifty will drop down to the third 25 percent, and fifty will hit the bottom 25 percent of the barrel. Random redistribution. What worked in the first period will have no bearing on the next period. The past is not predictive of future success.

The logical fallacy we commit is that we only look at the behaviors and theories of the winners, not the losers. We want to know what the winners did to win, and we want to believe that if we do the same thing, we'll win, too. This makes as much sense as taking financial advice from lottery winners. For every person who achieves "success" by buying lottery tickets, millions of others buy tickets and fail. It's that failure of the masses that creates the jackpots for the lucky few.

Why Gurus Can't Possibly Predict the Future

I have a friend who is the closest thing I know to a financial genius. He's a whiz with numbers and patterns. He can find fascinating trends in past data, but he can't get his financial models to work forward into the future. That's because no one knows what will happen next. We humans can only peek under a tiny corner of the infinitely huge rug that is reality. It's impossible to predict even the weather a month ahead of time. And the global economy is at least as complex as the weather, if not more so.

No one could have predicted that a phenomenon like Facebook would arrive overnight and not only change social networking but totally transform the way we advertise, organize, and communicate, and that this would, in turn, transform entire industries and the technologies that support them. We don't know what the next game changer will be, nor how it will affect the other moving pieces.

Look at John Paulson, who became famous for making the so-called "greatest trade ever," which was celebrated in a book by the same name and the subsequent 2015 movie *The Big Short*. During 2005, Paulson had a notion that the housing market would soon collapse, so in early 2006 he set out to borrow money to create an investment product that would bet against the real estate markets. He had a hard time finding investors because everyone thought real estate was only going to go up. Long story short, when the housing market collapsed in 2007, Paulson's investment strategy made $15 billion almost overnight — $4 billion of which was his alone. After his gargantuan success, new money *poured* into his company. The next year those new investors lost half of what they'd added. Even Paulson's record-breaking past performance could not guarantee future success.

It's possible to be successful for short periods of time, and some runs can go on for quite a while, but they *always* end. Often in spectacular fashion. Just ask Bill Miller, who is known for having had one of the longest market-beating runs in financial history when he was investment manager at Legg Mason. He beat the S&P 500 for fifteen years in a row, but then he went supernova and plunged almost to the absolute bottom.

What virtually *never* happens is that a manager bests the financial markets successfully for an entire lifetime.

Even if some financial guru did continue to be right year after year, trying to follow that person for the long term wouldn't work. Why? Because the more assets that follow a particular guru, the less his or her idea can produce big payouts. In order to beat the market, a guru's hot idea has to be a bit of a long shot. The smart money has to bet against that person. The more successful and popular an idea becomes, the more the guru has to spread those amazing returns across a greater number of dollars, so those returns spread more thinly. Tremendous success ends up diluting the investment's performance.

It's a lot like playing the ponies. When we bet on a long-shot horse and it wins, we make a lot of money. But once that horse becomes a favorite, the odds even out, and we only make a little money when it wins.

There is one sure thing, nonetheless. Some of those gurus *are* going to be right. Some of them, in fact, are going to make a killing. We just won't know which ones until after the fact. But we can't second-guess ourselves, or we'll be left in a perennial state of *non*-buyer's remorse, always wishing we'd bought something that we didn't. That's no way to live.

Skip the Guru and Find a Financial Adviser

Most of the time we can accomplish our long-term financial goals if we put in place our own simple investment program and follow it consistently, whether the market goes up, down, or sideways and regardless of what any pundit tells us.

Want help designing your investment program? My advice is to skip the guru and look for a financial adviser. An internet sensation with a strategy for generating market-beating returns knows virtually nothing about the financial circumstances of the nameless, faceless strangers following the blog. An adviser who takes the time to understand his or her clients' entire financial picture can be extraordinarily helpful. A good adviser won't have all the answers, and he or she will be honest about that. A good adviser will know and acknowledge his or her own limits; that person won't claim to be able to beat the market. Nonetheless, a good adviser can play a crucial role in helping clients define their dreams, create a financial vision for the future, and understand the trade-offs necessary to bring that vision to life.

This book also provides some of that practical financial advice. Particularly in section 3, I'll describe in detail my approach to investing.

However, almost any disciplined savings and investment program will work over time, if you stick with that program mindfully, calmly, and nonreactively. Being nonreactive is the key. All investment approaches will stop working at some moment in time, but history shows that the sound, logic-based ones eventually recover. Will we ride out the storm in the face of those gurus telling us to jump ship now? Can we leave our money where it is and be patient? That is our true test.

Mindful Money Practice

In today's hyperconnected world, it's not hard to become a bit of a media junkie, and most of us have our drug of choice. Some folks hit the financial pundits on cable TV every night before bed and then wonder why they can't sleep. Others get amped up by talk radio jocks on the drive to and from work every day. Still others, myself included, spend a fair amount of time on the internet mainlining any financial news we can get our hands on.

What or who is *your* drug of choice? Suze Orman? Jim Cramer? Barry Ritholtz? For the next month, go cold turkey. That doesn't mean you can't turn on the television, but avoid the financial channels. When the nightly newscaster on your local station starts preaching financial Armageddon, either change the channel or press the "off" button. The same goes for the radio. Switch to country, classical, or pop music for a month. If the web is your weakness, divert your attention to something more soothing, like crazy cat videos or food blogs. As for the newspaper? Pretend the *New York Times* doesn't have a business section for the next thirty days.

Write this resolution in your notebook, and stick to it. After a month, you may feel so much better about the world and your investment portfolios that you decide to make a permanent lifestyle adjustment.

CHAPTER 5

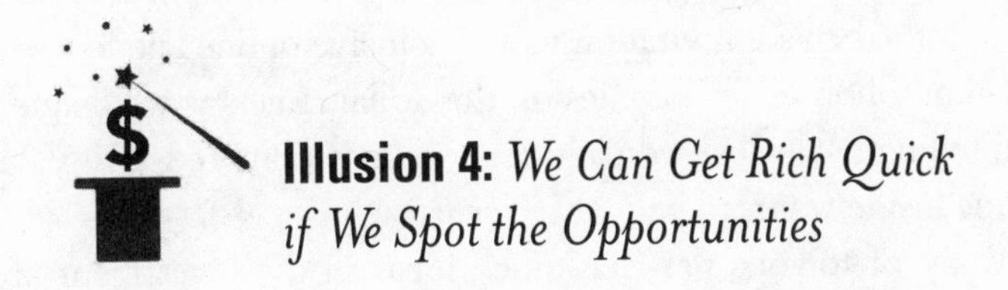

Illusion 4: *We Can Get Rich Quick if We Spot the Opportunities*

> Overconfidence is a very serious problem. If you don't think it affects you, that's probably because you're overconfident.
>
> — Carl Richards

The Get Rich Quick illusion is a kissing cousin of the Guru with the Secret Sauce illusion. This illusion is such a cliché that it should be unnecessary to include it at all. After all, everyone knows that getting rich quick is a foolish pipe dream. Right?

Perhaps, but the problem with illusions is that they don't dwell in our conscious, rational mind. They reside in our *unconscious*, where they wreak havoc on our emotions. Ask ten people whether it is a good idea to chase a get-rich-quick scheme, and ten out of ten will say *no*. But deep down inside, millions of us are secretly hoping to be the exception who wins ten thousand dollars a month for life on Powerball.

The Get Rich Quick illusion has probably been with us since the dawn of commerce. But in the past, opportunities to act on it were fewer. The Gold Rush of 1849 is one of the most famous get-rich-quick schemes in not-so-recent history, but just making it to California to pan for all that gold took months of preparation and arduous travel. Today, gold, money, business, and ideas travel at the speed of light. Day traders are able to move millions of dollars with the click of a mouse. Instant billionaires are created almost on a weekly basis. And we hear about these things in real time, online or on TV.

Schemes and ideas for making easy money bombard us from all angles, from the Nigerian potentate offering to wire us untold riches to the private invitation to an exclusive online auction where we can buy houses for pennies on the dollar. Even as we delete the email telling us we just won a lottery we never entered, a tiny flame of hope inside wants to believe it's true.

Many of today's get-rich-quick ideas in the investment arena are based on gaming the system without creating any value. We see hedge funds making millions by betting on companies to fail, traders exploiting inequities in global prices for quick killings, and young entrepreneurs selling hot business ideas before their companies have proven they can make a dime. The new wealth fantasy is not about developing some great new product or service that adds value to human life, but finding some clever way to skim the cream off the system in a huge lump sum. With today's technology in our hands, that seems tantalizingly possible.

But it isn't. As with the success of gurus, it's only *after the fact* that get-rich-quick stories reveal themselves. They are not replicable or predictable. Luck and timing are always huge factors. For every person who gets superrich by creating a Facebook or an Amazon, there are hundreds who try similar ideas and don't quite make it. The right set of conditions just don't materialize.

In Buddhism, the concept of karma reminds us that everything arises as a result of prior causes and conditions. If those underlying causes and conditions are altered even slightly, the results will change, too. We can implement the exact same behaviors and strategies as a Richard Branson or Mark Zuckerberg, but we don't have the same underlying circumstances in our lives, so we won't get the same results. Period.

While it's true that there are predictable things we can do to increase our odds of success, it is not true that there are known paths to *quick* success. The only *reliable* route to wealth is a consistent, disciplined, long-term saving and investing plan, and we will have to accept some risk if we hope to see our assets grow.

One Illusion, Many Faces

The Get Rich Quick illusion appears in many guises, but beneath each is the same idea: for no effort, and in no time, we will get rich. Here are just a few:

- Our genius idea will sell for a fortune. There is a popular illusion that a great idea alone can attract the investment of venture capitalists. The truth is, ideas are cheap; everyone has one or two good ones. The concrete execution of ideas is what adds all the value for investors. If we are not willing to invest some time and money developing our idea into something more proven and practical, such as a product, a service, or at least a detailed business plan, we can't expect others to invest either.
- We can buy a system that will make us rich. Television and the internet are full of systems that purport to teach "secret" methods for getting rich quick, from building websites that generate automatic income to software that exploits the foreign exchange market for quick profits. The question we need to ask anytime someone tries to sell us a wealth-making system is "Why would they sell it to *me*?" If the system really worked, then its originators would keep the secret to themselves. Why sell the system to others for $79.95? The answer: their wealth-creating system is designed to make *them* wealthy, not us. That's the plain *what is.*
- Super high-yield investments exist, and we can find them. One of the most persistent moneymaking fantasies is that if we look hard enough, we can find some

> high-yield, low-risk scheme that will turn a small investment into a pile of cash. Stock trading is a common version of this illusion, but other fantasies are investing a few thousand in a start-up company that goes intergalactic and exploiting currencies and other vehicles.

The bottom line with any moneymaking idea is that if it seems too good to be true, it is. When we wipe the dust from the mirror, it's plain to see that there is no incentive for anyone to share their wealth-making secrets unless they're going to make money *on* us.

The Boring, Plain Vanilla Approach

I have a close friend whose approach to financial health could serve as a model for most of us. If everyone did what he does, they'd have plenty of money in retirement. Spoiler alert: what he does is boring and unromantic.

He works at a decent-paying job; nothing extraordinary. Every paycheck, he puts the maximum allowable into his 401K, like he's been doing the last fifteen years. He invests in a plain vanilla portfolio that tracks the global equity market, and he keeps a toe in a portfolio that tracks the bond market. He doesn't move his money around, except to rebalance his portfolio every year. He drives a solid nonluxury car, and his family goes on vacations. They don't lack anything important, but they don't buy stuff they don't need.

When he retires, my friend will be set for life. Like I said: boring.

But beautiful. He doesn't worry about whether the market is hot or cold. His mind is not hooked by it. He follows his routine steps and forgets about it. By contrast, many people can't stop working their money. They're on the phone with their broker every few weeks, or every few days, anguishing over whether to make this trade or that trade.

As I see it, the quicker we seek a payoff, the lower the probability of success. But if we slow way, way down, we can and will make a profit. We may not get rich quick, but we *can* get rich slowly. All that's required is to be disciplined, mindful, and nonreactive. Never too excited, never too depressed. The middle path.

Mindfulness is a crucial quality for financial success. It allows us to stick to the big plan and ride out the day-to-day turbulence without panicking. Meditating for fifteen minutes a day, I promise, will do more to build a portfolio than attending trading seminars. Meditation empowers us to just *be* with whatever discomfort arises without feeling the need to push buttons or move game pieces around. Slow and steady wins the race. Corny but bankable.

Down to Business

It's not just in our investments that we look to make a killing. Many of us look to our careers for fast wealth, too. There's nothing wrong with wanting to earn good money, of course, but when the *primary* motivation for working is monetary, we miss the point. Focusing on the reward instead of the service we provide mixes up the means and the ends. It's a bit like living to eat instead of eating to live. Food is a wonderful and enriching part of life, but if life becomes all about food, it turns into a sickness. Money is similar. It can be rewarding and delicious, but if it becomes an end in itself, that's also a kind of sickness. Money should be the food that fuels us to keep doing what we are here on Earth to do.

Nowadays, the attitude many have toward work is to find something they can do for the shortest possible time and get paid a lump sum so they don't have to do it anymore. I often see this with young entrepreneurs starting their first business. They're looking for an exit plan, not a satisfying career. Their whole goal is to build a business as quickly as possible and then sell it, rather than figuring out how to build a thriving, long-term enterprise that creates an income stream for their family and provides value for the world.

I believe a value-based, customer-centric approach is more personally and financially rewarding than a big-payoff approach. Serving customers in a caring, attentive manner pays much more reliable dividends in the long run. It also makes our day-to-day work meaningful and engaging. In fact, if I were asked the secret to starting a successful business, I'd say it's finding a way to use one's passions in a way that serves others. Everything else will take care of itself.

My own experience in business echoes this theme. In my first seven years in the financial industry, I had one great year and six not-so-great ones. I blew myself up more than once chasing the lure of the big deal. Finally, in 2001, I started again completely from scratch. This time I committed myself to being client-centered, rather than transaction-centered. As a result, my firm grew faster than I could ever have imagined. I have almost doubled my business goals and have exceeded every metric I set for my own success. Just by taking care of people, one client at a time. No desperation, no goal anxiety, just a present-moment intention to serve.

Tilting at Windfalls

Perhaps the craziest aspect of the Get Rich Quick illusion is that huge financial windfalls are even desirable to begin with. There is plenty of anecdotal evidence to suggest that they are not. For example, it is well known that many lottery winners end up broke, miserable, in legal trouble, or divorced within a few years of winning. Many young people who rocket to fame and fortune end up self-destructing, and we've all heard stories about the children of the über-wealthy falling into bad company and worse habits. That is largely because they acquire their wealth without the values and lessons hard work teaches.

Slow earners have respect for their money because they know what it took to earn it. Read the biographies of business greats like the Carnegies and the Vanderbilts. It took them *decades* to build their fortunes. In the process they learned values like persistence, service-mindedness, self-belief, humility, courage, and discipline. Living according to these values is what leads to happiness. Not money.

When we concentrate on using our gifts at the highest possible level and serving others, we reap happiness even if we don't find ourselves rolling in dough.

There simply is no known reliable *and* fast way to wealth. If there were, everyone would do it, and then it wouldn't work anymore.

There is a reliable, *slow* way to wealth. That is by creating value for others in our own unique way, and by investing in a portfolio designed to capture the long-term growth of our country's — and the world's — top companies. Why worry about speed? If getting rich is part of our destination, we don't have to get there quickly. Life is long. Take your time and enjoy the ride.

Mindful Money Practice

Once we set aside the Get Rich Quick illusion, how can we start to work mindfully right now toward achieving our financial goals over the long haul?

Let's revisit the "Setting an Itinerary" exercise in chapter 3. Turn to the page where you wrote down the three lists in that exercise. Now divide a new page into two columns; label one column "Here" and the other "Present." In the first column, take another pass at describing your "Here" from the "Itinerary" exercise; feel free to add, subtract, or clarify anything from your previous list. Now, turn to the "Present" column. For each item under "Here," identify at least one simple, concrete action you can take to improve that thing in the present moment. Then, tear this page out of your notebook, write "TO DO" across the top, and put this list in a prominent place, such as on your desk or tacked to your refrigerator, where you'll see it at least once a day. Set the intention to implement each and every action in your "Present" column over the coming twelve months. Don't rush to accomplish all of them at once. Take your time turning these actions into a daily practice.

CHAPTER 6

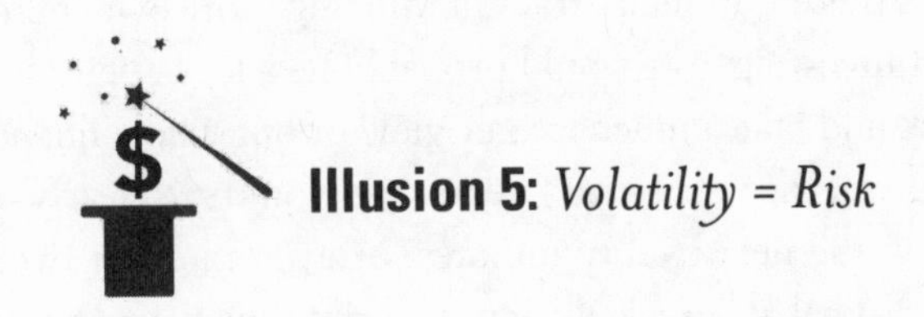

Illusion 5: *Volatility = Risk*

> Investing should be more like watching paint dry or watching grass grow. If you want excitement, take $800 and go to Las Vegas.
>
> — Paul Samuelson

This story or koan, attributed to seventh-century Buddhist monk Hui-Neng, may be the most famous Zen parable of all time:

Two monks are standing outside a monastery on a breezy day. One points to a flag dancing overhead and says to the other, "Look at how that flag is moving!"

The other monk replies, "It is not the flag that is moving. It is the wind."

"No, it is the flag," argues the first.

"The wind!" insists the second. Back and forth they argue.

A Zen master happens by and hears the bickering. The monks ask him to settle the debate. One asks, "Master, which is really moving, the flag or the wind?"

The master sighs and looks up at the unchanging blue sky. "Neither," he replies. "It is only your *minds* moving." Smiling, the master walks on.

The human mind loves to create conflict, worry, and anxiety. It likes to artificially divide the world into separate parts and pit those parts against one another. Will A or B win? Which is right, C or D? Instead of looking at the whole, the mind pays attention to the little pieces, drawn to the drama of whatever piece appears to be winning or losing today. The mind assigns great importance to these small wins and losses, becoming emotionally invested in the outcome and causing endless anguish.

Nowhere is this emotionally fraught thinking more evident than in the world of investing. We would probably be a lot happier if we could step back and take a much longer view of our whole financial picture — say, over the next twenty years. We would see clearly that what happens in the next twenty minutes, or even the next twenty days, is not as critical as it feels during the brief time we're panicking over some perceived financial disaster. Inevitably, we focus on the minuscule individual pieces that torture our brains and nervous systems, but what feels like a huge tidal wave right now might not even appear as a ripple two decades out. The whole appears just fine when seen from a distance.

Like life itself, our investment strategies may be most effective when we walk away from the microscope and take a less-is-more approach. There is a true Zen aspect to long-term investing. When we are doing our best *work*, we are often doing the least. In fact, the closer we come to doing almost nothing at all, the more that is accomplished *for* us, and the better we do as investors. By keeping our hands and minds off the moving parts and letting the whole do its marvelous thing, we empower whole economies to go to work on our behalf.

In order to surrender to this flow, we have to tackle a few more illusions. The next three chapters build upon one another like bricks. The first illusion at the bottom of the pile is this: stock market volatility equals risk.

Crashing and Burning

One common fear is that we can lose our money if we "risk" it in the stock market. This fear can stem from a bad investment experience.

Perhaps our parents, or their parents, lived through the Great Depression. Or perhaps our portfolio took a huge hit when the dot-com bubble burst in 2000, or when the world economy seemingly imploded in 2008. In these moments, people can decide to get the hell out of the stock market and stay out.

It's true that there is genuine risk in the stock market. People *can* lose money, especially when they panic. Yet how we think about and act with our investments can make a big difference in our actual level of risk, and the generalized fear that the market will crash and burn and take all our money with it is based on a deep misunderstanding or false belief. This fear misinterprets the normal ups and downs of the market as a clear and present danger to our financial safety and can cause us to act against our own best interests.

Risk is a fundamental *what is* in all of life. There is risk inherent in driving, eating red meat, swimming, crossing the street, and getting out of bed in the morning. We take risks every day. Mood swings are the simple *what is* of the stock market, ones we should accept, rather than regarding them as life-threatening experiences to be avoided at all costs.

Although the ups and downs in the market are often referred to as *risk*, the proper term for these zigs and zags is *volatility*. And volatility is nothing more than a natural pattern of growth.

Take the weather. Each spring, it grows warmer, but this doesn't happen in a smooth upward slope. Rather, it's 50 degrees one day, 42 the next, 55 the following day. We climb toward spring, and then summer, through peaks and valleys. A lifelong marriage weathers both better and worse to make it to the finish line. A winning baseball season always includes a few losing streaks. We seem to accept this jagged trajectory in most areas of life, but when it happens in the stock market, we panic.

In my favorite financial dictionary, Investopedia.com, *volatility* is defined as "a statistical measure of the dispersion of returns for a given security or market index."

Notice the absence of the word *risk* in that definition.

Where *does* the concept of risk enter the picture? Well, if a single company's stock price is highly volatile, with returns that shoot up and down unpredictably, we'd be right to consider that a risky investment. This company may close its doors due to poor management or struggle with heightened competition, putting their investors at genuine risk of losing most or all their money. In this example, risk *is* very closely tied to volatility.

On the other hand, when we own stock in a large *set* of companies, the overall risk generated by any one of those securities is greatly reduced. We've spread our delicate nest eggs into several baskets. Even if one or two of the baskets go south, it's unlikely that all the other baskets will as well.

This is why, as interesting as it can be to follow the stock price of the Apples and Amazons of the world, I am not a fan of investing in individual companies. I think it makes a lot more sense to invest in an exchange-traded fund or mutual fund stock portfolio designed to either participate in the whole global economy or to track a broad index. And by broad, I mean a lot broader than the ever-popular S&P 500. Since it is the inherent nature of companies and economies to rise and fall, diversification can help us decrease our risk.

Those who are too afraid to commit their hard-earned dollars to any investment campaign usually commit a logical error that goes something like this:

1. Volatility equals risk.
2. The stock market is volatile.
3. Therefore, investing in the stock market is risky.

The fallacy? Investing in the stock market has yet to prove all that risky over the long term. Yes, there has always been and always will be volatility in the *short term*, but volatility is not the same as risk in the long term. When we zoom out and look at that big picture, the history of the whole stock market has been one of slow, quiet expansion over time, much like our expanding universe.

Of course, it's rarely wise to have all of our money invested at any given time. We often have certain immediate-term goals that could be greatly impacted by market volatility. When that's the case, I suggest putting the money for those immediate goals in an old-fashioned savings account. Retirement funds we won't begin using for thirty years can ride out a lot more volatility than the down payment on the house we hope to buy next year.

A Better Definition of Risk

If we accept the premise that it's a good idea to invest in the whole stock market basket, rather than in just a few cherry-picked companies, risk takes on an entirely different meaning.

I am convinced that true risk is actually a product of our own behavior as investors rather than the behavior of the markets. A better definition of risk might be this:

Risk = Volatility + Surprise + Reaction

Behavioral risk plays out via two standard scenarios:

1. We see an unexpected *downward* spike in the stock market, we are surprised by it, and we panic. We sell when we should hold or buy.
2. We see an unexpected *upward* spike in the stock market, we are surprised by it, and we get excited and greedy. We buy when we should hold or sell.

We react in the short term when patient belief in the long-term prospect of growth is what's really needed. A rock-solid belief that the economy as a whole will continue to grow in due course allows us to have faith in our future and relax as we continue to follow our investment program *in the present*. In my view, it is not risky to "bet" on the world's economies, especially those as robust and innovative as ours. In fact, this is the single investment thesis that seems most prudent to me.

Reducing Risk

If much of our investment risk is created by our own reactions to sudden changes in the markets, then the solution for dealing with risk is built into the definition. That is: *expect* volatility, don't be surprised by it, and as Douglas Adams advised in *The Hitchhiker's Guide to the Galaxy*, DON'T PANIC.

Volatility is a nonnegotiable. It just happens. When we group a thousand companies together, each with varying amounts of individual volatility, and we throw in variables like the emergence of new technologies, surpluses and shortages of global resources, global weather and climate factors, the behavior of investors, political instability, international conflicts, new scientific discoveries, and unpredictable world events, it is inevitable that the market will react with ups and downs. It is also a given that volatility will increase at certain times. Since World War II, there have been thirteen separate periods when the market dipped by an average of 30 percent. On average, these "events" happen every five or six years. Sometimes events surprise us. We can't predict or control them. All we can control is our response.

Change is the only constant. *Know* that volatility happens. We need to expect it and accept it as normal. We must resist panic when we see stock prices and our account balances receding. Once fear kicks in, the human brain is at its worst.

Fear Shuts Down the Brain

We've all heard of the fight-or-flight response. When the brain perceives a threat, it reverts to primitive responses. Sensory input bypasses the normal thought pathways that lead through the prefrontal cortex, where higher-level thinking takes place. The input instead shoots straight to the limbic system, or amygdala. This is the part of the brain that processes emotion. In the limbic system, decision making becomes very fast, black-and-white, and emotion driven. The panicked brain does whatever it thinks it needs to do to remove the perceived threat as quickly and efficiently as possible. It doesn't care about the big picture or the long term; it just wants to feel safe again.

If we suddenly see the monetary value of our stock investment portfolio shrinking overnight, and we do not understand what is happening, we're apt to forget Douglas Adams's warning and to panic. This money, after all, represents our safety and security. When our ability to reason and think logically is compromised, we're vulnerable to making fearful (flight) or aggressive (fight) decisions. These might include dumping a long-term investment when we see its price plummeting or taking an ill-advised gamble on a hot stock for fear of missing out on an opportunity.

As Daniel Kahneman points out in his excellent book *Thinking, Fast and Slow*, our instinctive brains are much more motivated to avoid loss than to pursue gain. That's why the limbic system should never be our portfolio manager. We can avoid this pitfall by determining our reaction to volatility long before it hits. A big part of that discipline is training ourselves to recognize that each instance of volatility will undoubtedly seem different than the last time. And a lot more scary.

Whenever our stocks go down, we can channel our response to the prefrontal cortex by asking ourselves questions like "Is this a pattern I have seen before?" and "When I was making my financial plan, how did I say I would behave when the market took a dip?" Instead of choosing panic, we can choose to take a deep breath and then stick to our plan. Mindfulness — not reactivity — is generally the best approach in most situations. Not just financial ones.

Loss and Gain Only Occur When We Take Action

Dwindling numbers can sure look frightening in black and white. But when looking at a "loss" we've suffered as a result of a stock market dip, it's important to understand that a paper loss is not the same as an *actual* loss. Yes, today's selling price of our portfolio has dropped, but that only affects us *if* we sell today. Actual losses occur only if and when we take action. If we patiently hold on to our investments and allow the market to rise again, no actual loss takes place. In fact, odds are good that an eventual *gain* will take place. If we're brave and smart enough to *buy* stocks when the market is low, rather than sell due to fear, our potential for gain will be even higher.

When faced with market turmoil, in the famous words of meditation teachers worldwide: Don't just do something. Sit there. Like Warren Buffett.

On October 19, 1987, the infamous Black Monday, the Dow plummeted 508 points. Buffett's Berkshire Hathaway investments lost an astonishing $347 billion *on paper*. Did Buffett jump out a window? No, because he knew that he had not actually lost anything. If he had panicked and *sold* his shares at fire-sale prices, he would have lost in historic style. But Buffett was not surprised by the crash, and he didn't react. He kept faith with his belief that what goes down must come up. And it did.

I repeat: The biggest risk is not what happens in the market as a result of natural volatility. The biggest risk is a function of our own behavior. Are we taking the right actions, or nonactions, in response to market stimulus? That's what makes a loss or gain final.

Excitement can be just as dangerous as panic. If we see a particular investment or market sector shooting up in price, many of us are tempted to jump on the bandwagon and buy it, with sometimes disastrous results.

When the housing market was going crazy in 2006, for example, everyone bought real estate. The same thing happened during the dot-com bubble. In the late nineties, all of the money fled traditional value-based companies and chased sexy, high-tech stocks. Historically solid companies like GM and Chicago Bridge & Iron (CB&I), which were selling at bargain-basement prices, were all but deserted by investors. A dust-free mind could have seen that a bubble burst was coming, but everyone convinced themselves that high-tech prices would keep going up indefinitely. Of course, the bubble eventually burst in spectacular fashion. That's when all the money went scurrying back to companies that were producing real value, not theoretical business ideas and gimmicks.

Our job is to keep our eye on the whole picture and not worry about the rapidly moving parts. The simple truth is we can't afford *not* to accept today's volatility if we want tomorrow's opportunity.

Mindful Money Practice

The illusion that volatility equals risk causes people to be either too aggressive or too timid with their money in the moment, so they lose out on the opportunity to slowly and patiently grow their wealth over the long haul. Take a few minutes to consider how your mind and emotions move when you see the stock market and your account balances rise and fall.

Divide a fresh page in your notebook into three columns, and title these "Events," "Feelings," and "Reactions." In the "Events" column, list recent economic, political, or world events that caused volatility in the stock markets *and* triggered an emotional response in you. Some recent examples include Brexit (or the United Kingdom's 2016 vote to leave the European Union), the Great Recession, the 2015 terrorist attacks on Paris, and so on. In the "Feelings" column, describe how each of those events made you feel about your financial (and human) condition. Nervous? Frightened? Excited? Feelings are complicated, so use more than one word to capture your emotional response. In the "Reactions" column, list what actions you took (or didn't take) in response to market volatility. A few examples might be "Stopped contributing to my 401K," "Sold every international investment I owned," or "Checked my account balances obsessively." Hopefully, none of the above.

Looking forward, make a conscious decision to "just sit there," rather than react, the next time the market dishes out more volatility than you can handle. Decide in the relative calm of today how you are going to react when turbulence hits tomorrow. Write a behavioral prescription for yourself in your notebook, and then follow those "doctor's orders" religiously. Some helpful prescriptions include: turn the computer off, put walking shoes on, stop checking account balances daily, and breathe!

CHAPTER 7

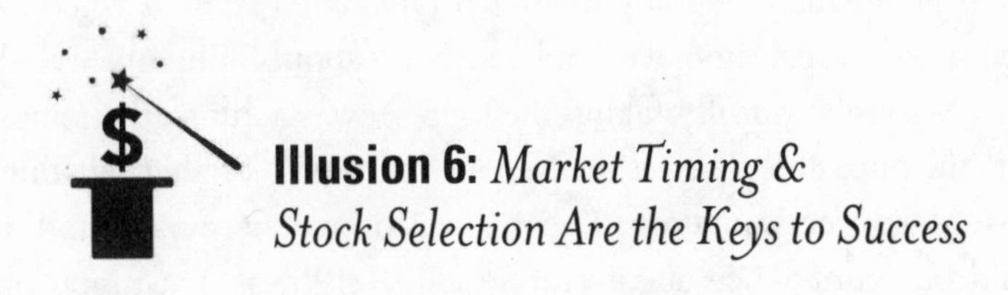

Illusion 6: *Market Timing & Stock Selection Are the Keys to Success*

> Don't look for the needle in the haystack, just buy the haystack!
>
> — John Bogle

Many people think they can't avoid risk, but they also think they can beat risk by using the right tactics. This leads to another big illusion. Namely, that market timing and stock selection are the most critical factors in investing. We mistakenly believe the goal is to beat the market and that there are two ways to do that:

1. Pick the right investments (selection).
2. Buy and sell those investments at the right time (timing).

Neither strategy works with even a modicum of reliability. Instead of worrying about timing and selection, we should calmly and consistently invest in the long-term growth of the whole market.

This constant emphasis on gains and losses encourages anxiety and short-term thinking. People are making money *right now*, and we want in. We also want to outperform our neighbor, and the only way we think we can pull that off is to make better choices *and* time them better.

However, just like coping with market volatility, patience and nonaction make the smartest financial approach, and the side benefit is that this creates peace of mind. This is the key to the Taoist concept of *wu wei*, or intentional nonaction. Doing without doing. A hands-off, patient, and nonreactive approach to investing is much easier on us mentally, emotionally, *and* spiritually. While everyone else is panicking, watching the ticker tape, and deciding whether to buy or sell in real time, we can happily go about living our lives because we are mindfully taking the long view. Each failed attempt to time the market and select the best stock leads to further self-doubt, anxiety, and recrimination. The rewards of patient nonaction slowly build our confidence and foster serenity, stillness, trust, and optimism, which are the key ingredients of happiness.

Gaming the Market Is a Loser's Bet

Despite what they say on the airwaves, research strongly indicates that timing and selection don't work. One thing, and one thing only, makes a *major* difference in our success as investors. That one thing is the answer to this simple question: Are we in the market or not?

Do we have the faith, patience, and discipline to keep our money in the stock market? Yes or no? According to research and theories developed in the 1950s and 1960s by Harry Markowitz and William Sharpe — who, along with Merton Miller, won the 1990 Nobel Memorial Prize in Economic Sciences — the lion's share of long-term returns can be attributed to the decision to invest and stay invested, rather than to any particular stock we've selected. There will always be folks who were lucky enough (yes, *lucky*) to stumble upon a stock like Google before it became big, but most of us don't.

Here's why. The big problem if we try to *game* the market, jumping in and out as we attempt to stay ahead of that timing and selection curve is this: our brains. The human brain has a notorious knack for impulsively doing the wrong thing at the wrong time. As discussed in chapter 6, this is often due to our instinctive reactions to fear. Yet many people harbor the illusion that successful investing is a highly active, anxiety-prone, adrenaline-driven process of buying and selling stocks like crazy, punctuated by sleepless nights spent staring at the ticker tape. It isn't.

The best investment strategy is patience, since real money growth proceeds from holding a steady course despite whatever volatility occurs. Over time, the gains will slowly win out. If growth is our goal, we must accept that *whatever* we're invested in will most certainly lose money at some point. This mindful, measured approach does not make for good movie plots, and it doesn't sell hot investment strategies, but if we're more interested in building wealth than creating drama, it's the best ticket in town.

Many folks don't get this, but the one thing we should absolutely *never* do is sell the losers and buy more of the winners. This is a sure recipe for failure. In fact, if we do anything when market volatility strikes, the only correct play should be the exact opposite: buy the losers and sell the winners. We can accomplish this easily through an annual rebalancing of our portfolios, which is nothing more complicated than selling a bit of the current winners to buy more of the current losers.

Timing the Market Is a Loser's Bet, Too

The idea that we can somehow have the savvy to make great timing decisions about the market is pure illusion. Timing is the belief that we can get a better price on a security than the market is currently offering *if* we can identify the "right" time to get in or out of that particular investment. For example, after we buy Apple when it dips to an all-time low, we romantically believe we have the superior knowledge, research charts, or pure investment acumen to sell it on the day it hits the highest price ever. This is impossible *even in principle*.

Eugene Fama won the Nobel Prize in Economics in 2013 for his work on this topic. In his oft-cited paper, "Efficient Capital Markets: A Review of Theory and Empirical Work," Fama introduced the so-called "informational efficiency" of the market. What that means, in simple terms, is that virtually all stock market participants have access to the same currently available information that could affect the potential price of a stock at any given time. There is nothing you or I can know that the millions of other investors in the market haven't accounted for.

Nothing remains hidden, and there is no place outside the collective minds in the market where secret information resides. We must stop driving ourselves crazy searching for an information edge and humbly accept the limits of our knowledge. Even if it were *theoretically* possible to consistently beat the market with timing, we'd have to be God to do it. Literally.

Why Selection Is More Luck Than Skill

Everyone dreams of getting in on the ground floor with the next Microsoft or Nokia. Who doesn't fantasize about buying a stock for 20¢ a share that ends up trading for $750? As with timing, successfully selecting the next great stock is an unlikely gambit. All available information about any publicly traded company has been researched inside out and backward by many, many sharp people who do nothing but analyze stocks from morning till night. Even if our neighbor told us some inside information about a great *new* company about to go public, we would not legally be allowed to use it. There are strict laws against insider trading.

Of course, it's quite possible that we could have the foresight or luck to make a great stock pick. Many people do. But the likelihood of our doing this *consistently over time*, without picking more duds than winners, is remote. Over time, the odds are overwhelmingly against us if we're relying on stock selection as the key to our investment success. Sure, we may pull the lever and hit triple cherries now and then, reveling in that rush of excitement. But the house always wins eventually.

Some folks who are wise enough to recognize the limitations of their own stock-picking skill will commit yet another form of selection: choosing the "best" *money manager* or *money system* for investing their dollars. When we climb aboard the bandwagon, we're gambling that the manager's luck today will continue into the future. Odds are just as high, though, that the person's luck will inevitably run out, if it hasn't already, but that's another thing we can't know until it's too late.

Mindful Money Practice

Take a look at your current investment approach. Keeping in mind that market timing and stock selection are not successful long-term investment strategies, ask yourself: What am I *doing* to manage my investment portfolios that is counterproductive to my present happiness and long-term goals? Obsessively researching stocks? Keeping my cash on the sidelines until the timing is right? Losing sleep at night when the market takes a dip? Relying on the opinion of someone who has never met me to direct my investment decisions?

On a fresh page in your notebook, list *everything* you've done (or are still doing) in your investment accounts to game the market, time your purchases, or pick the best stocks. Here are a few examples to get you started: Did you sell all your investments and stay in cash during the dot-com bust? Have you waited to buy or sell a particular stock until after an election? Do you subscribe to an online stock-picking newsletter?

Once you've finished your list, at the top of this page, write "Not Do List." These behaviors are based on self-defeating illusions. Let them go and embrace the following discipline instead: start adding the same amount of money to an investment account every single month, and invest that money in a broadly diversified portfolio of exchange-traded funds or low-cost mutual funds. Sometimes you'll buy a little higher. Other times you'll buy a little lower. Research indicates you'll come out ahead in the long run. This discipline is called dollar-cost averaging, and we'll explore it further in chapter 24. It is one of the most direct routes to long-term financial success. Timing and selection are just detours.

CHAPTER 8

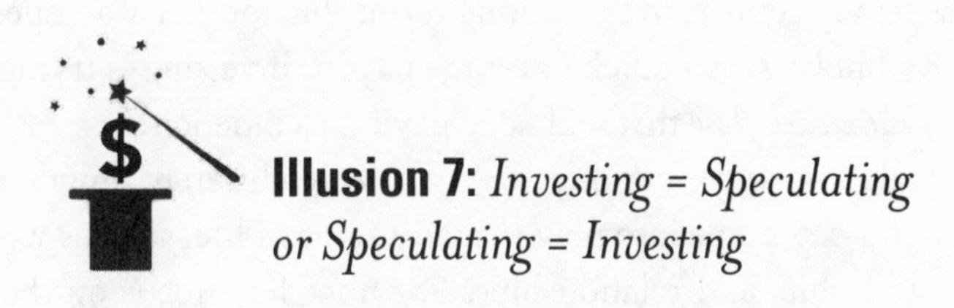

Illusion 7: *Investing = Speculating or Speculating = Investing*

Patience is bitter, but its fruit is sweet.

— Jean-Jacques Rousseau

Many people view investing as a sophisticated form of gambling in which the croupiers wear three-piece suits and use fancy terms like "market cap" and "alpha." They're convinced that buying stocks is the same as placing a bet at a blackjack table, a bet that may or may not pay off depending on what cards you draw. In other words, they're under the illusion that *speculating* and *investing* are the same thing. This illusion manifests itself in two distinct ways, leading to two different forms of dysfunctional investor behavior:

1. Speculating is investing. This person constantly plays the market, hopping from transaction to transaction and stock to stock, mistakenly believing that this is investing. For reasons far beyond the scope of this book, I think this may be a peculiarly *male* tendency.
2. Investing is speculating. This person steers clear of the stock market and wrongly views all investing as a risky act of speculation in which you will inevitably lose your shirt.

Before we explore this pair of illusions, let's clarify our terms. *Speculating* means buying something (stock, real estate, a tulip bulb, and so on) in the hope that the price will go up, preferably quickly, so that the something can be sold again for a profit. *Investing* means putting money, energy, and attention into something (stock, real estate, and so on) with the goal of keeping that something and cultivating steady returns over the long term. Put another way, speculating is gambling on a quick one-time payoff; investing is trying to build a *future cash flow* that will keep paying us indefinitely.

Speculating and investing are two very different mind-sets. These mind-sets come into play in many areas of life, such as work, home ownership, and relationships. For now, let's focus on the *financial* realm and explore the difference between speculating with our money and investing our money. Confusion about the two causes plenty of problems.

Speculating Is Not Investing

Speculating, or "playing the market," is an aggressive, short-term, goal-oriented pursuit. The idea is to buy something at a relatively low price and sell it at a relatively high one. Price is the only concern. Get in. Get out. Make a profit.

Speculators seek a big bang for their buck. In the midst of the hunt for the next killer deal, excitement can cloud their judgment. This often causes them to chase after hot stocks, even when doing so defies common sense.

For a good example, let's consider the dot-com debacle of the late nineties. During those days, greed and what Alan Greenspan called "irrational exuberance" led everyone to pour money into any and all internet stocks. Even theoretical companies that had never produced a product or made a penny of profit were wildly overvalued. Believing in the inflated value of their dot-com stock portfolios, a lot of people overextended themselves financially. The "paper profits" on their internet stocks made them feel rich, but they had little cash in the bank, so they began borrowing money to take lavish vacations and to buy new cars and vacation homes they couldn't really afford. They made plans to retire at fifty.

Then the whole thing imploded. The market realized how overvalued dot-com stocks were, speculators sold them in a panic, companies went bankrupt, and all those "paper profits" turned into real losses. Those real losses were compounded by all the debt people could no longer manage. Some folks lost homes and cars. More than a few dot-com workers lost their jobs and had to move back in with Mom and Dad. One couple I know had to come out of their early retirement in Mexico to return to work at age sixty. Ouch!

The dot-com collapse also illustrates another tactical blunder that a speculator mind-set encourages. When people see prices dropping in a given company, sector, or index, panic ensues and they bail out. Hoping to cut their losses, they are the first to jump on the sell bandwagon, completely forgetting that the famous axiom is to buy *low* and sell *high* — not the other way around. Not every dot-com stock was a dud, and there were plenty of *investors* with catcher's mitts waiting to catch deals on the solid internet companies *speculators* were frantically pitching out the window. An unfortunate consequence of the dot-com bust is that some of those speculators now dismiss investing altogether because they view the markets, rather than their own behavior, as the problem.

Once we truly understand the difference between speculating and investing, we can appreciate the essential role patience plays. With speculating, we quickly know whether or not our big play is going to work. *Investing* requires time and stamina. Value reveals itself on a longer schedule. We have to wait for it.

As mindful investors, we need to constantly return our attention to value, rather than letting our focus drift to price.

Accumulation, Not Speculation

Because speculators focus on price, they're forever scrambling to figure out which stock will go up the fastest. But as I've said, the market already knows more than any individual can ever hope to, so speculators are reduced to betting like sports gamblers. They furtively look for any informational edge that might help them predict the future.

The investor doesn't care about short-term fluctuations in price. What the investor buys is future cash flow. Value. The investor wants to acquire something that's going to *keep* paying, not just provide a one-time bump. *Accumulation* is much more compelling to an investor than making a quick killing.

Why does Warren Buffett own so much stock in Coca-Cola? It's not because he thinks he can turn around and sell his Coke stock next month for 20 percent more than he paid for it. The reason Buffett holds Coke is that he likes what the company does — it makes a product that people love, and it puts the product in as many places as possible — and he likes its business plan and management team. He sees it as a company that will continue to make money and pay dividends well into the foreseeable future. When asked, Buffett says his favorite holding time for a stock is "forever." He is focused on accumulation opportunities. Future growth. Not just price.

In the world of investing, the Buffett school says, "Buy and hold. Buy and hold." There is another school that says, "Don't buy and hold. Look for good deals and trade." However, *my* favorite school says, "Buy and buy and buy and buy. Then rebalance." It's easier to implement. And it works.

In other words, invest in your diversified portfolio every month, and rebalance that portfolio once a year. That is the secret to successful accumulation versus speculation.

Not All Investors Can Be Warren Buffett

Investing is a mind-set. That doesn't mean that all investors are the same. If, as I suggest, investing in diversified vehicles that capture the growth of the whole world economy is the way to go, then why do great investors like Warren Buffett acquire stock in individual companies? You could do the same, of course, but Buffett has a lot more money and expertise than most of us do. He can afford to buy entire companies — not just their stock — and he does a great deal of research before he buys. He and his partner eat, sleep, and breathe investing.

We should all take Buffett's lead and spend most of our time doing what *we* love. For most of us, that won't be analyzing stocks. It's not our passion. Instead, we should do what makes us happy and let our money handle itself by investing in a balanced, diversified portfolio designed to capture the long-term growth of whole markets. Then we need to leave those investments alone. Remember the concept of *wu wei*? For most people, especially those whose primary occupation isn't being an investor, actively choosing not to pursue timing and selection will likely achieve a better result than *they* would if they micromanaged their accounts.

The market may fluctuate from year to year, but there is no precedent in history where investors who've left their money in the market in a balanced portfolio for twenty years have lost money. Even through the Great Depression. According to 2014 data from the Center for Research in Security Prices at the University of Chicago's Booth School of Business, for any historical twenty-year period, annualized returns on a balanced portfolio have been somewhere between 2.8 and 15 percent. Even if you look at any historical ten-year period, annualized returns on a balanced portfolio fall along a range of −.06 (or basically flat) to 16.5 percent.

Ultimately, it's not the rate of return that determines the success of our investments. It's the money we leave in and the money we *keep putting* in. Great investors like Buffett keep *adding* to their investments, rather than playing chess with them. They add whatever they can afford to add, whether it's ten dollars a month, a hundred dollars a week, or ten thousand dollars a year. This is something that any investor can do: keep putting more money in, and let dollar-cost averaging work its slow magic.

Great investors focus on their pay-*in*, not the pay*out*, and their wealth quietly grows like a spring-fed lake. To paraphrase John F. Kennedy, "Ask not what your *investments* can do for you. Ask what you can do for your *investments*."

Why Investors Need Volatility

When we truly understand the nature of the stock market, we realize that investors actually make their money at the expense of speculators.

To understand this principle, let's circle back to volatility. Volatility is not just a phenomenon to be endured with white knuckles and an iron will. It is the very key to long-term returns. We *need* volatility in the market because that's the only way to get returns. Volatility, in fact, is the engine that drives returns.

Any investment vehicle that is stable, predictable, and guaranteed has a low rate of return — cash in a savings account, for example. The stronger the guarantee, the lower the payoff. For investors to be willing to take more risk, they need to be paid more. As a general rule, the higher the risk, the greater the potential payoff. Very safe and stable investments, such as government bonds, have a low associated risk, so their rate of return is relatively low. Shares in a brand-new company have a high associated risk because there is a good possibility that the company will not make it. Thus, the payoff is relatively high, so long as the company doesn't lose everything. As one would expect, riskier investments tend to be more volatile.

Shares in *any* single company are risky by nature. This form of risk is sometimes called *idiosyncratic* risk because it's particular to that specific company. One way to spread out our risk is to invest in many companies at once, or even in whole economies. This approach makes our risk more *systemic* than idiosyncratic. Systemic risk is generally less hazardous because whole economic systems include both relatively stable companies and relatively risky ones, at various stages of growth and maturity. Whole economies can be volatile at times, but their tendency is to grow over time to keep pace with the needs and desires of their growing populations. When we put our money into a portfolio focused on the whole global economy, we are investing in the premise that markets will continue to grow in the future. To me, based on history, that sounds like a reasonable assumption.

Speculators don't take the long view, though. When volatility occurs, their fear and greed kick in. A certain percentage of folks inevitably chase the next hot stock and/or bail out on the current cold one. Predictably, they do so at unwise times and to an unwise degree. They lose money by buying too high and selling too low.

That's where we investors are at a true advantage. Since we are smart enough not to equate volatility with risk, we *don't* act out of fear and greed. We invest every month, simply because that's what we do. While the speculators are frantically placing the wrong trades at the wrong times, we investors patiently place the *same* trades at the *same* time every month. If their dysfunctional behavior drives the markets up, we'll pay a bit more that month for each share and buy fewer shares, but the total value of our portfolio will rise as well. If their panic drives the markets down, we'll pay less that month for each share and buy more shares with our usual monthly investment, which will give our accounts a bit of extra lift when the market climbs back up again. Because we dollar-cost average money into our accounts every month and rebalance once a year, no matter what's going on in the markets, we are well positioned to benefit from the avarice and desperation of speculators. The loss of the impetuous becomes the gain of the patient.

Investors *embrace* volatility, rather than fear it, because we understand volatility is the very source of long-term returns.

The Mattress

Still afraid of volatility? Arguably the safest thing any of us can do with our money is sew it up inside a fireproof mattress. We won't lose a penny that way. But we won't gain anything, either. We can also put our dollars in a savings account or CD (certificate of deposit). Our rate of return may be minuscule, but at least our money will be more or less safe. Won't it?

Nope. Protecting money in the bank is another illusion. Thanks to inflation, the only thing such measures ensure is the guaranteed loss of buying power over time. Sometimes we think we can't afford to ride out our losses when stock market volatility hits and wait for markets to recover. The truth is that we can't afford *not* to stay on the horse. It won't cost us anything to lose a little money *on paper* from time to time, and the long-term benefits are worth some short-term discomfort. We'll explore why in the next chapter.

Mindful Money Practice

As complex humans, our approach to life, and investing, is usually multifaceted. Most of us have inside at least some of both the speculator and the investor. Hopefully, more of the latter than the former. The purpose of this exercise is to help you examine your investment style by casting it in black and white. Divide a fresh page in your notebook into two columns. Label one column "Speculator" and the other "Investor." Leave a few inches open at the bottom of the page and label it "Prescription."

Now, take a moment to reflect on your past investment behavior. In the "Speculator" column, list three to four instances where you behaved like a speculator in your investment accounts. Describe any positive and/or negative results you experienced with this approach; consider the emotional *and* financial impact speculating had on you and your portfolio. Next, in the "Investor" column, list and describe three to four instances when you behaved more like an investor. As before, describe what did and didn't work for you.

Finally, in the clear space at the bottom of the page, write down the following "prescription," which is exactly the same no matter what your investment style: "Invest more and speculate less." This prescription can be a lot harder for speculators to follow, especially if they've had some success playing the market. I know it feels counterintuitive to stop doing what's worked well at times and to take a different approach. And I know being an investor isn't the only viable path. But the research about long-term investment success and the anecdotal evidence I've gathered while watching clients blow themselves up with speculative trading strategies have convinced me that investing is the *best* path. Commit to taking a walk on the less wild side!

CHAPTER 9

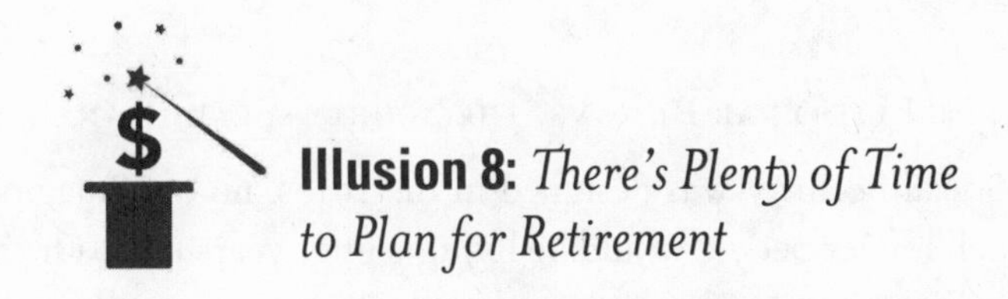

Illusion 8: *There's Plenty of Time to Plan for Retirement*

He who has begun has half done. Dare to be wise; begin!

— Horace

Retirement isn't what it once was. Fifty years ago, in the United States at least, the cultural expectation was that retirement was a time of nonstop golf, world cruises, and bingo, followed by death a few years down the road. That was our grandparents' reality. Our grandparents retired with fully funded pensions, they collected a monthly Social Security check, and most importantly, they only lived about five years after retiring. Their savings were better funded, and that money didn't have to last very long.

Today, few of us have pensions, and we will probably receive less Social Security than we expect. We may also live thirty years, or *more*, after retiring — not five. For some people, their retirement years may be nearly as long as their working careers. That's the new *what is*. Our retirement may include putting greens and plaid pants, but it's a different animal, and we need to approach it in a very different way.

Most folks know they need to save for their future, but few

understand what their actual retirement *income* needs are going to be. This is brewing perhaps the largest financial crisis in our country. We need to redefine retirement for today's realities or we will face a gigantic problem. There is a universe of difference between planning for a five-to-ten-year retirement, as previous generations did, and planning for a "third life chapter" that could be thirty-plus years long.

The Five-Year Plan vs. the Thirty-Year Plan

When Social Security was designed in the 1930s, no one imagined how much longer people would be living eighty years later. Or that we'd be living longer, but not *working* longer. Current data published by the Social Security Administration (SSA) indicates that a man who is 65 today has a life expectancy of 84.3, and a 65-year-old woman can expect to live until 86.6. The SSA data also suggests that one out of four 65-year-olds today will live past ninety. And it's a neat trick of statistics that the longer we live, the greater the odds that we'll live even longer.

At the same time, according to a 2014 Gallup report, the average retirement age in the United States is 62. With more of us living into our nineties than ever before, we need to rethink that time frame as well as our approach to retirement planning.

The old retirement recipe — getting by for five to ten years on a combination of Social Security, a job pension, and some modest savings — no longer works. Social Security is hanging in there, but company-funded pension benefits have gone the way of the VCR, and the dynamics of saving have changed radically. We need to save *much* more money for retirement than ever before, and we need to be much more investment-minded with our savings if we hope to sustain our current lifestyle.

In the past, people took a cautious approach with their retirement savings. Understandably so. The last thing they wanted to do as they neared retirement was put their savings at risk by placing their money in volatile investments. Many people left their money in the bank, which was easy to do when savings accounts were paying 4 percent interest or more and generally keeping ahead of inflation.

Further, in the past, our working years were many times longer than our retirement years, which made it easier to save enough for retirement without making huge trade-offs. For example, say someone in 1940 started working at age eighteen, retired at sixty-five, and died at seventy-three. That person would have worked for forty-seven years and spent eight years in retirement. That's nearly a 6:1 ratio of working years to retirement years. With those metrics, taking a yearly vacation and still saving enough for a decent retirement wouldn't be terribly hard.

Today, the common scenario looks a lot different. Assuming someone goes to college, he or she would start working at twenty-one and retire at that current average age of sixty-two. Using the SSA's calculator, if that person is a woman, she will likely live to age eighty-seven. That means she would work for forty-one years and spend twenty-five years in retirement, resulting in a very scary 3:2 ratio of working years to retirement years. Not a math person? Bottom line: a twenty-five-year retirement is three times as long as an eight-year retirement.

Next we have to consider inflation. Inflation has now become the *number-one factor* when planning for retirement. The cost of living keeps going up, and it is going up faster than the rates paid by CDs and savings accounts. The longer we spend in retirement, the more inflation matters.

There are two distinct time frames we need to consider when it comes to inflation. First, we need to calculate how much the cost of living will increase between now and the day we retire. Second, we need to anticipate how much the cost of living will increase between the day we retire and the day we're pushing up daisies.

Of course, it can be uncomfortable to consider when we will actually die, but because of longevity, we can no longer think of our retirement as a static endpoint to aim toward. Now, the day we retire is actually the *beginning* of a new, decades-long era — an era that will have its own inflation scale. To put it in perspective: In January 1985, the average cost of a half-gallon of ice cream was $2.28; thirty years later, in January 2015, the cost had risen to $5.09. In thirty years, ice cream more than doubled in price. If we live for thirty years after our retirement, will our postworking, retirement income be able to keep up with that rate of inflation?

If we want to keep enjoying our pie à la mode, it has to.

Currency and Money Are Not the Same Thing

One big reason people do not adequately plan for retirement is that they confuse currency with money. This can get them in a world of trouble.

The ten-dollar bill in my wallet is not money. It is *currency*. Currency is a note with a specific figure in a specific denomination. It doesn't change. In 1960, if someone stuffed two thousand ten-dollar bills in that fireproof mattress, then today that person would still have two thousand ten-dollar bills, or twenty thousand dollars. The amount of the currency would remain the same. In name, a dollar is always a dollar.

However, the *value* of those dollars would have decreased due to inflation. This is the crucial difference between currency and money. *Money* equals purchasing power, or the value in goods that our currency can buy. When we look toward retirement, *money* is what we need to think about, not currency.

The price of goods always goes up over time. We can count on it. For people in their twenties today, the products and services that now cost $20,000 a year might cost $50,000 a year by the time they retire. And the things that cost $50,000 a year on the day they *retire* might cost $125,000 or more by the time they *die*.

The only way we can protect and grow our *money* for the future is if we are willing to risk our *currency* today. That's because these days the traditionally "safe" ways of saving currency do not keep up with inflation. Given the current low-interest-rate environment, vehicles like savings accounts have become the equivalent of a fireproof mattress. They are surefire methods for *losing* money against inflation, even as they protect currency.

Real Returns vs. Nominal Returns

Among the many, many things we are not taught in school about money is the concept of real returns versus nominal returns. Real returns represent an actual increase in our purchasing power. Nominal returns represent merely an increase in the amount of currency we possess. The only way we can grow our money / purchasing power is to get *real* returns.

For example, say we decide to place our money in a vehicle that pays something close to "risk-free" rates, such as a certificate of deposit (CD) or money market fund. The risk-free rate is the investment return one might expect to receive from an investment that theoretically carries no risk of losing the original principal, although in reality no investment is truly risk-free. Not so many years ago, risk-free rates were in the neighborhood of 4.5 percent. Today, these rates are almost zero. A CD might pay 1 percent. Savings accounts pay far less than 1 percent.

The problem is that the inflation rate is usually equal to or higher than what "risk-free" investments offer. If our rate of return is less than the rate of inflation, then whatever returns we get are *nominal*, not real. Even though we may be gaining currency on paper, we are losing money in reality.

For instance, let's say we're earning 2 percent in a savings account, but the inflation rate is 3 percent. Inflation rates vary annually, and have been lower recently, but this is about average. If we place $1,000 in that savings account, in a year it will earn $20, giving us $1,020. Yet the 3 percent inflation rate means we need $1,030 to buy the same amount of goods and services as when we made our initial $1,000 bank deposit. What we gained in currency did not keep up with what we need in *money*. Our gains are nominal, not real.

In order to grow our money, not just our currency, we need to make real returns. That means keeping ahead of the inflation leviathan.

There Is No Magic Number

A lot of folks attempt to identify the "magic number" they will need to save while they're working to maintain their lifestyle during retirement. Yet the confusion of currency with money causes them to vastly underestimate the amount of capital they will need. There is no single, simple magic number we can calculate that will match our needs over time. If we rely on a single earning goal, we are likely to fool ourselves by a landslide.

For instance, say we are forty-three, and we want to figure out our retirement numbers, or the amount we need to save by the time we retire in twenty years (around age sixty-two). We might be tempted to start with the monthly amount we currently spend. Let's call that $3,500, and let's say that Social Security promises to pay us about $2,000 a month when we retire. Easy math, right? That leaves us with a gap of $1,500 per month at retirement, which means we'll need $18,000 a year in additional income during retirement (which is $1,500 times twelve months). Assuming we're one of the lucky one-fourth of Americans destined to live past age ninety, we will need an additional $18,000 a year for thirty years to bridge the gap. Multiplying $18,000 by those thirty years gives us $540,000, which is a pretty hefty sum to save over the next twenty years. But at least now we know the "magic number" we need to reach, right?

Nope. Perhaps not even close. We have drastically underestimated our retirement needs by making three errors:

1. We have not accounted for inflation over the course of our working career. The $3,500 per month we currently require to support our lifestyle will increase substantially by the time we retire. If we assume a 3 percent annual inflation rate over twenty years, our per-month expenses on day one of our retirement could be $6,321.39 or more. Nearly double!
2. We have neglected to account for inflation *during* our retirement years. If inflation remains at 3 percent annually during our retirement, our income will need to

keep growing by 3 percent every year to keep up. The $3,500 we needed to maintain our lifestyle when we made our original calculation at age forty-three would become $15,343.67 by the end of our life, which is more than four times the original amount. That's with *no* upgrade in our lifestyle for fifty years.

3. We may underestimate our longevity. Thirty years of retirement sounds like a long time, but today's mortality rates may not reflect tomorrow's. Medical advances continue to push life expectancy upward. If that trend continues, fifty years from now people will be living even longer than they are now. One estimate is that by 2050, 10 percent of US senior citizens will be over ninety. If we were to surpass that estimate and live to one hundred, it would add an additional decade of income needs and inflation we didn't account for at age forty-three!

Successful Retirement in the Face of Inflation

By presenting the immense financial challenge of retirement, I'm not trying to instill panic or discourage anyone. Still, inflation is a relentless force we must contend with every day. Inflation was not such a huge problem in our parents' and grandparents' era of relatively short retirements and relatively high interest rates on savings. It is critical now.

We can no longer think of retirement income as some fixed monthly amount. Fixed income in a rising-costs world is a recipe for failure.

To me, the first and most important solution is to accept the risk of investing as a hedge against inflation. But even this alone might not be enough. There are other options we can consider if we anticipate an income shortfall when our retirement day comes. Sometimes it works best to use some combination of all of them.

1. Reduce expenses. We can plan for a more modest lifestyle. Perhaps we give up on annual vacations and lavish

holiday spending. However, while cutting back on luxuries is doable, basic necessities will cost more, due to inflation, and we may add expenses we don't have now, such as for medical care. None of us can totally control our costs.

2. Depend on others or the government. If we don't have enough to live on during retirement, we may need to rely on family members or public assistance programs. This is rarely a choice we want to make, and it's not always wise to plan on needing outside resources, since they may not be there when we need them.
3. Retire at a later age. We can also delay retirement. I've heard countless people say, "I'll work into my seventies." If we're able to pull that off, it can help us a great deal, both financially and mentally. But we don't always get to choose our retirement age. The decision to stop working might be made *for* us, whether because of health, ageism, or other factors. Simply planning *not* to retire may not work.

Planning for our retirement is daunting. This is why, if we haven't already, we should start doing so now while we still have enough time to control our retirement destiny.

Mindful Money Practice

Take a moment right now to do some simple math. Since the average age most folks retire is sixty-two, subtract your age from sixty-two. The difference is the number of working years you have left to accumulate money for your retirement. Remember that number and bring it to the front of your mental closet whenever you are considering any major short- or long-term financial decision.

If you are already sixty-two, lucky you! You get to do another simple math problem. Subtract your age from one hundred. That is how many years you should plan on stretching your retirement assets, which you're hopefully still accumulating. Let that number inform pretty much any financial decision you make in the coming decades.

Ready for extra credit? Skip ahead to Step 5 of the appendix, "Your Financial Action Plan" (see page 262). There you will find a step-by-step gap-analysis exercise and helpful retirement income–planning tools.

SECTION TWO

Finding Your Happiness

CHAPTER 10

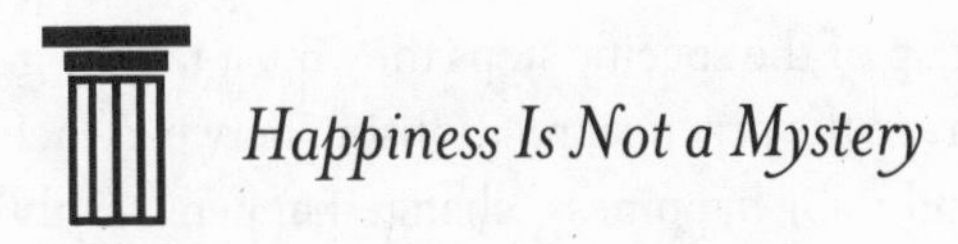

Happiness Is Not a Mystery

> A man wants to earn money in order to be happy, and his whole effort and the best of a life are devoted to the earning of that money. Happiness is forgotten; the means are taken for the end.
>
> — Albert Camus

As we move beyond our illusions about money, we see more clearly the direct connection between our personal behavior and our financial outcomes. Money touches every aspect of our lives — from how we feed and clothe ourselves to the opportunities we can afford our children — so financial outcomes have a significant impact on our long-term well-being. Making thoughtful, proactive money choices is how we foster the conditions that lead to happiness.

The first step is pledging to do a better job managing our money. Yet good intentions are rarely enough to motivate us to effect meaningful change, even when accompanied by a profound understanding of any financial failings we may have. Perhaps it is simply human nature: we often continue practicing bad habits long after we realize they are self-defeating. If I am offered a big bowl of ice cream before bed, I will almost never say no, even though I know with absolute certainty that it will keep me up at night. The lure of immediate gratification and the momentum of habit are just too powerful to make me put the spoon down.

If understanding isn't the key to action, what does motivate us to alter our behavior? Working toward personally meaningful goals. Each June, as I try to fit into last summer's swim trunks, I find it a lot easier to resist those three scoops of rocky road.

As a financial planner, I have found that my clients won't quit their financial misbehaviors until they have defined what makes them happy and how they can use money to support their happiness. To change bad habits, they need a compelling vision of a brighter future and a map of the specific steps they must take to get there. Once clients embrace the practical relationship between their money, their behavior, and their happiness, change happens. Only then do they willingly make the necessary trade-offs and create a financial plan that they can *own* and implement.

The purpose of this section of the book is to help you clarify what makes *you* happy. We'll explore what makes human beings happy in general — and I'll help you define what that means for you in particular. Then you'll be ready to apply that knowledge to the financial plan you'll create in section 3.

Symbols vs. Substance

In *The Nicomachean Ethics*, Aristotle famously declared that the chief aim of life is happiness. Happiness should also be the primary goal of financial planning.

That said, many people have even more illusions about happiness than they have about money. Chief among them is the hope that material comforts will provide inner satisfaction. This hope drives the advertising industry, which works overtime to market enticing material *symbols* of happiness: the fastest car, the biggest house, the newest gadget. These symbols are designed to appeal to our primal desire for happiness. Yet any happiness we feel when we acquire more stuff is inevitably fleeting. It can take a long time, and a lot of cash, to realize that things are just the symbols of what we really want and that substance and meaning arise from who we are and what we do, not what we have.

Most of our material desires arise out of a wish for greater happiness, but not every desire is what some Buddhist teachers call a *skillful* desire. Skillful desires are those that actually *do* bring us happiness. *Un*skillful desires are those that lead to dissatisfaction, such as the constant craving for bigger, faster, newer, more.

There are primary ingredients of happiness that are common to all human beings in all cultures, and those ingredients have little to do with owning *more* of anything. Happiness derives not from our possessions, but from small daily pleasures that don't cost much money, such as a full belly, the sun on our face, and the smile of a loved one. Skillfully pursuing these moments of bliss is a lot more rewarding than unskillfully pursuing symbols of wealth and prestige. It's also a lot more affordable.

When we do decide to plop down cold, hard cash on an object or experience we desire, we will get a much greater return on our investment if we spend that money on something that fuels our own unique idea of happiness, rather than the generic version sold in the marketplace.

For example, I have a client who is an avid bibliophile and lifelong learner. He has this great, well-worn T-shirt that reads: "When I have money, I buy books. When I have a little more money, I buy food and clothes." On the other hand, I know another guy who lives in a modest house but once spent more money on a car than I ever would because driving a Porsche gives him unadulterated joy every day — the very definition of a *skillful* desire.

If autos truly are your thing, there's nothing wrong with this. The key is figuring out your thing, considering what trade-offs you may need to make, and spending your money accordingly. But I know people who buy the newest Mercedes or BMW or Tesla because they think someone at their income level is supposed to own a nice car. They don't really care about cars, and they would be better off spending thousands less on a reliable automobile to get them from point A to point B. Then they could use the money they save on something that's a skillful desire for them. There's nothing wrong with a BMW, but we need to consider the trade-offs we're making with our tomorrow before we write the dealer that big check today.

When we splurge only on things that truly matter to us, and forgo those things that don't, there is a positive ripple effect. Of course, spending money on things that are personally meaningful makes us happier. But we also experience happiness when we show restraint, since we know we are freeing up money to fund our *future* happiness. Rather than making us feel impoverished or lacking, saving for our future fulfillment also substantially increases our happiness in the here and now.

Eight Pillars of Happiness

So what *is* happiness, anyway?

There's been an explosion of interest on the topic in recent years. In fact, a whole field of research evolved in the 1990s to explore what makes folks feel satisfied and fulfilled: positive psychology. Rather than focusing on mental illness, some psychologists are trying to solve the puzzle of human happiness. Every week, at least one new study, article, book, TED Talk, or PBS special about human happiness is released. While there isn't a perfect consensus among researchers, some common elements pop up over and over again.

Happiness appears to be closely correlated to simple factors like health, optimism, meaningful relationships, and generosity. Happiness has also been linked to the habit of mind Zen practitioners call present-moment awareness — the ability to remain rooted in whatever experience we are currently having, rather than getting caught up in worries and desires about the past and future.

Money also factors into the psychology of happiness, but only in a tangential way. When we don't have enough money to meet our daily needs for food, clothing, shelter, and a little fun, it causes more stress than enjoyment.

How much money is enough? In their oft-cited 2010 paper "High Income Improves Evaluation of Life but Not Emotional Well-Being," psychologist Daniel Kahneman and Princeton economist

Angus Deaton concluded that Americans need a household income of about seventy-five thousand dollars to enjoy a "comfortable standard" of life. People with lower incomes are measurably less happy the closer they get to the poverty line. But here's the kicker: above the seventy-five-thousand-dollar watermark, further boosts in income created little or no increase in day-to-day happiness.

Not surprisingly, when we struggle to get our basic needs met, we are unhappy. But once we feel secure and reasonably comfortable, we reach what Deaton and Kahneman describe as a "happiness plateau." Any additional income beyond that comfort zone becomes part of our psychological status quo.

Regardless of our income level, there are some essential elements that can add real and lasting happiness to our lives. I have distilled these elements down to what I call the Eight Pillars of Happiness.

You may identify seven, nine, or even more pillars of happiness, but I find myself naturally drawn to the number eight, perhaps because of the famous Eightfold Path that leads to awakening. Although some of my pillars correspond with aspects of the Buddha's teaching, I've tried to make them universal, so they don't reflect any particular faith tradition.

These are the eight elements I believe are essential to a happy life, no matter what your belief system or culture:

1. health
2. engagement
3. relationships
4. meaning
5. accountability
6. generosity
7. optimism
8. gratitude

Everyone interprets these elements in their own way, but they invite all of us to live more mindfully. How do *you* define health, generosity, and gratitude? Where do *you* find meaning? What is essential to *you*? Your financial decisions should be based on the pillars that support and sustain your unique version of happiness.

A Balancing Act

Money is not one of my Eight Pillars of Happiness, but it *can* strengthen the foundations of a happy life.

Aligning our financial actions with what makes us happy isn't easy. We often need to choose between two competing priorities: our happiness today and our happiness tomorrow.

Some choices lead to happiness in the present moment, such as a fancy dinner out to celebrate a special occasion. Other choices lead to happiness in the future, like driving an old car another year or two to save more money for retirement. Striking a balance between our *now* happiness and *later* happiness requires walking the middle path. Too much deferred happiness — all old cars and no fancy dinners — robs life of its vibrancy. But too much indulging our appetite for immediate gratification can compromise our long-term prospects for a happy and secure future. Mindful equilibrium should be the goal.

Maintaining our pillars of happiness also requires a balancing act between now and later. We must keep them front and center in the present while leaving ample room for them in the future. As we explore happiness in the following pages, look for ways to make these eight essential elements your own.

CHAPTER 11

Happiness Pillar 1: *Health*

If you haven't got your health, you haven't got anything.
— COUNT RUGEN, *The Princess Bride*

Health is so integral to our lives that many people view *good* health as the physical embodiment of happiness. When we are blessed with good health, we are enthusiastic, self-confident, and powerful. Our cells crackle with energy, light shines through our eyes, and the world is our proverbial oyster. We feel *alive*!

The critical role our health plays in happiness cannot be overstated, as anyone who has ever been leveled by the flu for a few weeks can attest. So why is health one of the first things people are willing to sacrifice when they manage the financial aspects of their lives? They will work extended hours, endure constant deadline stress, and subject themselves to long commutes that leave no time to take proper care of themselves — all so they can pay for a lifestyle they're too tired to enjoy.

Our health should be the bedrock on which we build our lives, not just forty-five minutes we spend on the elliptical machine if/when we can find the time. Eating right and getting enough sleep and exercise are important, but we also need to factor our physical and emotional well-being into the money and career decisions we make.

Where do we begin our quest for a happier, healthier life? In Buddhist philosophy, the *mind* is considered the source of both health and illness. Attaining good health is seen less as a function of treating physical symptoms and more about cultivating healthy thoughts. The principle is that healthy beliefs lead to the healthy thoughts that lead to the healthy behaviors that lead to good health. It's simple cause and effect — the very definition of karma. Nowhere is our karma more evident than in the tremendous power our minds have over our bodies. We literally *become* what we think and how we act.

Good health is both the alpha *and* omega of a happy life. It supports the other seven pillars of happiness, and it is strengthened by those pillars at the same time. The more engaged we are with who and what make us happy, the healthier we feel.

Our health also dictates how effectively we can work, which influences how much we can earn, which impacts our sense of security, which affects how happy we are. Without ample energy reserves to propel our career and life forward, we'll find ourselves operating at a deficit that drags us down financially *and* emotionally.

Reclaiming My Health

There's a huge difference between running on empty and firing on all cylinders, as I know from firsthand experience. After hitting an energy bottom about ten years ago, I launched a fitness campaign to reclaim my health. My slow but steady transformation gave me personal insight into the undeniable connection between better thinking and better health, and it taught me how better health can trigger a far-reaching chain of positive effects — many of them financial.

This isn't an inspiring tale of overcoming some major, life-threatening illness. My health merely followed the typical trajectory of a Midwestern American male. During high school I was in amazing shape. I played soccer, skied, road my bike, and rock climbed with my friends. My physical activities commanded the lion's share of my mental attention. When I got to college, I still found time for athletic endeavors, but I also had a full course load, a part-time job, and a blossoming social life. My hours on the soccer pitch dwindled, as other interests captured my attention.

Then I embarked into the working world, and I became a business owner, husband, and parent in rapid succession. I quit exercising, became overworked, and developed horrible eating habits. This happened not because these new roles *caused* my unhealthy behavior, but because *I* let other priorities push my well-being to the back burner.

In the winter of 2006, I had a fairly mundane experience that made me realize just how far I'd let myself go. My wife and I were heading to the ski slopes for the day. As we dropped off our son, Eli, at my parents' house, I discovered I'd forgotten my ski pants. My dad offered to let me borrow his, but my dad's a pretty big guy. Just to be polite, I agreed to try on his pants, thinking, "What a crazy guy! There's no way Dad's pants are going to fit me." They fit like a glove.

That was my wake-up call. Eli was two years old, and we had another baby on the way. I *had* to get fit if I wanted to keep up with two children and live long enough to meet my grandkids. My height had helped me hide the truth, but my dad's ski pants laid it bare. I was no longer healthy, and it wasn't just a weight issue. I'd lost the flexibility, strength, balance, and energy that were vital to my sense of self.

I began to make my health a priority. Not *the* priority, but *a* priority. I made a conscious decision to exercise every morning, and I followed through on that commitment to myself. Soon everything shifted. I felt better physically and mentally, which encouraged me to exercise more and eat less. The pounds started melting away, and I felt even *better*, which made my 5 AM workouts a little easier every day.

The changes in my life wrought by this small shift in focus have been remarkable. Reclaiming my health made me feel more attractive, which has done wonders for my relationship with my wife. My increased self-esteem makes me project a more confident image, giving my business a boost and feeding my confidence even more. As my business continues to grow, I am more financially secure, so I can make the career choices *I* want to make, not ones I feel pressured to make. I now have more freedom to pursue my passions, which have included writing this book.

Most importantly, my improved physical and mental fitness lets me work more efficiently, freeing up time to spend with my family. Since I have the stamina to run around with my kids, we can enjoy a wide range of indoor and outdoor activities together, opening up new venues of intellectual curiosity and adventure for all of us, which makes me tremendously happy. The happier I am, the greater my capacity to be present for my friends, colleagues, and wife, which makes them happier in turn.

One simple, conscious decision a decade ago — making my health a priority — continues to lead my personal life and career to places I never imagined.

First Instead of Last

My experience is far from unique. The life-altering properties of making healthier choices are widely known, as evidenced by the hundreds of articles and books published on the subject every year. In addition to the proven physical benefits that I registered — like enhanced appearance, higher energy levels, and improved resistance to illness — there are many other well-documented mental and emotional payoffs:

- improved mood
- higher self-esteem
- enhanced brain function
- reduced mental fatigue
- diminished anxiety

Studies have even linked exercise to higher salaries. According to Vasilios D. Kosteas of Cleveland State University, in his 2012 paper "The Effect of Exercise on Earnings: Evidence from the NLSY," workers who exercise at least three hours a week earn an average of 9 percent more than workers who don't. An economist might say that the labor market values a healthy employee more than an unhealthy one.

We should value our health, too. When we ignore our health or put it last on our priority list, the cause-and-effect cycle becomes a downward spiral. We run out of juice sooner, making us less effective, so we're forced to push through longer and harder workdays. As a result, it becomes nearly impossible to find those three hours a week to exercise, which translates into less *natural* energy. Then we start relying on artificial stimulants like caffeine and sugar, which depletes our energy more.

We can reverse this trend by making a conscious decision to put our health first, and then converting that thought into action. We will see a dramatic shift in our physical and mental well-being if we start doing three simple things every day:

1. exercise
2. put good things into our body
3. get enough sleep

The increased happiness and vitality that result from better health are available to anyone who takes these three easy steps. We don't need fancy equipment or mental gymnastics or monk-like devotion to a physical ideal. We just have to cultivate a few good habits and to remember that good health isn't only about being able to touch our toes and do a few jumping jacks. We must keep our minds toned and flexible as well. Once our health becomes a daily practice, the benefits will flow.

Health Is True Wealth

Learning how to get healthy and stay healthy serves as a blueprint for setting and accomplishing other happiness goals. When we take command of our physical and mental health, we internalize a template for success that we can apply to every aspect of our lives. The skills we rely upon to sustain a daily exercise regimen parallel the skills we must hone if we want to build a business, attend graduate school, or learn to play a musical instrument. There's something about a dedicated workout routine — the discomfort and temptations we must rise above, the mental discipline we need, the rewards we earn from sticking to a plan — that makes maintaining physical fitness a master class in goal achievement. We can harness that same focus, commitment, and consistency to realize all of our goals, especially the financial ones.

Since our physical and mental well-being are fundamental to our happiness, our financial goals must include our health as a primary consideration. From a practical standpoint, that means making sure that the *conditions* necessary for supporting and sustaining good health are present and accounted for in our short- and long-term financial plans.

We can't base the success of our financial plan on a precarious work/life balance. While toiling away sixty-five hours a week might help you further your career or earn more money, overworking leads to decreased health, which may eventually lead to *lower* income. Therefore, overworking should not be part of a financial plan. Other things that have no place in a viable financial plan include the following:

- choosing to buy a house that's two hours from your job, which ensures an exhausting daily commute;
- working eighty hours a week when you're forty in the hope that you will earn enough to retire at fifty;
- accepting a job doing something you hate for people you don't respect simply to bring home a big paycheck;
- adding a prestigious project or part-time job that takes away the time you'd normally spend exercising; and
- any goal that adds more stress than joy to your life.

In the long run, all of the above choices will be self-defeating: we will wind up too busy, tired, and miserable to enjoy our home, family, career, and self. Instead of working longer and harder to acquire brownie points at the office or new stuff that won't make us happier, we should ask ourselves what we can do without, so that we have more time and energy to invest in ourselves and those we love. Each moment in life should count toward a lot more than the bottom line on a bank statement.

Speaking of the bottom line, did I mention that good health is also extraordinarily efficient from an economic standpoint? A healthy lifestyle increases our income potential *and* reduces our illness and injury-related costs, leaving us more money to spend on our skillful desires. It eliminates the need for many of the pricey consolation prizes we buy ourselves to compensate for the general malaise and listlessness we experience when we *don't* feel good. Good health is its own reward — and it's free to anyone willing to put in a little sweat equity.

Like happiness, we each have our own personal ideas about what constitutes a healthy lifestyle. There is no uniform, one-size-fits-all definition of good health. For some folks, leading a healthy life means taking a long walk most mornings and enjoying a glass of red wine each night. Others don't feel mentally or physically fit unless they're running marathons, scaling mountains, or swimming a mile every day. Still others — myself included — need to meditate daily to stay energized and maintain our sense of well-being. What we do to stay healthy is far less important than remaining consistent and *mindful* about what we do.

We may each have our own unique expression of health, but there is one universal truth: health is *true* wealth, and we should never take ours for granted. We must do everything in our power to support the central pillar of a happy life.

Mindful Money Practice

Our health should be a primary consideration in our life plans, not an afterthought, so let's move it front and center for a few minutes.

Start by thinking about yesterday. How did you feel — both physically and mentally — at the end of your day? Healthy, energized, and strong? Sick, tired, and weak? None of the above? Some mix of the above? Write down how you felt, and take a moment to reflect on the conscious and unconscious financial choices you made yesterday that affected your health. What nurtured you? What sabotaged you? Make a list.

Now think about *today*. How do you feel right this moment? Again, put pen to paper and assign words to those feelings, then compare how you feel today with how you felt yesterday. Is it better, worse, or the same? Consider today's conscious and unconscious financial choices, and compare them to the choices that impacted your health yesterday. How is today different? Have any of your choices worked better or worse for you today? Make another list.

Finally, take a moment to *decide* how you want to feel *tomorrow*. Review your evaluations of the past two days and identify three conscious financial choices you can make tomorrow to support your decision and your health. Perhaps that means bringing a homemade lunch or leaving work on time. Jot down your choices on a sticky note, and leave it someplace, like a bathroom mirror, where you'll see it first thing tomorrow morning. Start each day with a conscious reminder to turn your healthy choices into deliberate actions.

CHAPTER 12

Happiness Pillar 2: *Engagement*

> When I learn something new — and it happens every day — I feel a little more at home in this universe.
>
> — Bill Moyers

Happiness studies reveal that the happiest and healthiest people are those who are actively engaged in the world. They continually seek new experiences and strive to learn new things. By comparison, there appears to be little evidence indicating that owning a lot of stuff contributes to long-term happiness. This suggests that choosing to acquire more life experiences is a more skillful desire than choosing to accumulate more possessions. We should keep this in mind as we consider our life goals.

Engagement is both a pillar of happiness *and* a core element of mindfulness philosophy. Buddhists believe that the secret of human happiness lies in detaching from our desires for the transient — whether objects, people, or outcomes — and remaining fully engaged in whatever is unfolding for us in the present moment. The guiding principle is that everything in the universe is impermanent. Therefore, we should endeavor to "be here now" because now is the only certainty.

Humans are happiest when we are learning something new that transports us into the world, or we are doing something we love that demands our unwavering focus and attention right this minute. Seizing the day is a great mantra, but we can't rely on spontaneity to deliver enough intellectual and emotional stimulation to keep us engaged. We must deliberately choose to schedule fun, wonder, and excitement into our lives; we must build ample opportunity for pursuing our passions and interests into our short-term and long-range plans.

Making the conscious choice to leave ourselves room for engagement requires a significant shift in how we approach many of our basic life-management decisions. Whether we work for someone else or run our own business, most of us are in the game of trading our time for money. Engagement offers us a much better deal, if we're willing to break out of this rut. We'll give up less time and gain more satisfaction by concentrating on acquiring new and improved experiences, rather than working extra hours to bankroll our next big purchase or pay for our last one.

The Case for Lifelong Learning

I'm no neurologist, but I've read enough popular science to know that learning something new boosts our brain power — both literally and figuratively. Engaging and stimulating the brain doesn't merely expand our knowledge base, improve our reasoning, and elevate our thoughts. Flexing our mental muscles also builds new neural pathways, making our brains sharper and healthier. The brain is no different than any other part of our body. The more exercise it gets, the more likely it is to last a lifetime.

While there's no scientific proof that a healthier brain is a *wealthier* brain, every other week someone publishes a book or article maintaining that rich people think and act differently than the rest of us. Depending on who's talking, there are anywhere from five to twenty habits wealthy folks cultivate that lead to increasing their riches. What one habit makes every list? Reading. But not just reading for pleasure or entertainment. According to Thomas Corley, the author of the bestseller *Rich Habits: The Daily Success Habits of Wealthy Individuals*, the richest of the rich are voracious readers of nonfiction books and articles that explore the big ideas and challenges shaping contemporary society. The über-wealthy don't log as many hours in front of the TV as the average American because they'd rather spend their time with a book expanding their understanding of history, science, and human nature.

In addition to reading more, Corley found that wealthy folks — compared to individuals who haven't enjoyed financial success — are more likely to listen to books on tape or take courses on a topic that interests them. Rich or poor, all of us are granted just twenty-four hours in a day. When it comes to leisure time, most of us bust our butts to carve out more space for R&R, but the rich are busy "sharpening the saw," as my father used to say — pursuing opportunities to learn more, do more, and engage more.

I'm convinced that this elevated level of engagement is the primary reason the wealthy report higher levels of life satisfaction. My theory is that folks who are rich enough to buy anything they want are often a few steps ahead on the financial learning curve. By virtue of having more than enough, many have already figured out something others haven't yet had the chance to learn: It's not *having* more that makes people happier. It's *engaging* more. That's why many rich people place such a high value on lifelong learning.

Just like the positive chain of life events we activate when we focus on our health, there is a cause-and-effect relationship between lifelong learning and enhanced earning that can snowball into an avalanche of unexpected benefits.

Anyone who has ever seen the Bureau of Labor Statistics chart on salary versus education level knows that the more years people spend in college, the higher pay they tend to command on average. As we deepen our knowledge in our chosen field and further develop our problem-solving skills, we're able to make even more money. As we make more money, our increased earnings afford us opportunities for more education, more travel, and a broader array of life experiences. Expanding our horizons allows us to meet other interesting and engaged people like ourselves and uncover personal interests and professional prospects we didn't know existed. This, in turn, leads to even more earning, which, in turn, opens up even more avenues of learning, which in the long run makes us happier humans.

A disciplined practice of lifelong learning supports the conditions that increase our happiness by promoting the following:

- Greater engagement: Exposure to new ideas fosters professional and personal engagement. The most game-changing innovations in business, the arts, and our day-to-day lives often arise when ideas from different cultures, industries, or historical periods are joined together by a curious, creative mind.
- Better problem-solving: Learning about how our world works improves our ability to solve problems, which makes us more valuable family members, employees, business owners, neighbors, and citizens.
- Higher self-esteem: Acquiring more knowledge helps us feel wiser, more competent, more effective, and more powerful. When others treat us in kind, our self-respect, income, and happiness dividends go up.
- Inspiration: Being introduced to brilliant, innovative art, music, literature, and business ideas can change our lives and motivate us to reach new heights of human potential, teaching us that more is possible.
- Ability to zoom out: When we move beyond our limited perspective, we view our lives and the world with a wider lens, and we are better able to see the interconnectedness of all things. When we make the shift from "I" to "we," our lives gain more meaning — another vital pillar of happiness.

Lifelong learning provides the context to understand and interpret the world around us. Learning starts with our formal education, but it certainly doesn't end there. We learn by reading, observing, listening, and watching. Most importantly, we learn by *doing*. Experience is the master teacher.

Experience: The Gift That Keeps On Giving

One counterintuitive finding in happiness studies, such as Paulina Pchelin and Ryan T. Howell's 2014 report "The Hidden Cost of Value-Seeking," is that relatively brief life experiences provide greater long-term joy than do seemingly permanent *things*. A shiny, new object can be an active source of pleasure for anywhere from a few minutes to a few weeks. But our most meaningful experiences — climbing a fourteen-thousand-foot mountain in Colorado, seeing a great play on Broadway, or volunteering at a local soup kitchen — will stick with us indefinitely. This is not merely because these experiences create memories we will cherish forever. A meaningful experience changes something fundamental inside us and alters how we interact with the world.

Raising two children affords me almost daily opportunities to watch someone's world be blown wide open by new experiences. For example, my son recently attended a birthday party where all the kids got to take turns "flying" in a wind tunnel. The ten minutes Eli spent in that tunnel got under his skin in a way that no toy or object ever has. He is now, for the rest of his life, a person who has experienced the feeling of flight. Who knows where that might lead him someday?

Nonetheless, adults tend to hunger for possessions more than experiences, and some may even believe that money spent on intangibles is wasted. Part of the reason is that advertisers do a masterful job making their products seem like defining aspects of our identity. But something else is also at play, according to Pchelin and Howell.

Their research suggests that we intuitively believe permanent objects offer greater financial value than fleeting experiences. During their three-part study, participants were polled before and after making a purchase or having an experience. Before making a purchase, most participants thought it made more financial sense to buy a material item, even though they believed the experience might make them happier. But *after* a purchase, they tended to see an experience as being a better value than a material item. It seems that once we *have* an experience, we recognize its true worth.

How can we apply this research to our financial lives? By mindfully shifting our focus from accumulating possessions to gaining meaningful life experiences and allocating our dollars accordingly. Most of us have limited resources and unlimited desires. That means we need to make trade-offs. Recognizing that a new life experience may be a more skillful desire for us than a new "toy" helps us make those trade-offs in an informed way.

Those trade-offs aren't just about how we spend our money, however. They are also about how we invest our time. As we formulate our life plans, we must remember to leave room in our busy schedules for the mundane but meaningful experiences that bring us closer to the people we love, such as taking a weekly walk with a close friend, enjoying a leisurely breakfast with our significant other, or helping our kids or grandkids with their homework. Shared experiences create the deepest human bonds, and those bonds are essential to our happiness.

That said, we do live in a material world, and there will obviously be many times when we choose to spend our money on a *thing* that we need or want. Before we open our wallets, we should take a few moments to consider whether that particular purchase satisfies a skillful desire *and* will stimulate more opportunities for engagement.

For example, when buying birthday presents for our children, we can choose gifts that will lead them to new experiences, such as a bicycle, ukulele, or backyard gardening tools. When we want to treat ourselves to something nice, we can indulge in the latest book by our favorite author or a fancy chef's knife to enhance our culinary adventures. When we go shopping for big-ticket items, such as a new car or our first home, we can prioritize features that will improve our day-to-day life more than our standing in the neighborhood. We can buy a small house in a good school district, or rent an apartment that's walking distance from work, leaving us more time and money to engage in who and what matters most to us. Instead of splurging on a luxury sedan, we can choose a modest four-wheel-drive station wagon that will make it easier to take our dog and/or family up to the mountains on weekends. We can use the leftover money to pay for even more engagement opportunities — like our next big outdoor adventure or the piano lessons we've always wanted.

In Buddhist philosophy, always and now are one and the same, so don't wait until tomorrow to call that piano teacher. There's never going to be a better time to focus on your happiness than today because the present moment is all any of us truly have.

Mindful Money Practice

Remember kindergarten? The structure and rigid routine provided a well-defined framework for engagement that stimulated your curiosity and developed your competence. Now you're old enough to design your own engagement plan tailored to your specific interests. The tools you need for this undertaking are simple: a calendar, a pencil, and an open mind.

Open your calendar and block off thirty minutes each day for the next thirty days to initiate your lifelong learning campaign. Ideally, reserve the same slot every day, but choose a time that fits into *your* schedule and lifestyle. What and how you want to learn something during those thirty minutes is up to you. You can take up knitting, start reading poetry, or seek out nonfiction books on topics that are fascinating but foreign to you. Spend money on a class or take a free crash course on the internet. The only constraints are thirty minutes of "homework" every day and subject matter that is brand new to you.

Next, block off a two-hour slot each week during this same thirty-day period for acquiring meaningful experiences. Look for opportunities to be an active participant rather than a spectator. Do something like hike in nature or volunteer at a senior center, instead of having something *done to* or *for* you, like a pedicure. Perhaps your meaningful experiences will overlap with your lifelong learning campaign, or perhaps they will launch you into entirely different directions. Maybe the experiences will require a financial investment in athletic equipment or a new cake pan. The one requirement is that you make a conscious decision about what you want to do, and then *do* it.

At the end of the thirty days, assess your approach to engagement. What did and didn't work? What came more easily to you: learning or experience? Where did you get the most value for the time and money you invested? What can you do better in the future? Like all mindfulness disciplines, lifelong learning and meaningful experiences will deepen and grow with regular practice and commitment — as will your happiness.

CHAPTER 13

Happiness Pillar 3: *Relationships*

> Plant a seed of friendship, reap a bouquet of happiness.
>
> — Lois Kaufman

No one needs a book to tell them that meaningful relationships are vital to happiness. Nor do they need scientific proof. Still, in their 2010 paper "Social Relationships and Health," Debra Umberson and Jennifer Karas Montez cite numerous studies that confirm what we already know from personal experience: those who make time for others and maintain close ties to friends and family report fewer illnesses, less depression, greater happiness, and longer life spans than those who don't. The old Yiddish expression "Life is with people" says it all.

Buddhism adheres to the same philosophy. The very idea that one can lead a truly independent existence is considered an illusion. This illusion, perhaps more than any other, can be a tremendous source of suffering in our lives. Since everyone and everything in the universe is connected, we are actually nothing *but* our relationships.

This knowledge should have vast implications for how we choose to spend our money. But for some strange reason, money's powerful impact on our most important relationships is often left out of financial discussions. By doing so, we ignore a fundamental *what is* of life: true happiness derives from those relationships. Therefore, if we want to be happy, we must earn, save, and plan to utilize our money in ways that will increase, not reduce, our togetherness with our nearest and dearest. Too many people waste their energy and money chasing superficial desires to fill an emotional void, when spending time with friends and family would fill that void to overflowing.

Relationships Are Good Business

Focusing on our relationships isn't just good for our emotional well-being. It's good for our careers. People with a satisfying home life tend to enjoy more *professional* success as well. Likewise, the ability to forge strong bonds with colleagues and clients leads to greater productivity, increased sales, and enhanced job performance, which leads to better career opportunities.

Hiring and firing decisions, and decisions about who gets promoted or who wins the company's business, often come down to a feeling of personal connection between the individuals involved. Customers want to buy from salespeople they like, and colleagues tend to present new opportunities to people they know and trust. In his book *Vital Friends: The People You Can't Afford to Live Without*, Tom Rath notes that people are *seven times* more likely to be engaged at their jobs if they have a meaningful relationship with at least one person in the workplace.

Cultivating healthy relationships needs to be an integral element of how we run our businesses and handle our customers, coworkers, and colleagues. While we don't want to view any relationships solely through a lens of dollars, we should be mindful that maintaining close personal ties enriches virtually every aspect of our lives. It's all connected.

Connectivity vs. Connection

Even though we know that meaningful personal relationships are critical to our happiness, we don't always do a very good job of *living* this truth in the modern Western world. We spend lots of money on *technology* to facilitate human connection, but we're increasingly missing out on the real thing.

"Connectivity" has become the buzzword of our times. Smart devices allow us to stay connected to one another almost constantly. Many of us have phone and email contact lists that number in the hundreds, not to mention all of our Facebook friends, Twitter followers, and LinkedIn connections. And yet, according to Matthew Brashears in his 2011 report "Small Networks and High Isolation?" Americans have fewer close friends than they did before the era of social networking began. In 1985 the average person reported having three close friends they could confide in and go to for help or advice. By 2010 that number was down to two. We may have dozens, even hundreds, of Facebook "friends," but we have fewer true *friends.* When it comes to relationships, we've traded connectivity for connection and quantity for quality.

A few months ago, I had an experience that really drove this point home for me. I was at my favorite Berkeley restaurant, Saul's Deli, with my kids. A family of six — representing three generations — came in and sat in the lobby waiting for a table. Immediately, *all six of them* pulled out their smartphones and started pushing buttons. These family members were *physically* together and about to drop a hundred dollars on a great meal, but they were not sharing the experience with one another. The kicker? I was about to make the same mistake. Witnessing this moment prompted me to pocket the phone and give Eli and Annie my full attention. We need to put down our devices and engage with those we love.

How Close Is Close?

No matter how large our extended circle of family and friends, the folks we're closest to have the most profound effect on our happiness. Instead of leaving something so important to chance, we should make a conscious effort to build and sustain close relationships in our life that share these key characteristics:

- You confide in one another.
- You understand something about each other's inner life.
- You believe the person has your best interests at heart.
- You feel and express love and affection for one another.
- You honor each other's desires and preferences.
- You share emotional intimacy.
- You trust and solicit the person's opinion.
- You can call each other if you are in trouble.
- You challenge each other when you're being foolish, dishonest, or untrue to your goals and principles.

Close relationships add value and vitality to life. It's easy to lose sight of what matters most when we're caught up in the hustle and bustle of our busy lives. We get so overwhelmed by the ritual of earning our daily bread that we can neglect to feed our relationships. We must never forget that the *real* riches we seek come from those who know and love us well.

I/Thou Relationships

We can greatly increase the depth of our closest relationships by adopting what the Austrian-born Jewish philosopher Martin Buber called the "I/thou" approach. This I/thou approach refers to when we respect and honor others, which affirms and strengthens our common ground, as opposed to a "me/you" point of view, which is what we adopt when we mentally separate ourselves from our fellow creatures and turn them into little more than means to our ends.

Buber's I/thou philosophy dovetails with the Buddhist understanding that we are all inextricably connected. We arise together amid the same sea of causes and conditions, so any actions I take in my life will affect others in seen and unseen ways, and vice versa.

In fact, the very consciousness that flows through me is the same essential consciousness that flows through all beings.

That's why Buddhists are advised to treat everyone, including our enemies, as our own mother — or, better yet, as divine. The familiar greeting from yoga class, "*Namaste*," literally means "the divine in me bows to the divine in you." When we adopt an I/thou approach to relationships, we honor the other person as a complete and sacred being with his or her own unique self-worth, distinct from our own self-serving desires. Empathy, respect, and genuine love flow as a result.

If we can develop an I/thou connection with everyone, from family members to bosses to the guy who runs the coffee truck, we will unlock the *intrinsic* value of those relationships and can stop pursuing costly and empty substitutes that will never make us happy.

Investing in Friendship

What will make us happy? More friends! In a 2013 paper, John F. Helliwell and Haifang Huang examined data from a Canadian survey of five thousand people and came to the conclusion that doubling one's number of friends has the same effect on one's sense of well-being as a 50 percent increase in income. In other words, if we have today's average number of two close friends, we'll need to earn 50 percent more money (and work 50 percent harder) if we want to enjoy the same benefits that adding two more close friends would provide.

It comes as no surprise that when people are asked why they don't have more friendships, they say the main reason is lack of free time. What would happen if we tapered back on our work hours and spent some of that time with friends? If the research is to be trusted, we'd come away feeling richer than if we'd pushed ourselves to earn the extra income. And with any luck, those friends will still be close in years to come — such as after we retire.

Close friends prove valuable throughout life, but never more so than in retirement. That's why we must invest in our friendships, and not just stocks and bonds, while we're planning for our future. Although we may get by without many close friends during the hectic working and family-raising years, friendship takes on a primary role once we retire. Comfortable, well-worn friendships are what bring us the most joy. If we don't spend time and lunch money developing those relationships now, they won't be there when we need them most. As we plan for a happy old age, we must also be mindful of what will make us *un*happy. Lack of friendship has a debilitating effect on our mental, physical, and spiritual well-being, especially as we grow older. As Umberson and Montez noted in their 2010 study (cited above), folks without friends get sicker and die sooner.

Who'll be there to help us navigate through the rough patches? The difficult *what is* of the entire aging process is something many of us are afraid to face head-on, but ignoring the issue won't make it go away. Old age is when we start losing spouses, siblings, and our closest confidants to death and diseases such as Alzheimer's. We should make time today to develop an extended network of friends who share common bonds and interests, so we'll all be there to entertain, delight, and care for one another during our golden years. If we have only one close friend, and he or she passes away, we may face the prospect of many lonely and isolated years at a time when we need community in order to thrive.

Loneliness and isolation can undermine our *financial* health as well. Folks with an inadequate support system often have greater need for expensive personal care and medical intervention. Many things we might have to pay for, friends would be willing to do for free. As you work on your financial retirement plan, it's a good idea to think long and hard about who you can lean on and laugh with in your old age. Perhaps you'll reconsider turning down the next invitation to lunch with a pal or your neighborhood book club.

Time Is More Valuable Than Money

We've all heard the saying "Time is money." I disagree. Time is far more valuable than money. It's the one natural resource that is completely nonrenewable. We're each granted just a limited amount — and we won't know how much that is until it's over.

When someone devotes an hour to us, they give us something irreplaceable. Yet, despite its tremendous value, time is the one gift we all have to give, no matter what our financial circumstances. Being *present* for our loved ones, spending a few precious moments together with no pressing agenda, is the most powerful investment we can make in our relationships. But we have to pay careful attention, or we'll miss the opportunities for connection that come our way. My meditation teacher calls this practice "slowing down the frames of the movie," so that we can truly see what's going on in our life and in the lives of the people we love.

Last year, I spoke at a conference in Hawaii, and my family came along. We had a great time together, but Hawaii is two hours behind California, and the day after we got home was a school day. I knew my daughter would have a hard time navigating the time change, so instead of shouting my usual wake-up call, I went up to Annie's room, sat on her bed, and gently rubbed her cheek. She woke up, stretched, purred, and dozed off again. I whispered to her, stroking her cheek until she gradually came around. Her eyes fluttered open, and then she gave me the biggest smile ever. That smile was more memorable than our entire trip to Hawaii, and it was earned simply by spending a few unhurried minutes together.

Mindfully slowing down the frames helped me capture Annie's smile forever. That brief moment of bliss cost nothing but time, yet many of us are convinced that we need to *buy* life's valuable moments. We'll plan a three-hundred-dollar dinner-and-theater evening with our mate, when a game of Scrabble and a pizza on our dining room table might make us just as happy, and no one would have to pay for parking or a babysitter. Not that there's anything inherently wrong with spending money on an amazing experience we share with a friend or loved one. My wife and I save all year for the one big ski vacation we take every February, and I wouldn't miss it for the world. But we both understand that many of life's indelible memories are born of those unplanned moments of just plain *being* together, so we budget for that, too. No reservations. No expenses. Just two humans taking time for each other — something we all need.

The Myth of Independence

We Americans often have difficulty accepting this genuine *need* for others in our lives. Perhaps this is due to the sense of rugged individualism that marks our national character. But since everything is connected, independence is a myth.

The happiest cultures in the world appear to be those that cultivate a strong sense of community and *inter*dependence and that encourage lifelong close relationships within families. Maybe it's time we reconsider the notion that we are designed to fly solo and instead embrace our inestimable need for human connection — especially when making a lifetime financial plan. The planning process in section 3 of this book will help you weigh factors like when and where you want to retire, what hobbies and interests you'd like to pursue, and how much disposable income you wish to have. It's equally important to plan how you'll maximize the time, money, and experiences you share with your children, grandchildren, friends, mate, and members of your chosen community. The stronger your relationship pillar, the happier you'll be. Not a single human being, on his or her deathbed, ever said, "I wish I'd spent *less* time with the ones I love."

Mindful Money Practice

Money touches every aspect of our lives. Although relationships aren't *about* money, our relationships often affect our finances, and vice versa. We want to be conscious of these connections when making a financial plan.

This is another three-column exercise. At the top of a sheet of paper, write the following headings: "The Bad," "The Good," "The Better."

In "The Bad" column, list recent instances when money proved problematic in a close relationship. Be as specific and honest as possible. What caused the conflict? Was it a question of how much you spent? How little you had? What you chose to do with your money? Disappointing results?

"The Good" column is a lot more fun and will hopefully be longer. List recent instances when money benefited a close relationship. Why was it helpful? How did you use it? Did you buy something? Do something? Give it away?

In "The Better" column, brainstorm ideas about how money can better serve your relationships. List ways you can start mindfully using your money to support the conditions that will foster happiness in your closest relationships today and in the future.

Once you're finished, test-drive a few of the "Better" ideas with the significant people in your life. Remember to slow down the frames and enjoy the ride.

CHAPTER 14

Happiness Pillar 4: *Meaning*

> The least of things with a meaning is worth more in life than the greatest of things without it.
>
> — CARL JUNG

There is a deeper dimension to happiness that transcends mere joy and zest for life. A dimension that sustains and inspires us through the best of times as well as in the periods when happiness feels like a distant memory. That dimension is *meaning*.

Meaning supercharges our joy when life is good and keeps us moving forward when life is painful and difficult. Such transient conditions may send ripples across the surface, but meaning provides a bottomless substrate of happiness that is independent of the ebb and flow of fortune.

For many, family is the foundation that gives existence its meaning. For others, meaning comes from engaging in artistic endeavors or working to make our world a better place for all of its citizens. Still others rely on their faith in a higher power. No matter how we define it, or where we find it, meaning is essential to a satisfying life. When we believe that what we are doing has a purpose and importance greater than ourselves, we do it with care, conviction, and passion, and we take far more pleasure in the success of our endeavors.

For Buddhists, the ultimate meaning of life is to attain enlightenment. As this highest of goals may not be achievable, or even comprehensible, within a single lifetime, Buddhism recognizes the importance of assigning *relative* meaning to our lives. We must each discover the purpose that speaks directly to and for *us*.

One of the fundamental tenets of financial planning is to "put your money where your meaning is." In other words, we need to harness our money in service of what we consider most important. A hundred dollars spent mindfully provides far more value than a million bucks frittered away on dazzle. Once you've identified *your* meaning, you should make it the primary *focus* of your financial plan.

When we align our financial decisions with our values, we become "stewards" of money, not just users. It's a rare soul who can nurture, grow, and shepherd capital so that it serves the greatest good, but it's something to aspire to.

The Meaning of Meaning

The most admired figures in history — such as Jesus Christ, Rosa Parks, Gandhi, Mother Teresa, Abraham Lincoln, Harriet Tubman, and the Dalai Lama — have all been driven by a profound sense of meaning. Often, meaning-driven people do not lead what we would consider happy lives. They may be imprisoned, persecuted, or live in conditions of extreme poverty and violence. Yet something indestructible in their nature allows them to triumph over impossible odds and overcome seemingly spirit-breaking obstacles.

A life imbued with meaning isn't just the provenance of the great. In many poor Buddhist societies, this unwavering devotion to a higher purpose allows people to be happy in the face of crippling scarcity and deprivation.

If we subtract meaning from our day-to-day existence, we humans disintegrate, no matter who we are or how comfortable our circumstances. Even folks who are quite wealthy become depressed, listless, or suicidal when they feel their lives lack meaning. Acquiring material things and achieving social status just won't fill the void. We need a central, unifying theme to flourish.

Since meaning is the very engine of profound happiness, the

search for our higher calling is not something we can afford to put off until tomorrow. Rather, we must seek out meaning every day. A purpose-driven life takes a far more satisfying trajectory than one guided by hedonistic pursuits or aimless wandering.

Finding Meaning in the Modern World

For much of human history, meaning was woven into the tapestry of daily life. From birth, our ancestors tended to live reverent lives filled with ritual and tradition. And once folks reached the "fourth quarter" of life, they often became respected community elders whose job was to ensure that meaning was honored and preserved for posterity.

In many Asian cultures, it is still common for a person to renounce creature comforts and material possessions to devote their final years to God or enlightenment. But in much of our secular, youth-centric, technology-driven modern world, we no longer value tradition or honor our elders in their fourth quarter. We are now each individually responsible for blazing our own path to meaning, with no guides and few trail markers. Should we find our way — and we must, if true happiness is what we seek — our efforts will be rewarded with the untold riches meaning offers:

- Meaning provides significance. We have a deep need to believe that what we do matters. Linking our actions to a personal "cause" informs and elevates everything we do. Mundane tasks like going to the office every day take on a significance far greater than just earning a paycheck. Living with purpose inspires us to dedicate our time, our talent, and our treasure to the world.
- Meaning motivates us. Meaning is what gets us out of bed in the morning. It answers all our big "whys." Why am I doing this work? Why am I making this sacrifice? Why am I saving instead of spending? Without motivation, we default to what feels good right now or to what brings the least amount of pain, which gets us nowhere.

- Meaning gives us a moral compass. If life lacks meaning, there is no reason to act with integrity or do the right thing. Self-interest, habit, and fear can become our only moral rudders. Meaning provides a framework for making moral decisions.
- Meaning makes life richer. Those who discover their true calling find that life acquires a rich new flavor. A few years ago my close friend Scott became connected with PAWS, a charitable organization whose mission is to help "preserve, support, and nurture the human-animal bond." That mission is now Scott's mission, and PAWS is now central to his life. The people and animals he's met have transformed him, and his volunteer work has made Scott a happier, brighter guy.
- Meaning makes us better people. Having a higher purpose lifts us up as human beings, enhances our sense of self-worth, and encourages us to become better versions of ourselves. Yoking our individual purpose to a meaningful cause calls forth our best traits. As we strive to represent that cause with integrity, we become a model for others. I have seen this very change in Scott. He's always been a great guy, but now he's also a leader and inspiration to others. He's grown into the role he chose for himself.

There's More to Life Than Us

In the modern West, we may cherish the illusion that each person is an independent being, but we are immutably connected to all other creatures and things. The Buddhist concept of *dependent origination* holds that all beings are caused to come into existence *by* other beings and forces, and that all beings depend on other beings and forces for their continued existence. A human being is born of parents and survives by breathing oxygen, which is supplied by plants, which are nourished by soil, which consists of decomposing animals, which were brought into existence by other animals, and so on. *Inter*dependence, *not* independence.

This isn't just some esoteric theological construct. Scientists tell us that when we zoom in and look at the world very closely at the atomic level, the separation between objects disappears and all that can be seen are pulsating points of energy in a vast field of empty space, nothing distinct from anything else. We are each just a tiny facet of something much larger than ourselves.

Every human being exists on two levels: as a unique individual and as part of that larger whole. The cells of the human body illustrate this phenomenon perfectly. Each cell lives its own independent life. It eats, reproduces, defends itself, and may even move about autonomously. But each cell also serves the larger body. At a moment's notice, it will mobilize with ten trillion other cells to help the whole body pluck a guitar string or fight an infection. The cell sustains itself, but its true devotion is to the whole. It will readily give up its life for the whole's well-being.

In contemporary Western culture, we are trained to operate as solo cells. Strong individualism is honored, while holistic thinking is viewed with distrust. But both aspects are critical to our happiness. In order to live a fulfilled life, we must do something vital to contribute to the whole. Meaning connects us to the body human.

Financial Stewardship

If we accept that everything and everybody is connected, our entire relationship to money shifts. Money is no longer defined by what's mine or yours. It's no longer a tool we use to survive, care for our family, and occasionally have a little fun. We view it more like a natural resource that we must nurture and preserve for posterity. We become money's caretaker, not its owner. Money becomes a river that widens and deepens as it grows, not just a cache of cash.

Becoming a steward of capital means that we adopt a conscious intention to use money meaningfully while we are here on Earth, and we aspire to leave a legacy that will continue to produce value even after we die. Because we don't feel we *own* money, we are freer to deal with it intelligently and unemotionally. As a result, we become simultaneously more connected to money *and* more detached. When we're inspired by a motive larger than self-interest, we can kick ego out of the driver's seat and let our values drive the car. This shift ignites the prefrontal cortex of the brain, enabling us to make wiser, more mindful financial decisions that don't just benefit our investment portfolio. They also benefit humanity.

The true litmus test for a meaning-driven life is an unwavering commitment to being a force for good in the world, even if no one acknowledges us and we know we may never see the effects of our actions. Financial stewardship won't bear fruit overnight. But every time we plop money into our legacy account, we are quietly contributing to something bigger than ourselves. Whenever we make the trade-off to forgo a momentary pleasure so we can save still more, we are affirming our personal values. There is no more meaningful use of our money than serving others, and nobody else needs to know what we're up to for us to reap the sizable happiness dividend that comes from paying it forward.

Of course, informing how we choose to use our money is only a tiny facet of the powerful role meaning plays. Meaning also strengthens every other pillar of happiness in our lives, but we need to do the groundwork. Meaning won't be *given* to us. We must find it for ourselves. Maybe it's this quest to *find* meaning that makes meaning so *meaningful.*

Mindful Money Practice

Before you can put your money where your meaning is, you must determine your higher calling and clarify who and what matters most to you. The answer to those questions may shift over time, so use today as your starting point for an exercise you may want to revisit every year. *I* do.

Start by listing ten things that are very important to you, keeping in mind that those things may not be *things*. They may be people, projects, problems, causes, concepts, entire geographic regions, or the divine, as you define it. This list may take you a few minutes or a few hours to complete. If you quickly list twenty things, pare them in half; if you have a hard time coming up with more than one, keep at it till you have ten. Be patient but disciplined with yourself. The search for meaning can be an arduous task.

Once you've listed your top ten, identify the three things on that list that mean the *most* to you. Draw a circle around each of them.

Finally, look for a unifying theme between your three most important items, and write down that theme. It may not be readily apparent, but I guarantee you'll find a connection if you look long and hard enough. To start, describe each of the three most important things separately, whether in a paragraph or a single word. Then, as you identify the connection, distill this unifying theme into a single, crystal-clear sentence. This sentence is the "meaningful purpose" that describes your life's higher calling.

This is also the same "meaningful purpose" that you will use to guide your entire financial plan. Write it on an index card or a sticky note and keep it someplace where you will see it every single day. I keep mine in my wallet, but I suggest you use yours as a *Mindful Money* bookmark. That way it will be right at your fingertips when you reach chapter 20 and start developing your vision for your Financial Action Plan.

CHAPTER 15

Happiness Pillar 5: *Accountability*

Eighty percent of life is showing up.

— Woody Allen

Accountability may sound like more of a chore than a pillar of happiness, but accountability doesn't only mean accepting responsibility for our behavior toward others. It also means holding ourselves accountable *to ourselves*. Since the only reliable way for us to realize our heart's desires is through our personal actions, accountability is actually a prime mover of happiness.

Happiness doesn't just happen. It requires conscious effort. Meeting the high expectations we have of life takes hard work, discipline, and concrete steps. Before our reality can live up to its potential, we must identify the values and desires that are most important to us and translate them into specific goals and behaviors. Then we must practice those behaviors consistently over time, committing all the resources at our disposal to fulfilling our deepest desires and advancing our values.

Those who take happiness into their own hands are happier than those who wait for fate to intercede on their behalf. Accountability helps us midwife our dreams from the nebulous region of vague hope into the realm of tangible results.

According to Buddhist philosophy, each of us is exceedingly fortunate to be granted the gift of a human life. This gift is inconceivably rare in the grand, eternal scheme of things — no matter what faith tradition we follow. We can't squander our once-in-a-lifetime opportunity by living passively and noncommittally. We must passionately embrace every moment and strive to make it count.

The ABCs of Accountability

If we want to get from Here to happiness, we must follow a rigorous four-step process that is equal parts self-reflection and forward momentum. I call this process the "ABCs of Accountability":

- Identify desires and values. We thrive when our lives have purpose, and we flounder without it. In order to create a meaningful existence, we must clearly identify our desires and values and pursue them relentlessly. We can't let fear of failure make us hedge our bets.
- Create goals. Once we've set our sights, we need to translate those desires and values into specific goals and supporting behaviors. For example, if we desire to become a better pianist, the goal might be to learn a certain song by month's end. Daily practice would be the optimum behavior to support that goal.
- Take consistent action. Yes, daily! Taking committed, consistent steps affirms the value and insures the attainability of our goals. Consistent action buoys our self-worth and bolsters our discipline, while rewarding us with incremental achievements along the way.
- Commit the resources. Nothing will get done if we don't devote the requisite time to achieving our happiness goals *and* "put our money where our meaning is." If the piano's our passion, that might mean weekly lessons.

A viable financial plan must recognize your desires, reflect your values, and support the goals you set for yourself. It needs to enable you to enjoy the life you want to live right now, sustain you until the end of your days, and see your legacy plans into fruition. Although it's incredibly empowering to realize that your whole world rests firmly in your hands, it is also an awesome responsibility. You are accountable for knowing what you want. You are accountable for setting your goals. You are accountable for taking the steps to achieve those goals. And you are accountable for committing the necessary time and capital.

The Hard but Rewarding Road to Happiness

Accountability is not an easy path. Relaxation, idle pleasures, silly distractions, and hedonistic pursuits beckon like sirens' songs. Staying true to our goals and values is often the harder choice in any given moment. But every act of accountability makes a deposit into our happiness account and compounds our lifetime benefits.

Accountability also serves as a rudder, guiding us steadily toward our goals. Formulating an action plan for achieving those goals and following it gives us direction and stability. In that regard, a plan has much in common with a disciplined meditation practice. No matter what confusion or turbulence arises in our lives, we can rely on our plan to put us back on course. Like a Zen master who whacks his meditation students with a stick whenever their attention wanders from the correct focus, accountability returns our attention to the plan whenever we feel lost.

More importantly, accountability helps us build a track record of success. Each time we achieve a goal we've set for ourselves, we increase the likelihood of succeeding the next time around. We also become a model for those around us, especially any children in our life. When kids see adults realize their goals through consistent, disciplined behavior, they internalize a template for success.

The primary reason accountability is a pillar of happiness is because it delivers tangible results. We actually lose the weight, build the retirement account, and grow the business as we planned.

One great way to hold ourselves accountable is to make sure that all the goals we set pass what is popularly called the SMAC test. This means that goals are specific, measurable, achievable, and compatible. *Specific* means that each goal should be concrete. A few examples might be: "Celebrate my fortieth birthday by hiking to the bottom of the Grand Canyon," "Save fifty thousand dollars to make a down payment on a cabin in the woods before I retire in five years," or, "Pay off my student loans by the time I am thirty." A goal like "Be healthier" is vague, but "Lose ten pounds" is specific. "Save money for a down payment" is vague, but "Save fifty thousand dollars in five years" is both specific *and* measurable!

Measurable means the goal names or establishes an unambiguous metric that defines success. In the above scenarios, we will know we've attained our goals when we've lost those ten pounds, arrived at the bottom of the Grand Canyon on our fortieth birthday, put fifty thousand dollars for a down payment in our investment account by the time we get our gold watch, and reach age thirty with no student loan debt. A measurable goal will have a specific timeline, amount, or finish line that needs to be crossed before we consider the goal completed. Planning to go back to school "someday" is not a measurable or specific goal. Planning to enroll in accounting courses at the local community college by next year is *both*.

Achievable means the goal is something we can realistically hope to accomplish in the time frame we've established. For instance, say I set the goal "Become president of the United States by the time I'm fifty." This is clearly out of reach for me, since I'll be fifty in five years and I've never held an elected office — although I did run for student council unsuccessfully several times in high school. A more achievable goal might be "Run for *city* council next year," except that my wife wouldn't be supportive of that idea. On the other hand, in 2014 I set a goal for my firm: "Move into new offices in 2016." This was specific, measurable, and achievable, though it required setting and meeting a series of other SMAC goals along the way:

1. We hired a commercial real estate agent and toured only buildings that met our *specific* square footage, location, and aesthetic requirements until we found a beautiful office with the elevator we needed.
2. We negotiated a lease within the *measurable* metrics I had established for the new office, including rental price, availability, and zip code.
3. Ultimately, my goal was to better serve our clients, which was not *achievable* without moving. Though I loved our existing office space, I chose to move to a new space I liked less well because it had the elevator and the room to grow that we needed to achieve our main goal.
4. Originally, my goal was to buy a building, but we decided to lease offices when we realized that the goal to own commercial property was not *compatible* with our other primary goals.

Compatible is perhaps the hardest of the SMAC metrics to evaluate, since it requires comparing how well all our life goals mesh with and support one another. Inevitably, we will need to make trade-offs among our goals, such as happened when my firm moved offices. These adjustments may be small or large, temporary or permanent, depending on the situation. For me, even if I wanted to run for elected office next year, I still wouldn't because it is not compatible with other key goals that I consider more important — like working out every day, picking up my kids from school three afternoons a week (so that my wife can meet her goal of spending three days a week at her office), and coaching my kids' soccer teams. We might long to save enough money to retire at age fifty, but that goal wouldn't be compatible with our family's other SMAC goals, such as paying off our mortgage before retirement, replacing our roof next year, going on vacation to Hawaii next month, or taking our spouse out to an amazing dinner next week.

Only the Best Intentions

True accountability isn't just ticking off boxes on our SMAC checklist. Each of us must be accountable in a way that is personally meaningful and authentic. As important as goals are for motivating our behavior, they don't provide a moral framework or remind us how to *be* in the here and now. Mindfulness alone is not enough to keep us on the straight and narrow, either. That is why having what Buddhists call "right intention" is a critical component of accountability. True happiness comes from honoring our intentions as well as our goals. *Intention* serves as an inner guide for our behavior, while at the same time connecting us to that mysterious divine something *outside* ourselves.

Living with *right intention* is essential to a fulfilling and purposeful life. We must do our best to come from the "right place" every waking moment. In Buddhism, this right place is defined by three closely related intentions:

1. Do no harm. Every human interaction must be entered into with a firm intention to harm none of the parties directly involved or any other beings.
2. Radiate compassion. We must bring loving-kindness to all of our actions and carry an intention of happiness and peace for all beings in our hearts.
3. Be unattached. We must detach ourselves from our personal desires.

Detachment isn't the same thing as abandoning one's goals. Rather, it means recognizing that we only have control over our inputs, not the outcomes. Therefore, we can only be accountable for our own thoughts and actions, *not* for particular results. Letting go of attachment helps us treat others kindly, take specific steps toward our goals, and allow the results to happen as they will. We let go and trust. We surrender to the *what is*, accepting that we don't run the universe — and aren't the center of it either!

The concept of right intention is eminently applicable to money. Every financial action we take should be accompanied by an intention to further the greater good of all beings. Each action should also carry an intention to let the universe handle the results. We may be exceptionally prudent and intelligent with our money, but we are still powerless over what happens day by day. We must not be attached to specific outcomes, since we can only truly control our plan and our behavior. The markets will behave as they behave, and our financial situation will change in unpredictable ways. If we know our plan is sound, we must stick to it, regardless.

We can and should augment these three classic intentions with intentions of our own. It is not enough to strive toward our goals. We must deliberately incorporate our values into our day-to-day behavior, even though we know we are destined to fail at this endeavor on at least an hourly basis. Happiness in the future flows from being accountable to our goals, but happiness in the present moment flows from being accountable to our intentions.

It Is What It Is, It Is What You Made It, It Changes When You Change

At the heart of accountability lies acceptance: acceptance of the world as it is and acceptance of our part in it. Acceptance is also the heart of mindfulness.

For years, I have worked with a business coach who has turned out to be a brilliant *life* coach as well. He has a simple but effective philosophy that I have wholly embraced and keep on an index card by my desk. His three core principles capture the essence of accountability, and they are as applicable to life and love as they are to money:

1. It is what it is. Before we can change any part of our life, we must fully accept our *what is*. It doesn't matter what we *expected* our financial situation to be or *hoped* it would be or think it *should* be. It is what it *is*. We need to completely accept our present reality — "I'm overextended," "My earning power has gone down," "I charged too much on credit cards" — before true change can occur.

2. It is what you made it. There is one person who has been present for every financial decision in your life, and that person is you. Each of us is the protagonist of our own life story. If we have persistent challenges in certain areas, it's because of something we are doing or failing to do. Our current financial picture is the sum total of every choice we've made so far. While it may feel better to blame circumstance or others, accepting *full* responsibility for our financial state is the one thing that will empower us to change it.
3. It changes when you change. The notion that our luck is bound to change *someday* is fantasy. Our financial reality is a reflection of our inner state. The way we change our reflection in a mirror is not by manipulating the mirror. We must each, as Gandhi said, "*be* the change we wish to see in the world." The knowledge that we are solely responsible for changing our financial situation may seem like an onerous burden, but it is actually tremendously liberating. Since we hold all the cards, we also have all the power.

The Buddy System

Staying true to our goals and intentions often proves difficult without a little extra support. One good option is to work with an accountability partner who encourages us to stick to our plan.

The right financial adviser can serve as a great accountability partner for folks who have the inclination and money to hire a professional, but you may also ask a friend, relative, or colleague to be your money buddy. Significant others can also make wonderful accountability partners, since they share your life and your responsibilities. What you need is someone willing to help you stick to your plan once you've identified your major desires and values, translated them into specific goals and behaviors, and set your intentions. Whatever approach you choose, hold yourself accountable to yourself. Commit to the things you deeply desire and incorporate those desires into your financial plan. Nothing less than your happiness is at stake.

Mindful Money Practice

I call this practice "Walk the Talk" because it's designed to propel you from thought to action in four deliberate *baby* steps. On a sheet of paper, create four columns, and label them after each of the ABCs of Accountability:

1. Desires & Values
2. Goals
3. Actions
4. Resources

As with similar exercises, tackle each column one at a time. In the first column, describe one desire and/or value that feels compelling to you at the moment. If nothing immediately comes to mind, feel free to brainstorm some ideas until you settle on just one of your heart's desires. For example, perhaps you value animal rights or desire to improve your fitness level.

In the next column, translate your desire or value into a SMAC goal, that is, a goal that is specific, measurable, achievable, and compatible. For example, this could be lowering your resting heart rate five beats per minute over the next two months.

In the "Actions" column, choose a simple action that you can and *will* follow consistently. No need to go crazy. This could be something simple like taking a thirty-minute walk around the block every night before dinner or volunteering once a week at the local shelter.

In the "Resources" column, identify the resources you'll need to fulfill your chosen desire. Put your time and money where your meaning is: buy a pair of walking shoes or reserve two hours on your calendar to volunteer.

Your intention? Hold yourself 100 percent accountable to your action plan!

CHAPTER 16

Happiness Pillar 6: *Generosity*

> Since you get more joy out of giving joy to others, you should put a good deal of thought into the happiness that you are able to give.
>
> — Eleanor Roosevelt

We live in a culture that glorifies getting and spending. No public figure commands a brighter media spotlight than the self-made millionaire who started with nothing and now owns a private jet and Malibu beachfront estate. Yes, we also admire those who generously give away their money, but philanthropy doesn't garner as much press as personal acquisition. Bill Gates got *a lot* more attention when he was building his Microsoft fortune than he does now that he's giving it all away.

If we listened only to the press, we'd define success only in terms of getting, not giving. Yet as Bill Gates is demonstrating, giving is an essential part of a successful life. The most enlightened beings to ever walk our planet have emphasized generosity as an essential ingredient of true happiness. Jesus Christ constantly urged his followers to put others before themselves. The Buddha did the same. Although many folks believe meditation to be the foundational practice of Buddhism, the Buddha taught the principle of generosity to his students *before* he taught mindfulness. In fact, he named generosity as the first step on the path to spiritual enlightenment.

According to Buddhist philosophy, suffering in human life is caused by a misguided emphasis on the self. We futilely attempt to serve our self-interest by clinging to things and conditions — all of which are hollow and ephemeral. The most efficient way to rid ourselves of this attachment is to practice generosity. Generosity instantly shifts us from solo cell awareness to a holistic perspective, and by doing so, eases our suffering and the suffering of others.

We've all experienced this principle in action. Think back to an act of generosity and how great it made you feel. Perhaps you helped a stranger stranded by the side of the road, or gave ten dollars to a young mother in the grocery store who'd lost her wallet, or surrendered your seat on a crowded train to someone who clearly needed it more than you. When we're distracted by our own self-interest, it's easy to miss the small opportunities for generosity that present themselves on a daily basis. The loss is very much ours.

Not a Zero-Sum Game

Generosity is not a zero-sum game like poker or Monopoly, where one person's loss is another person's gain, and vice versa. Instead, contemporary research suggests that generosity is actually a win/win proposition in which *both* parties — the giver and the recipient — gain something valuable. That makes generosity an *added*-sum game. Since it also happens to be the most evolved way for us to behave as a species, generosity should be an integral part of our lives and financial plans.

Science supports what our hearts already know. In one experiment (published in 2008 as "Spending Money on Others Promotes Happiness"), a team of researchers randomly handed out envelopes on the street. Each envelope contained a five-dollar bill and a brief note. Half of the notes instructed the recipients to spend the five dollars on themselves, and the other half instructed recipients to spend the five dollars on someone else or make a charitable donation.

When the test subjects were contacted later that evening and asked how they were feeling, those who'd spent the money on others reported feeling substantially happier than those who'd spent the money on themselves, even though several hours had elapsed. Then researchers repeated the experiment, but they upped the ante by putting twenty dollars in each envelope. The results didn't vary. It didn't matter how much money the subjects received. Afterward, their levels of happiness reflected only *how* they spent it — on themselves or on others.

A survey of over six hundred Americans conducted as part of the same study revealed a parallel finding. Subjects' happiness levels did not appear to be affected by how much income they earned or how much they spent on themselves. The single greatest predictor of increased happiness was the amount of money subjects spent on others. The more they gave away, the happier they were. "'Tis better to give than to receive" is much more than a Hallmark platitude. It is a scientifically documented characteristic of how our brains work.

Of course, we don't need scientists to tell us that helping others makes us feel good. When we serve a fellow human being generously, we feel the unmistakable glow of happiness. Some people refer to this response as the "helper's high," but that is a facile, even dismissive characterization of something very profound.

The Gift That Keeps Giving

Generosity doesn't just impact the giver and the recipient — it can trigger ripple effects in the world at large. Witnessing even the smallest act of generosity may inspire observers to commit their own spontaneous acts of generosity, according to a 2013 study entitled "Social Contagion Theory: Examining Dynamic Social Networks and Human Behavior," which indicated that generous acts tend to inspire others to behave more generously. This study revealed that altruism, among many other positive and negative behaviors by folks in a social network, can radiate outward by as much as *three degrees of separation*. This implies that a single act of generosity has the potential to touch hundreds of people.

Generosity isn't merely contagious. It also conveys some terrific benefits:

- Generosity improves our physiological health. Being generous with our time in the service of others has demonstrated health benefits, such as decreased stress levels, increased endorphins, and lower blood pressure. Volunteering also helps us live longer. According to a 1999 study "Volunteerism and Mortality among the Community-Dwelling Elderly," elderly people who volunteer for two or more organizations are 44 percent less likely to die within the next five years than those who don't volunteer. Where do I sign up?
- Generosity activates the Law of Reciprocity. According to Robert Cialdini, author of *Influence: The Psychology of Persuasion*, folks are more likely to show generosity to a person who has already given *them* something, especially if the original gift was offered with no expectations of reciprocity. Apparently, generosity creates a psychic "debt" that recipients feel motivated to repay. I learned about this firsthand when I had to drive across the Bay Bridge to San Francisco every morning. Every now and then a complete stranger ahead of me would pay my toll. This unfailingly compelled me to do the same for the person behind me. After this happened a few times, I began randomly paying for others. It always made me inexplicably happy.
- Generosity triggers the Ben Franklin effect. One unexpected consequence of generosity is that our regard for the *recipient* of our kind gesture increases. This notion

> seems counterintuitive at first, but it does make sense. It was dubbed the Ben Franklin effect in honor of the man who once said, "He that has once done you a kindness will be more ready to do you another than he whom you yourself have obliged." Why? Because we prefer doing favors for people we like, so the very action of doing the favor retrofits our attitude toward the recipient of the favor. We effectively *make* the recipient deserving in our minds, as researchers Jon Jecker and David Landy concluded in their 1969 paper "Liking a Person as a Function of Doing Him a Favour" — published a few hundred years after Big Ben. We can transform our entire attitude toward humanity simply by performing small acts of kindness for others.

Of course, right intention is essential. Acts of generosity that are genuinely unselfish have great power to heal and inspire others. But giving solely out of the expectation of a returned favor is not generosity. Nor is giving out of guilt or a sense of martyrdom. A gift that is given for the wrong reasons makes everyone involved uncomfortable.

Generosity of intention is much more valuable than a generous gift. There are two Buddhist terms that describe this principle: *dana* and *caga*. *Dana* is the literal *act* of giving. It refers to the behavior. *Caga* refers to a "heart intent on giving." It is *caga* more than *dana* that fuels our happiness.

A Perpetual Giving Machine

A fundamental concept of economics is that every transaction in a free market is voluntary. A transaction occurs only when both parties feel they are getting something valuable out of the deal and the price is right. Every trade that takes place is an equivalent trade on some level because both parties believe they are getting separate but equivalent benefits.

Charitable giving is no different. When we see a person donate a large sum of money to a worthy cause, we tend to view it as a noble sacrifice. But the giver receives an equivalent benefit or the person wouldn't do it. "Want to feel like a million bucks? Give away a million dollars," as the saying goes. We may not have an extra million to allocate to charity, but generosity should play a pivotal role in our financial plan.

For many of us, the initial impetus for creating a financial plan is self-protection rather than philanthropy. We want to hang on to what's ours for dear life. While meeting our current and future financial needs is critical, I believe the *highest* purpose of a plan is to create a legacy. A well-crafted financial plan will allow us to do two things related to this:

1. Determine the amount of time, talent, and treasure we can afford to give away during our lifetime.
2. Leave enough wealth behind after our death to generously support the causes, people, and organizations that are meaningful to us.

If you start your retirement planning early, and mindfully follow the money goals you set for yourself, you can evolve into a true *steward* of capital. Your investment portfolio will become a growing *source of income* that you tap as planned, rather than a pie you continually nibble from. An income-generating account is like having a goose that lays golden eggs. If you eat only the eggs, and not the goose itself, you'll never run out of eggs.

By saving generously for your own future now, you'll enable yourself to be far more generous toward others at the end of your life. With careful planning, discipline, and a little good fortune, your generosity will reach its peak at the time of your death and continue into perpetuity. The happiest and most empowered clients I service are those whose financial plan is so robust they know they will exit this world leaving a generosity-driven, perpetual giving machine in their wake.

Mindful Money Practice

At my firm, we encourage team members to keep an eye out for opportunities to perform simple, meaningful, random acts of generosity for clients and colleagues. Those acts have ranged from forwarding articles that a client might find interesting to chipping in as a team to rent a Corvette for a coworker celebrating a milestone birthday.

For this exercise, we're taking a page out of the five-dollar generosity-experiment playbook. For the next thirty days, set the goal to perform at least one deliberate but unexpected act of generosity each day with the conscious intention of surprising and delighting the recipient. Once you start paying careful attention, countless opportunities will present themselves: an ice-cream cone for the office receptionist on a hot afternoon, a chocolate placed on your spouse's pillow before bed, a five-dollar tip for the barista who makes your cappuccino each morning, a pair of warm socks for the homeless person you pass every day near your office. Choose the same recipient every day or mix it up. Select someone in your inner circle or a complete stranger. There's no limit to the creativity you can invest in these acts of generosity, but limit your spending to five dollars or less per day (in keeping with the study "Spending Money on Others Promotes Happiness"). Since spending five dollars on someone can be just as rewarding as spending twenty, focus on your *intention* rather than on whatever dollar amount equates with generosity in your mind. Even giving a dollar can be a generous act, depending on the circumstances — such as paying the bus fare for a woman wrestling with a stroller and two small kids as she flounders for her wallet. Generosity isn't about how *much* we spend, in other words; it's about the *doing*. It's mindfully taking the time and effort to extend kindness to a fellow human.

List each act of generosity in your notebook. Perhaps you'll be inspired to start a running tab of potential random acts of generosity you can commit if and when the time is right.

CHAPTER 17

Happiness Pillar 7: *Optimism*

> When we meet real tragedy in life, we can react in two ways — either by losing hope and falling into self-destructive habits or by using the challenge to find our inner strength.
>
> — The Dalai Lama

Another persistent finding of happiness studies is that the happiest people are those who unabashedly profess optimism. Like the other seven pillars of happiness, optimism alone isn't enough to sustain a happy life, but it certainly improves our likelihood of success. Just the ability to visualize a better, brighter future gets us more than halfway there. In my experience as a financial professional, an optimist is also much more likely than a pessimist to create a financial plan and stick to it. For this reason alone, I view optimism as vital to achieving financial goals.

Optimism has countless other subtle and not-so-subtle financial benefits. An optimistic outlook stimulates the energetic and committed behavior that leads to career advancement, which in turn leads to higher pay. The confidence optimists have in their own judgment makes them willing to take risks — an indispensable factor in creating cutting-edge businesses or groundbreaking art. Since optimists expect positive outcomes, they tend to be more engaged *and* engaging, which attracts *other* optimistic people. Optimists often form the kinds of unstoppable teams that win championships, eradicate illnesses, and make world-changing discoveries that alter the face of science and technology.

If You Build It

Optimism is an essential ingredient of any financial plan because we can only plan effectively if we have faith in the future. The big challenge we all face is that no one knows how that future will unfold, day by day and moment by moment. Optimism helps us maintain the perspective that things *will* work out in the long run, even if the present moment looks uncertain and volatility is reigning. That perspective gives us the resilience to be patient and disciplined with our money.

A workable financial plan isn't just *built* on optimism. It helps *build* optimism. The incremental progress we see when we follow our plan encourages us to stay the course. As small steps like saving money each week in our 401K bring us closer to our ultimate goals, we're inspired to redouble our efforts. But in order to take those steps, we must first be optimistic about attaining our goals. Then we must believe that the steps we've outlined will actually carry us across the finish line. Optimism and planning can only make the leap of faith hand in hand.

The very act of planning for the future makes the future feel more secure, and feeling good about the future injects positivity into the present moment. Many of my clients have told me that their sense of optimism increased once they began actively working on their financial plan.

Optimism Meets Mindfulness

At first blush, mindfulness and optimism might seem at odds. Mindfulness is full immersion in the reality of the present moment, while optimism focuses on an imaginary future. But planning ahead is an essential part of a happy life. Otherwise, how will we ever grow a garden or build a temple? If we choose to live mindfully, we must also choose to make planning a mindful activity.

Many folks imagine that optimism requires a degree of deliberate *non*mindfulness, as if we must tune out the world in order to be optimistic. Medical journalist Dr. Michael Mosley has suggested just the opposite. For his 2013 BBC program "The Truth about Personality," Dr. Mosley made himself the guinea pig for his own research into optimism and pessimism. After undergoing cognitive testing — including an electroencephalograph — to confirm his pessimistic tendencies, he consciously attempted to alter his mind-set, documenting his experience for his BBC program. Dr. Mosley learned firsthand how the daily practice of tuning *into* a mindfulness meditation can rewire a brain from a pessimistic orientation to a more optimistic one. We can *mindfully* choose optimism.

Happy, Healthy, but Not Necessarily Wealthy

Like the other pillars of happiness, the choice to embrace optimism can play a vital supporting role in our overall health. In a 2009 research study of nearly a hundred thousand women, led by the University of Pittsburgh Medical Center's Dr. Hilary A. Tindle, optimism was found to prevent coronary heart disease and improve recovery rates after surgery. The same study also revealed that optimistic folks are 42 to 55 percent less likely to die within a given time period than their more pessimistic peers — depending upon the time frame studied. As we've seen, good physical and mental health makes for higher wealth.

There are many other direct and indirect ways optimism can affect our earning power. We develop better coping skills when we're optimistic, so we're equipped to handle career changes when they arise. Optimism can also lead to more creative engagement on the job. The belief that problems *can* and *will* be solved inspires us to try multiple solutions and approaches, much in the same way Edison tried seven hundred different materials before discovering the one that worked as a lightbulb filament.

Despite its ability to influence our financial success, optimism does not appear to be related to the presence *or* absence of wealth. Some optimistic people own very little, some pessimistic people own a great deal, and vice versa. In 2013, Shane Lopez of the University of Kansas and his colleagues analyzed Gallup World Poll data on the life satisfaction of approximately 150,000 survey respondents from 142 countries. They discovered that neither individual income level nor the wealth of the person's native country had much effect on people's levels of optimism.

What is it that makes one person an optimist and another a pessimist? Excluding possible genetic and physiological factors, it appears to be a function of personal beliefs and mental habits:

- Optimists believe "I matter." Optimists see themselves as vital and important parts of the universe with unique contributions to make. This spurs them to higher levels of achievement and earning.
- Optimists believe "I can handle it." Optimists wake up in the morning believing they won't be given a problem beyond their ability to solve.
- Optimists don't globalize problems. When something goes wrong, optimists see it as an isolated incident. They don't view misfortune as a catastrophe with far-reaching domino effects or as part of a persistent negative pattern. This noncatastrophic attitude is absolutely critical to successful investing.
- Optimists look inward. Optimists tend to understand that solutions to problems lie within themselves, rather than without, which gives them a lot more control of their lives. Since they view themselves as part of any problem, they can own the solution.
- Optimists are realistic. Many pessimists are closet idealists whose high expectations have been dashed repeatedly. Optimists, on the other hand, try to extract

optimal results from any scenario, good *or* bad. It seems paradoxical, but optimistic people *expect* bad things to happen. They just don't let blips on their radar shake their trust in the universe. As investors, they understand that an average return is a combination of good years and bad years, so they are willing to ride out the bad times and hang on to their extra money in the good years.

- Optimists focus on the goal, not the obstacle. I once asked a friend who's a passionate mountain biker how he avoided hitting rocks when flying down rugged mountain trails. "I focus on the trail ahead, not on the rocks in front of me," he replied. What a powerful metaphor for business and life. If we can keep our attention on the destination, we will sail past obstacles with relative ease.

The Rational Case for Financial Optimism

Many believe that pessimism is the "rational" response to the troubled world we live in today, and certainly many stories we read in the media confirm that point of view. But Matt Ridley makes a very strong case for optimism in his 2010 book *The Rational Optimist*. He surveyed over two hundred thousand years of human history and concluded that previous generations of humans managed to find solutions to what were considered insurmountable obstacles at the time they happened. Today, we have even more knowledge and resources to combat many pervasive problems, although not everyone on our planet has equal access to things many of us take for granted, like clean drinking water, electricity, and three meals a day. There has always been and always will be bad news: wars, famines, natural disasters, plagues, and economic collapses. The Buddha called it impermanence. Economists call it creative destruction. Still, Ridley found, the overall trajectory of human history has always been onward and upward, and that trend shows no signs of stopping.

As I mentioned in chapter 8, the long-term trajectory of the stock market has *also* been onward and upward. Even when faced with huge chasms, like the Great Depression, humankind has evolved creative economic strategies to get to the other side. Many advances in the banking and investment world over the last few centuries make financial optimism the most rational mind-set, in my humble opinion. You don't have to look back a hundred years for evidence. Just last year the US stock market hit an all-time high. So, why isn't *financial optimism* at an all-time high?

To put my case for financial optimism into context, consider the evolution of three well-known financial products:

1. Bank savings accounts: A few generations ago, we saved money by stuffing it under the mattress. This solution didn't just prevent us from growing our money through compound interest. It also meant that we were one house fire away from losing everything. The solution? A savings account.
2. Stocks: One day someone realized that we could combine our assets, share ownership *and* our risk, and build something bigger — like a railroad company — and more profitable together than any of us could build alone, and *stocks* were born.
3. Mutual funds: Though plenty of folks have become wealthy investing in individual stocks, there has always been a lot of risk involved in putting money into just one company. Eventually, money managers offered financial products designed to spread out that risk by combining many people's money and investing in many companies at once, which gave us the market basket of stocks and/or bonds known as a *mutual fund*. Today we can spread out that risk even further by buying the entire global economy in just one mutual fund. This

> means that our individual stock risk (just one of the inherent risks of investing) has fundamentally been diversified away.

As far as I'm concerned, there is no rational reason for economic fear at this juncture in human history, and I don't believe we need to fear the future, either. When humankind is faced with extraordinary dilemmas, be they economic, political, or social, we strive to find extraordinary solutions. The same thing applies to our own lives. When we attack our personal and financial challenges with vigor, creativity, and an innovative spirit born of the optimistic belief that we can solve them, we *will* find the solutions we seek.

Directing Our Life Movie

What we choose to pay attention to frames and colors every experience we have and, ultimately, shapes the person we become. If we focus on what's troubling and problematic, our life will be troubled and problematic. How can it be otherwise? The brain is our primary interface with the world, and the only editorial control we have over the content of our lives is where we direct our attention. We must choose carefully if we want our story to be a happy one. For a truly masterful discussion of this topic, I recommend reading David Foster Wallace's 2005 commencement speech at Kenyon College entitled "This Is Water."

At the beginning of his address, Wallace says, "The most obvious, ubiquitous, important realities are often the ones that are the hardest to see and talk about." Since human beings are naturally self-centered, and since our reality is shaped by how we think and what we think about every day, we must consciously choose to look outside of our own limited perspective if we want to see the big picture.

Unfortunately, too often *what* we think about is everything that is wrong in the world. For reasons that escape me, many of us choose to begin and end our day watching the news on television. First thing in the morning and last thing at night, we are served up a concentrated menu of warfare, political unrest, vehicular tragedy, natural disaster, and crime. This steady diet of doom continues throughout our day via the real-time scrolling of internet headlines.

Yes, troubling events occur each day. But so do countless inspiring ones. Scientists make amazing discoveries, people experience spiritual breakthroughs, businesses find brilliant new ways to help humanity *and* make a profit. The fact that good news rarely commands headlines doesn't make it less important than conflict in the Middle East. The media trains its lens on the negative and the dramatic because that's what hooks our attention for advertising purposes. Bad news, as they say, makes good copy.

Dwelling on problems, both personal and global, pretty much guarantees we'll be overcome by anxiety and pessimism. On the flip side, turning our attention to what's going well in the world and our lives keeps everything in perspective. There will always be issues we need to address, but if we let them occupy only 5 percent of our attention instead of 95 percent, they literally become smaller.

My aunt Dot understood this principle better than anyone. During the last five years of her life, she was extremely ill and frail. She could barely move, and she had to wheel an oxygen tank behind her whenever she did. Her list of medical symptoms was a mile long. No one had more excuses to be miserable than Aunt Dot, but she was always the sunniest person in the room. Why? Because every single day Dot made the conscious choice to focus on what was still working. Not what was broken. She embodied the Buddha's idea, "We become what we think."

There Is No Absolute Truth, Just One Choice

Humankind has forever debated whether the optimistic or pessimistic view of existence is more valid. Neither is objectively true or false, in my opinion. Both are self-fulfilling prophecies waiting for us to embody them. If we believe we are an insignificant speck in a meaningless universe, we will behave consistently with that belief. If we believe we matter in the world, we will make "I matter" choices. As a result, we *will* matter.

In the same vein, those who believe in a positive future for the world *create* that very future by acting in accordance with that belief. Those who believe in doom and hopelessness construct that reality with self-defeating choices.

Each of us decides whether we matter by mattering. We decide whether life has meaning by living meaningfully. We decide whether the economic future is bright for us and our children by building a brighter future through our actions.

Fake It and You'll Make It

Although optimism makes up a huge portion of your happiness quotient, when it comes to financial planning, there's very little relationship between the size of your investment portfolio and your level of optimism. The factor that has the biggest impact on how optimistic you feel isn't what you own in your portfolio or how well those investments are performing. The powerful rush of optimism that hits when you open your monthly statement is the product of a few simple but meaningful actions you've taken on your own behalf: you have an investment portfolio, you're working on a financial plan, and you're taking small, concrete steps *right now* to ensure that your financial future is the one *you* choose. It doesn't matter *what* you did or *how* you did it. What matters is *that you did it*, that you're doing it now, and that you will keep doing it.

You don't have to be naturally optimistic for financial planning to enhance your life. Watching your assets grow over time to support your future can have a hugely positive effect on your thinking. Positivity reinforces your desire to save more and waste less, which in turn accelerates the growth of your money, which in turn generates even more optimism. Optimism doesn't have to be relegated to chance. It is something you can create and nurture through mindful money choices.

Mindful Money Practice

When I was in high school, one of my English teachers used to say: "If you take a walk to hunt blueberries, blueberries are what you'll find." He was trying to explain why there are so many interpretations of certain Bible passages, but I didn't get the point he was making until I was in college years later: Our search for meaning is prejudiced by our preconceived notions. If we've already decided that we're looking for blueberries, we will miss the huckleberries along the side of the road.

His argument was that we need to keep an open mind, but for the purposes of this exercise, I want you to do the exact opposite. For at least one week, restrict your media diet to nothing but positive, heart-warming, *optimistic* stories. I am not suggesting you settle for news that you would consider meaningless drivel. If your cousin posts sappy, sentimental links on Facebook that drive you crazy, ignore them. On the contrary, I recommend you ferret out stories about things that genuinely inspire you: perhaps the next life-changing scientific study, a profile about superhuman volunteers at the other end of the world, or exciting feats of derring-do. You get extra credit if you forward the article to friends or relatives who could use some sunshine in their life. The goal is to mindfully hunt for happiness and light, even if you're more at home on the dark side!

Get out of jail free card: if you're a political junkie (like me!), and you're reading this book during an election cycle, you have my blessing to save this practice for after the election.

CHAPTER 18

Happiness Pillar 8: *Gratitude*

Piglet noticed that even though he had a Very Small Heart, it could hold a rather large amount of Gratitude.

— A. A. MILNE

Gratitude is perhaps the simplest *and* the most profound of the eight pillars of happiness. Simple, because we can activate it in any moment by giving thanks for someone or something in our lives. Profound, because it unlocks our hearts and welcomes all the other aspects of happiness into our lives.

Gratitude has an almost magical power to flood the present moment with positive energy. In a 2003 research study, Robert A. Emmons of the University of California, Davis, and Michael E. McCullough of the University of Miami found that *habitual* gratitude leads to a happier, more cheerful outlook, while giving rise to better sleep patterns, improved mental health, fewer aches and pains, less stress, enhanced job performance, and increased optimism. Gratitude is like a psychological Aladdin's lamp. Rubbing it immediately summons up a healthier, happier mind-set.

The *what is* of daily life also has the occasional downside. That's why Buddhism teaches us to be grateful for our suffering as well as for our blessings. In fact, since suffering obliges us to grow more than pleasure does, we should strive to be as grateful for setbacks as we are for successes. Those who can learn to embrace both the negatives *and* positives in life are a giant step closer to personal liberation.

Defense and Offense

Gratitude can have a significant impact on our financial behavior, as well as on our overall well-being, according to a 2014 research study by David DeSteno and his colleagues entitled "Gratitude: A Tool for Reducing Economic Impatience." Test subjects were told that if they delayed payment for their participation in the study, they would receive an incrementally larger sum. People who were first instructed to recall an event that made them feel grateful were more willing to make this exchange than were subjects in the control group *or* subjects asked to recall an experience that made them feel happy.

In the Emmons and McCullough study cited above, subjects who were asked to keep a daily gratitude journal tended to be more optimistic and enthusiastic, more likely to exercise, and less prone to physical illness than those who were in a group instructed to document hassles they'd experienced, and those in the control group who were instructed to list recent life events without a positive or negative bias. The gratitude journal keepers were also more determined and more likely to take positive action toward their personal goals.

Such studies suggest that gratitude can be used as both a "defensive" and "offensive" tool. Defensively, gratitude can steer us away from damaging behaviors such as impulse purchasing and wasting money. Offensively, gratitude can give us the energy, determination, and motivation to take concrete steps toward fulfilling our goals, many of which have a financial aspect.

From a nonscientific perspective, anecdotal evidence suggests that gratitude can lead to an improved relationship with money. One popular exercise, which many consider transformative, is to pay one's monthly bills with a sense of gratitude for the service provided. Instead of harboring resentment, harbor a grateful heart: "Thank you, Verizon, for enabling me to talk to my wife on the phone this morning and for helping my mom find me this afternoon when she had good news to share." This simple intention encourages us to acknowledge and appreciate the resources we *have*, rather than focus our attention on what's going out the door.

When it comes to financial planning, gratitude can serve as the acid test for what we include in our plan and what we do not. One of the first steps of planning is to think deeply about what we're most grateful for in life: our family, our friends, our beautiful home, our health, the mountains, and so on. Whoever and whatever we love. Those are the values we should make the cornerstones of our plan and the things we should seek to protect and support with our money choices. It can be difficult to maintain the delicate balance between sustaining what we already have and facilitating what we want from the future. When we're guided by gratitude, rather than attachment, it's easier to find our equilibrium. That's why I keep a picture of my wife and kids front and center on my desk.

Seek and Ye Shall Find

Whatever we mindfully focus our attention on will manifest in our life. Like my high school English teacher said: if we go berry picking in the woods, berries are what we'll find. It's not that berries magically appear. It's that once we start paying attention to berries, we'll see them wherever they are. Likewise, if we look for things to be grateful for, that is what we will find. Like the Buddha said, "All that we are arises with our thoughts. With our thoughts, we make the world."

Ideas may buzz around our heads like bees, but it is the nature of our brains that we can only truly focus on one thought at a time. It is neurologically all but impossible for a brain to focus on gratitude and to simultaneously focus on complaints. The more we consciously choose to think grateful thoughts, the less mental capacity we'll have to dwell on the negative. If that sounds simple, that's because it *is* simple. Of course, that doesn't mean it's easy. The world is always happy to remind us of the negative.

To bring more gratitude into our lives, we may need to reprogram our thinking. Humans are more or less wired to be ungrateful. Our brains are designed to focus on what is *new* in our environment, not what is always present. Existing data fades into the background while our brains continuously scan for new data that might affect our survival or well-being. That's why we stop hearing a waterfall after fifteen minutes and our wife's snoring after fifteen years. In a very real sense, the brain filters out the familiar. It is hard to be grateful for something we've tuned out.

Fortunately, the brain is very user-friendly. It will apply whatever filtering criteria we tell it to use, thanks in large part to a section of the brain known as the reticular activating system (RAS). Called the brain's "attention center," the RAS helps control what we notice and focus on. We can easily program the RAS to scan for things to be grateful for, and it will happily comply. With a little practice, we can turn our brains into allies of gratitude.

Appreciation vs. Entitlement

The brain's tendency to notice what is different and unexpected is a hard-wired survival tactic. For example, one small item out of place when we get home from the grocery store might signal the presence of burglars. The faint smell of gas may mean danger. Unfortunately, our brain's focus on what's wrong, rather than what's right, can easily deteriorate into a mental state of entitlement rather than appreciation.

Entitlement's rationale is that we deserve to have our lives filled with convenience and perfectly functioning systems. Because of the high level of comfort most Westerners enjoy today, entitlement has become a curse of our era.

When entitlement becomes our mind-set, we notice only the things that don't live up to our expectations, so we miss out on the modern and timeless miracles that grace us every day. As the popular comedian Louis C.K. points out, people complain about poor internet reception on an airplane, while they fail to notice that they're sitting on a chair flying through the sky, being whisked away to an exotic destination halfway around the globe with a drink in their hand. "Everything is incredible and no one is happy," he jokes.

All it takes is the conscious flip of a mental switch to ignite the alchemy that turns the lead of entitlement into the gold of gratitude.

Enough vs. More

I recently had an illuminating conversation with a gentleman in his nineties. He told me that when he was a child, the only holiday gift he received from his parents every year was an orange. He looked forward to that orange for months and savored every bite of it. Now that oranges are a daily pleasure for him, he's lost none of his youthful appreciation. What a contrast to the countless children today who tear through a thousand dollars' worth of gifts in fifteen minutes and are bored with them by the next morning.

Once we cultivate an attitude of appreciation for the bounty that is right under our nose, we can't help but question our culture's obsession with *more*. The illusion that's marketed to us from toddlerhood to old age is that happiness derives from constantly getting bigger and better stuff. Ultimately, this obsession with more only brings us more *stress*. And a lot less appreciation. What most human beings truly want is *time*, not stuff: time to enjoy the things they already own, time to spend with friends and family, time to read a book or walk in the woods. Time brings peace, reflection, contentment, and happiness.

As you start planning your financial life in section 3, frequently ask yourself, "How much is enough for me?" This doesn't mean you need to lower your standard of living. You will actually *raise* it by spending *more time* with the people and things that genuinely bring you pleasure and *less money* on things that aren't central to your own idea of happiness, even if they add prestige to your life.

The Myth of Attraction

A lot of books and articles have been written lately about the so-called "law of attraction." Gratitude apparently activates secret forces in the universe that work in mystical ways to draw more prosperity to our lives. "Think grateful thoughts and good things will come to you," proponents claim. While this may or may not be true, hidden laws aren't necessary to explain how gratitude works its magic:

- Gratitude makes us receptive to the good that comes our way. We may be surrounded by bounty, but if we aren't ready to receive it, we won't reap the rewards. Gratitude opens our eyes to the abundance that's all around us, so it can flow *into* our lives instead of being ignored or denied.
- Gratitude motivates generosity in others. We all prefer giving gifts to someone who expresses their gratitude freely. When a person fails to appreciate what we offer them, we are less motivated to do them another good turn. Not because we selfishly require thanks. We'd just rather go to the trouble, time, and expense for someone who values what we're giving. Without a doubt, appreciative people receive more gifts and help from others, and they are happier. But that's the power of gratitude at play, not some secret handshake.
- We can't game the system. Like generosity, gratitude triggers cascading benefits, but we can't practice gratitude in order to *get* those benefits. There's no gaming the system. Only right intention and hard work succeed. This holds true for all eight pillars of happiness. We must practice them genuinely and mindfully for their own sake if we want to earn our happiness dividend.

Ready, Set, Go!

My hope is that the nine chapters of section 2 have deepened your understanding of what *really* brings happiness to a human life and to *your* life in particular — and that they've given you some concrete ideas on how you can use money to nurture the conditions that support a happy life. However, the eight pillars of happiness may not have addressed everything you need to keep your house in order. If so, I encourage you to spend ample time reflecting about exactly what you need in your life to be happy and fulfilled before moving on to the book's final section, "Making a Plan."

Most people are quick to say, "Money doesn't buy happiness," but many still act as if it does. A little mindfulness and a lot of discipline will vastly improve your personal and financial life. As you untangle your illusions about money from your ideas about happiness, and consider what genuinely makes you happy and healthy, you're ready to walk through the steps of developing a financial plan. Ready, set, go!

Mindful Money Practice

Instead of pen and paper, this exercise in gratitude requires nothing except your pillow and blanket. When you wake up tomorrow morning, allow yourself a few extra minutes under the covers to consciously take note of all the incredible blessings you typically take for granted. That's all.

For instance, you might express gratitude for a healthy body, with a beating heart and aware senses. Or the person sleeping next to you. Your comfortable mattress. Clean sheets and blankets. The roof and walls that keep the weather out. The heating and cooling systems that create the perfect temperature in your home. Electricity. Warm clothing. Indoor plumbing. Hot showers. Hot coffee. A fridge. A stove. A microwave. TV. Fresh fruit, year-round. Chairs. Windows. Forks. People who love you. The internet. A cell phone with more computing power than existed in the entire world a few decades ago. Also consider what awaits you once you step out the door: cars, paved roads, ATMs, convenience stores, a job that pays you money. Not everyone has everything you do, and many people in the world have far less, although they still have much to be grateful for as well.

When you finally climb out of bed, remember to bring your gratitude. And don't forget to keep it handy while you're working on your financial plan. Make this gratitude scan a daily practice, and your gratitude and happiness dividend will grow exponentially.

SECTION THREE

Making a Plan

CHAPTER 19

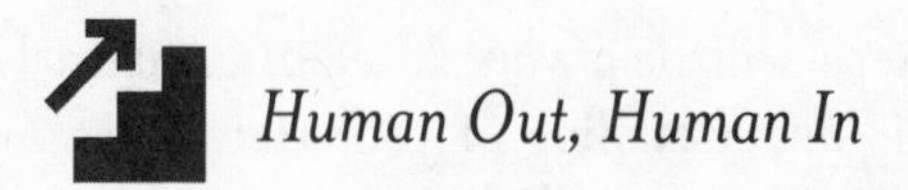

Human Out, Human In

> A garden is a grand teacher. It teaches patience and careful watchfulness; it teaches industry and thrift; above all it teaches entire trust.
>
> — Gertrude Jekyll

We've examined our illusions and we've looked at happiness. What's the true connection between the two? In a very real sense, they represent two sides of human nature: the problem side and the solution side. The inherent conflict between those two sides requires us to perform two key tasks when we create our financial plan: take the human out and put the human in.

Creating a financial plan is a lot like digging a garden. That is, we need to weed out the most problematic aspects of human nature — the panicky, fickle, self-defeating behaviors that can sabotage our long-term vision — and systematically exclude them from our financial planning and execution. Then we need to mindfully cultivate the highest, most-evolved, positive aspects of our humanity — our pillars of happiness — and plant them firmly in the *center* of our plan.

The following chapters of *Mindful Money* will guide you through eight basic financial steps you can take to grow your happiness dividend. These include the following:

1. developing your Vision,
2. starting the saving habit,
3. building an emergency fund,
4. eliminating high-interest debt,
5. investing for retirement,
6. eliminating low-interest debt,
7. increasing your emergency fund, and
8. investing in a taxable nonretirement account.

These eight steps will help you develop a financial plan that is based on a solid understanding of your Here and your There and that is informed by who and what matters to you most. The appendix in *Mindful Money* contains a very simple template ("Your Financial Action Plan," see page 255) that you can use to document your financial plan, and I'll ask you to turn to it periodically as you strategize your journey in section 3. In addition to walking you through each of your plan's eight steps, I will also explain the *least*-complicated approach to money management I know.

This simple and sane strategy will help you remain calm when markets are turbulent, so that you can stay focused on the things that bring joy to your life and so you can shield yourself from the panic, doubt, and mind-flipping that so often complicate money matters.

Failing to account for what really makes us happy when we create a financial plan leaves us vulnerable to advertisers constantly pitching their wares and to the panicked voices of financial pundits that barrage us every time we turn on the television or computer. Instead of picking a lane and driving calmly down the road, they encourage us to make one jittery financial maneuver after another: buy this car, sell that stock, jump in and out of the market, find a new guru, repeat.

We don't have to let unskillful desires, the financial media, or fear guide how we manage our money. There is a better way. A way based on trust, inner stillness, and confidence. That's the way we will go.

Tune Out the Noise and Keep It Simple

The financial world is a noisy place, full of nonstop chatter and conflicting advice. Can we *beat* the market or should we just *join* the market? *Avoid* bull markets or run with the bulls? *Buy* or *sell*? Invest *now* or *later* and in what? Whose advice should we follow? Some experts make economics sound more complicated than physics, and if even the experts can't agree, what chance do regular folks have of figuring out who has the right answer? Hint: it's probably not a pundit on the radio who doesn't know our kids' names, where we work, or how we like to spend our days off.

To make things still more confusing, Wall Street keeps changing its financial story so that it can create new products and services to sell us. As you may recall, the Buddha compared our minds to a monkey, constantly distracted, swinging madly from one branch to another, looking for new fruit. Managers and marketers on Wall Street *also* know that the human mind is fickle, so they jump up and down and make a lot of noise, hoping to lure us to the next bright banana they're selling. If that doesn't work, they try to undermine our confidence in our ability to make sound financial decisions for ourselves because we lack their experience and investment savvy. Another hint: investing isn't rocket science.

It is darn near impossible to discern any actionable message from the noise. My solution? Don't even try. *Tune out the noise completely.* Calm your monkey mind, walk away from the tree, and sit still. Stop constantly worrying about the who, what, where, when, and how of investing. This doesn't mean you should bury your head in the sand. Rather, in the coming chapters, I will explain the steps to take to make, document, and follow a mindful Financial Action Plan. This involves building a diversified, balanced portfolio — with the help of a trusted financial professional if you need it — and establishing a regular investment program that you stick to in good market times and bad. Then, you can turn your attention to what makes you and your family happy and focus on that instead. Pursue your pillars of happiness and stick to your Financial Action Plan. No matter what.

The bulk of what most of us should do with our money comes down to a handful of simple, timeless practices. Those practices worked a hundred years ago, and they still work today. Simplicity is the key. These eight financial steps don't require putting our faith in the "right" guru or oracle. The only leap of faith we'll need to make is *optimism*. We must wholeheartedly believe in just two things:

1. The future of humankind
2. The long, long–term growth of the global economy.

Once we accept the premise that global economic growth will continue its historical, slow, meandering, but inevitably upward trajectory, 90 percent of our financial and investment research will be done for us.

However, there *is* that remaining 10 percent. Like I said, we can't just bury our heads in the sand. The eight financial planning steps we'll walk through together follow the middle path between obsessing over money and ignoring it. They include some very specific practices that can be challenging to carry out — not because they're complicated or difficult (they're not) but because they require making trade-offs. For our long-term financial plans to succeed, we must often sacrifice some momentary pleasures. We must live within our means. We must earn enough. We must save enough. We must invest enough.

The path we're going to tread is about setting behaviors in place that can help us win the meet. The goal isn't to try to win every single race. At times, the entire economy will take a dive, and we will suffer financial setbacks, both real and on paper, both in our careers *and* in our investment portfolios. That's the cyclical *what is* of the stock market and of life. Setbacks happen. Expect them. Panicking during a downturn does not serve anyone's long-term financial plan.

Remember, investment losses only occur when we take action — that is, when we sell low because we're freaking out. When stressful times hit the markets, the economy, or your life, zoom out, remember your goals, and hold yourself accountable to your Financial Action Plan like that Zen master with a stick. Be patient. Don't lose conviction in the careful investment decisions you made with a clear head in calmer days. There's no good reason to be fearful or act mindlessly. Follow your plan and you'll be fine.

Part of being fine requires accepting that the *noise*, your *shenpa*, and that no-good monkey mind will never stop trying to play with your emotions. The pitchmen will continue to sell. The gurus will continue to preach. There will always be fascinating new voices with fascinating points of view. But those people with the bullhorns do not have crystal balls. Never did, never will.

Meanwhile, Back at the Garden

Family travel is one of my biggest pillars of happiness. So is our family vegetable garden. As I write these words, the four of us have just returned from a two-week trip to Greece, and I am blown away by what happened in the garden during our absence. Our return was met by two twelve-inch pumpkins that didn't exist when we left, along with a brand-new harvest of snap peas, pole beans, lettuces, and cucumbers. All of this bounty simply *arrived* because we took the correct steps early last spring.

Growing money is an awful lot like growing vegetables. We need to follow some very specific steps — and then do nothing but water. For vegetables, we must choose a sunny location, till the soil, plant the right seeds at the right time, feed and water the shoots, clear the weeds, erect a fence to keep out critters, and leave the vegetables alone till they ripen. Do those things and growth *happens*. On its own.

Anyone who believes they can grow vegetables without taking these steps is sorely mistaken. To complain that the rules of vegetable growing are too restrictive, or intellectually unfashionable, would be pointless. They are what they are. When we *do* take the proper steps, the results follow. Some growing seasons will be better than others, but over time our labor will be rewarded with copious amounts of fresh produce.

The principles of vegetable growing have not fundamentally

changed in ten thousand years. The steps are not glamorous or fun, but they're not complicated either. Do them and nature will handle the growth. Ignore them and all the advice we read from gardening experts is for naught. Investing is very much the same.

Another lesson from gardening? *Trust the process.* If we get nervous about how our seedlings are doing, we know we can't pull them up to check on them. That would only short-circuit the very growth we want and guarantee no fat, juicy carrots result.

Money is no different — although we can't expect satisfactory results if we bury our cash in the backyard. There are time-worn principles designed to help money grow like zucchini after a summer rain, although growing money takes *years*, not just weeks. In order to harness that growth potential, we must take the right steps, water regularly, wait patiently, and trust the process.

Don't Believe Everything You Feel

Anyone who ever heard their parents argue about the bills when they were growing up knows that money can be a touchy subject. In the coming chapters, we'll map out a *practical* route to get you from Here to There, but financial planning is often an *emotional* journey as well. While you methodically plot the course from your point A to your point B and beyond, tuning out media pundits and advertising soothsayers may not afford you enough peace and quiet to find your calm financial center. You might also need to dial down your personal fears about the future and regrets about your financial past. Some of those fears will manage to capture your attention or try to drag you back to some dark, scary cave in your head. *Don't go there.*

Sit with your fear out in the open, where you can examine it in the clear light of day. Accept it, acknowledge it, but avoid acting on it. The fact that your fear echoes so loudly through the corridors of your brain doesn't mean it's telling you the truth. It probably isn't. Don't abandon your Financial Action Plan. Don't tear up the roots to see if your plants are growing. Protect, nourish, and water your dreams, stay focused on your journey, and go about the business of being happy.

Mindful Money Practice

Before you turn to chapter 20, please take at least an hour to review all the hard work you've done in your *Mindful Money* notebook so far, especially the "Itinerary" practices in chapters 3 and 5, and the "meaningful purpose" practice from chapter 14. Have any of your responses to the practice questions changed now that you've completed the first two sections? What about your actions? Intentions? Goals? Allow yourself ample time to revisit each of the practices and your responses, and complete any "homework" you may have skipped. Even practices that seem tangential to the actual process of creating a Financial Action Plan will play a critical role in the coming pages. You'll want to have everything you've discovered about yourself, your money, and your happiness at the top of your mind as you begin drafting your Financial Action Plan.

CHAPTER 20

Step 1: *Develop Your Vision*

> I have noticed that even people who claim everything is predetermined, and that we can do nothing to change it, look before they cross the road.
>
> — Stephen Hawking

Imagine this scenario:

You wake up in a strange hotel room and have no idea what city or state you're in. Propelled only by the vague feeling that you need to get somewhere, you wander out to the parking lot where several rental vehicles await. You select one at random. In the backseat sit several strangers who know nothing about you, or where you're going, but they are ready to offer their "expert" commentary on how to get there. You slide behind the wheel, pull out onto the road, and begin driving with no specific destination in mind as these strangers bark out directions, all while hoping you'll eventually get "somewhere good."

Would you embark on a trip this way?

Oddly enough, this is how many folks approach their financial lives. They fail to acknowledge their present reality, don't know where they want to go, and give little advance thought to the journey they'd like to take.

You can't get "somewhere good" in your financial life until you understand where you are *today* and have a clear picture of what you want your life to be like *tomorrow.* Beginning with a range of probing, big-picture questions, this chapter will help you determine both of these things, so that you understand your starting point and your destination, and you can identify how to blaze your path between them.

Though at times philosophical, these questions are not rhetorical. All are meant to be answered, although how you answer them is up to you. To begin, just consider these questions, but if you prefer, you can write your answers and thoughts freely in your notebook. Many of these questions have been raised already in some form, and the answers may come easily. Others will require more thought. Then, once you reach the section "Develop Your Vision" below, you will be asked to commit your responses to writing as you define the Vision for your Financial Action Plan (for a complete template, see the appendix, page 255). By the time you finish describing your Vision, you should have a fully developed picture of the future you are working toward and know the specific financial goals you'll need to set and accomplish if you're going to get There. "Develop Your Vision" is Step 1 of your Financial Action Plan, but creating the Vision itself consists of five elements, and each of these parts consists of dozens of baby steps. If the overall process of creating your Financial Action Plan ever feels daunting, simply focus on the next small step in front of you and keep going till you finish!

Here

Making a financial and life action plan means embarking on a *conscious pilgrimage*, not a blind excursion. As discussed in chapter 3, in order to do that, you need to get clear about two things: Here and There. Where are you now and where do you want to go? Every trip starts with these two coordinates. A map is useless unless we know our Here and our There.

It is easy to lose sight of our Here or to miss it entirely. Caught up in our unfolding dramas and daily repetitive routines, we can forget to ask the most fundamental questions about our lives. Our Here is a thorough understanding of *who we are* and *what is important to us* at this time in our life. Take a moment to consider each of the following questions, either simply pondering them or writing your answers down:

- Who am I?
- How do I view my place in the universe?
- What matters most to me?
- Who matters most to me and how do I show that?
- What delights me and makes my life worth living?
- What are my greatest strengths and talents?
- Where do I derive my sense of meaning?
- What is the point of my life?
- What motivates me and makes me tick?

These questions, and others like them, are the stuff of Here. It is both pointless and impossible to try to make a financial plan without giving a lot of thought to your Here. Who is this person embarking on this pilgrimage? What matters deeply to this person? What satisfies, delights, and motivates this person?

Pinpointing your Here also means being honest about your financial reality. Take a moment to consider each of the following questions, focusing more on the *quality* of your financial life rather than on the quantity of your resources. In chapter 21, "Start the Saving Habit," we'll get specific about the actual numbers when we tackle Step 2 of the Financial Action Plan. For now, appraise your current financial circumstances in a more general way:

- How does my balance sheet look? Do I owe more than I own? Or am I on solid financial ground?
- How healthy is my asset base? Have I saved enough for current and future goals like retirement and helping my parents as they age?
- What is my income level? Do I earn enough to realistically save for those goals, given my present obligations?

You may not be happy with where you are financially right at this moment, so be gentle with yourself as you think about these questions. But be honest. Without a straightforward Here, you cannot possibly map a Route to a more secure There. If your Here is negative today, remember that impermanence is a constant. Things can and will change. *My* Here has been negative multiple times, but I did not despair. I decided on a better course, put one foot in front of the other, and kept walking.

There

It is equally important to know where your There is. Without a clear destination in mind, your journey will lack purpose and focus. To figure out where your There is, you must do some soul searching. Take a moment to consider these next questions very carefully, as the answers will be critical when it's time to finalize your Vision below. Again, you can either just ponder these questions or commit your answers to writing:

- What are the true goals of my heart?
- What is absolutely vital for me to achieve in this lifetime?
- How do I want to be remembered? That is, what do I want my legacy to be?
- What are my bottom-line requirements from life?
- What do I want my retirement to look and feel like?

We will only be invested enough to make a plan and stick to it every day, week, and month if we know where we want to be in life with absolute emotional certainty. Having a well-defined There gives us a sense of direction that will pull us through the dark times. It will spur us to make tough trade-offs and push us over difficult humps. Your There cannot be generic or borrowed from the pages of a magazine. It must be based on who you really are, what you really care about, and what truly makes you happy. In other words, your There must be firmly rooted in your Here *and* reflect your version of the eight pillars of happiness.

Finally, in my somewhat-biased point of view — I am a financial adviser, after all — your There should include an income stream you can't outlive in retirement.

The Route

As you define your Here and your There, you must also consider the journey between them. What *Route* will you take? In earlier practices, you were asked to consider a potential Itinerary, that is, places where you might need or want to stop along the way to your There. Now it's time to make the *where* and *how* of this journey concrete.

What quality of "travel" do you require? Do you prefer to take scenic byways or the express lane? What do you need to experience on a daily, weekly, and yearly basis in order to feel happy, renewed, and motivated?

Some people, for example, need to do work fueled by their passions. Others are happy with less passion-driven jobs, but they use their free time and income to pursue passions like theater or music or horses. Some folks *need* to live at the seashore or in the mountains. For others, scenery matters less than proximity to family. I know folks who choose to live like paupers in a part of Northern California that has few jobs because they absolutely love the natural splendor that surrounds them. Note that the Route we take can often impact our There, as we make trade-offs in our current lifestyle to accommodate our longer-term goals. For example, we may decide that we are willing to work a few years longer to fund our retirement — that is, *if* we can take three-week vacations annually instead of two-week vacations.

What are the major goals you want to accomplish along the way? There will undoubtedly be specific things you want to do and achieve in life, such as obtain a graduate degree or start a business. There will also be things you want to provide for your family, such as a comfortable home, a college education for your kids, and/or financial support for your aging parents. Life, for better or worse, has a built-in timeline. We must decide which goals along the way are critical to achieve and when they must occur. To accomplish those goals, we may need to trade off some things that are less important in the long run, as well as some nonessentials we crave in the present moment. If we're planning a big destination wedding in an exotic locale next year, for example, that will impact how we save and what we can buy right now. On the other hand, if another primary immediate goal is eliminating high-interest debt, then maybe we need to modify our wedding plans so we don't spend in ways that increase our debt.

It is imperative to pinpoint your big, time-sensitive goals because only by identifying them clearly will you be able to commit the resources and make the trade-offs necessary to ensure that they actually happen *when* and *how* you want.

The importance of trade-offs cannot be overstated. As you create your Financial Action Plan, you will list all the goals you wish to accomplish — including the overarching goal of creating an income stream you can't outlive. However, as you look at the assets you have now and are likely to have in the future, you may realize you're not going to have enough money to do everything you want.

In that case, you will have to make trade-offs, and you will have three choices to consider:

1. Invest more aggressively.
2. Increase your resources.
3. Modify some of your goals.

Of the three, investing more aggressively is my least favorite trade-off, as most folks (including me) can't emotionally handle the volatility or risk that entails (we'll discuss investment strategies in more detail later). To increase our resources, trade-offs we might consider include giving up a job we love to get a new job that pays more, working more hours at our current job, or getting a side job to earn a little money. The loss of leisure can be a manageable trade-off, especially if it's made temporarily to achieve a short-term goal. I know an attorney who took a weekend gig as a dog walker to pay off his student loans more quickly. We can start a home business or even make our home *into* a business. One client on a fixed income gets a great financial boost by renting out a room to visiting scholars, though this makes for a crowded house. Another client pays for vacations she couldn't otherwise afford by renting out her whole house on Airbnb one weekend each month.

Finally, modifying our goals can also be quite manageable and won't necessarily involve the dire choice of giving up a goal entirely. For example, if one goal is to pay for a child's college tuition, this can be modified by choosing a cheaper school (such as a state college) or planning to pay only part of the tuition (and use student loans for the rest).

The key thing to understand about trade-offs is that we all make them in life. The only difference is whether we make them consciously or unconsciously, actively or passively. The purpose of planning is to bring those trade-offs to the forefront so we can make them thoughtfully and realistically, ensuring that our most important goals are attained. In a way, the entire process of creating a Financial Action Plan involves taking a hard look at trade-offs and revising our plan till our goals, resources, and actions are aligned.

Develop Your Vision

In order to clarify your Here, your There, and your Route, you must develop a Vision. Architects call their vision a blueprint, mechanics call it a schematic, and cooks call it a recipe. I prefer "Vision" because it captures the forward-looking nature of financial planning. A Vision is a written document that serves as a rudimentary life and finance map. Putting our intentions in writing gives us the impetus we need to start *living* that map. Our Vision is at once the guiding force behind a financial plan *and* the entire reason for having a plan in the first place. In *Mindful Money*, developing your Vision is the first of the eight planning steps that make up your Financial Action Plan.

If you haven't already, now it's definitely time to take out your pencil and paper. In the rest of this chapter, as you tackle each of the five elements of your Vision, I suggest creating a draft version of each element in your notebook, so you can revise your responses as necessary. Then, once you've finished, turn to the appendix (page 255) and fill in "Step 1: Develop Your Vision" in the Financial Action Plan template. Or, if you prefer, use the template to create a final version of Step 1 in your notebook. Bottom line: do what works best for you.

The five essential elements of developing a Vision are these:

1. Identify your personal values.
2. State your meaningful purpose.
3. Picture your perfect life.
4. Develop your professional mission statement.
5. Set your personal goals and list your action steps.

Your Vision should be simple, clear, and specific. It will also be dynamic and changeable, just like life. I update my Vision every single year, and we advise our firm's clients to do the same. Instead of viewing the practice of developing a Vision as a one-and-done exercise, we encourage folks to think of updating their Vision as an annual financial physical.

1. Identify Your Personal Values

Every plan starts with Here. As you work to clarify your Here, the first thing you need to do is identify your personal values. Each question in this chapter — and every chapter in this book — is designed to help you home in on these values, so you should now be ready to answer these questions:

- What matters most to you?
- Who matters most to you?
- What are your passions?
- What are your desires?
- What are your pillars of happiness?

Identifying what we truly value gives us the impetus we need to create a long-range plan *and* live by it every day. Take as long as you need to reflect on your values before completing this element *in writing* below.

Element 1: Values

List the core values that make for a life well lived in your eyes, describing each value in as few words as possible. The goal is to capture the kernel of meaning. These values should align with *your* pillars of happiness, which may or may not correspond with the eight pillars I name in section 2, "Finding Your Happiness." For example, you might designate six values, such as family, spirituality, integrity, generosity, health, and self-determination. The key to a successful Vision is to name values about which you have strong convictions, so that you are motivated to structure your life and finances around them. Once you've listed your values, rank them in their order of importance in your life at this moment in time. Knowing where your priorities lie is critical when you're faced with competing goals that will require making trade-offs. If you find it impossible to prioritize one value over another, ties are perfectly acceptable.

2. State Your Meaningful Purpose

Next, turn your focus outward and consider your gifts, passions, values, and where you find and bring meaning to life. Each of us was born for a reason. We all have something unique and valuable to contribute to the world, and our happiness depends on making the most of that human potential. A meaningful purpose states your definitive answer to the question "*Why* am I Here?" If you completed the Mindful Money Practice in chapter 14, wrote your meaningful purpose on an index card, and used it as a bookmark, find that bookmark now. Here are some examples of how a meaningful purpose might read:

- I spread the message of nonviolence by writing children's books.
- I am here to make my community a better place.
- I teach peace.
- I seek beauty.
- I was born to inspire others with my athletic abilities.

Without a meaningful purpose, life feels flat or like a treadmill of obligations. We wake up, go to work, solve the day's problems, eat dinner, go to bed, wake up, and do it all over again. We can spin our wheels for fifty years and reach the end of our days wondering why we ever existed. Or we can strive to make a positive impact on the world and find meaning in even the most routine aspects of our existence. Modest acts performed with right intention are as powerful as grand gestures. We don't have to cure cancer or be the first human on Mars to make a meaningful contribution. We can plant flowers to bring beauty and happiness to our neighbors.

Element 2: Meaningful Purpose

Why are you here on this planet in this place at this time? Contemplate your reason for living and put that reason in writing. It may take you several passes, but clearly state your meaningful purpose in twenty words or fewer, similar to the examples above. If you completed the Mindful Money Practice in chapter 14, consider whether this statement still fits. If not, revise it or write a new one specifically for your Financial Action Plan. When you are tempted to stray from your financial plan or have difficulty choosing the right direction in your life, this meaningful purpose will be the beacon that guides you toward the best course of action. As in chapter 14, write your meaningful purpose on an index card and keep it where you will see it every day!

3. Picture Your Perfect Life

There's an old saying, "If you don't know where you're going, any road will take you there." People who achieve lasting happiness know exactly where they're going and exactly what There is meant to look like. They can clearly visualize the ideal There, even as they realize that the picture and destination *will* change over time.

If you want to earn *your* happiness dividend, you must unify your ideas about There into a full-color picture of your perfect life. By *perfect,* I do not mean imagining a fairy-tale life of leisure, complete with a thatched cottage in the middle of dwarf-inhabited woods. Don't imagine lording over a castle in the sky next door to heaven. There is nothing perfect about some romantic ideal no one could possibly reach. Then again, if things go well, where would you like to be? To use an example from chapter 15, aiming to become president and move into the White House is probably a stretch, but a life dedicated to public service is not. Some goals take longer to achieve, but *attainability* should be a key component of the picture you paint of your perfect life. Imagine a brighter future you can actively strive for, not the fantasy of winning the lottery.

This picture of your perfect life is not meant to be something you keep only in your head. Commit this scenario to writing in a present-tense, first-person narrative that describes what your life would be and *feel* like with as much emotional clarity as possible. Here's an example:

> My family is financially secure, physically fit, and emotionally close. I am self-employed and work out of our comfortable home on an acre of land within an hour's drive of the Pacific Ocean. Our home is light and airy with room in the backyard to garden and entertain. Pictures of my family adorn the walls. The sound of our children's laughter and the smell of my spouse's cooking fill the house. We have two rocking chairs on the front porch and a happy golden retriever.

The picture of your perfect life should reflect your deepest desires and values. As the focal point of your financial plan, it will provide the inspiration for sticking to that plan, day after day. When you feel down about temporary setbacks or frustrated with some aspect of your work or home life, picturing your perfect life will pull you through. If your picture is not compelling enough to excite and encourage you, it's not about you. Rework it till it is.

Element 3: Picture Perfect

Starting with pure stream of consciousness, write freely about what you would include in your perfect life. For the first pass, write as much as you need to get everything down. Ultimately, for the purpose of your Financial Action Plan, you want to capture this picture in far fewer than a thousand words, so that you can refer to it often. After that initial iteration, revise this description and sharpen your picture. Remove anything that feels superfluous, condense each vital attribute to its essence, and add any key factors you missed the first time around. The goal is to describe your perfect life in one vivid paragraph that moves and motivates you. After you've nailed down the key factors, polish your picture until it shines. I keep a copy of *my* picture on a laminated card. You can, too!

4. Develop Your Professional Mission Statement

The next task of refining your Vision is to develop a professional mission statement and put it in writing. This statement captures who you are in your professional life at this moment in time. Don't take the word *professional* too literally. If your full-time "job" is running a household or volunteering at a food bank, that vocation should be the focus of your mission statement. The same thing applies if you are a student.

This mission statement helps describe your Here, but it may also include There. For instance, if you are unhappy in your current employment, then your "professional mission" could be finding ways to make the best of that bad situation until you find another job that fits the type of work or role you want. If you're currently unemployed, your professional mission could be to excel as a job seeker! Finally, if you juggle more than one job, consider crafting a statement for each. One of my colleagues has two mission statements, since she is equally committed to her home and work life:

1. Bring love to the office every day.
2. Keep the household humming happily.

The central questions a professional statement should answer include the following:

- Why you are in business?
- Who do you serve?
- What do your clients need from you?
- What can your employers/employees reliably expect from you?

Developing a professional mission statement is a powerful practice — whether you are a business owner, volunteer, stay-at-home parent, or part-time employee — because ultimately each of us is in a "business of one," and we should run that business mindfully.

As an example, here's my professional mission statement:

> I inspire my clients to pursue their passions and make meaningful financial decisions that are firmly rooted in their values. I am trusted for my knowledge, integrity, discipline, and commitment to service.

Your professional mission statement can be as long as a paragraph or as brief as "I fix eleven-dollar haircuts." It should be something you can hold in your mind every day. While your meaningful purpose describes the fundamental "why" of your existence, your professional mission statement captures your conscious intention for approaching the central activity of your daily life and holds you accountable to that intention.

Element 4: Mission Statement

Put your professional mission statement in writing. You get bonus points if the statement is shorter than this two-sentence instruction!

5. Set Your Personal Goals and List Your Action Steps

The fifth and final element of developing your Vision is to set a series of goals and plan how you will achieve them. These goals will become the heart, soul, and driving force of your eight-step financial plan.

The picture of your perfect life describes your ultimate destination, but getting from Here to There will require taking a series of deliberate steps and staying true to your Vision, come what may. How many goals will this involve, how many steps will it require, and how will everything fit together over time? That is for you to decide. Since juggling multiple goals and weaving them into a single timeline is invariably complex, anticipate that finishing this step in your Vision will take the most time and effort.

In the chapter 15 Mindful Money Practice "Walk the Talk," this book guided you through the process of identifying and achieving a single goal. Now we'll use that same practice to complete the Vision that will guide your eight-step financial plan. If you haven't already, turn to the Financial Action Plan template in the appendix. The four-column "Set Your Personal Goals and List Your Action Steps" (page 257) element is similar to the four-column "Walk Your Talk" practice, but the column headings are a little different. For this activity, they are "Goal," "List Action Steps," "$ Cost," and

"Target Date." In essence, this element of your Vision asks you to name your large life goals, to specify the action steps that are needed to reach each goal, to calculate what the goals will cost, and to set a completion date for every goal. These last two data points will play a critical role as you work through the next seven steps of your Financial Action Plan. They will help you define how much cash you will need to save and/or spend by your target dates in order to achieve your goals.

Probably the best way to approach this process is to start from the picture of your perfect life and work backward. In order to bring that picture to life, what are the various discrete goals you need to accomplish? For example, if owning a home is part of your picture, then "buy a home" is one of your goals. Be as specific as necessary in characterizing each goal. For instance, do you want a historic home in a particular city, or a suburban home with a yard, or will owning an apartment or town house anywhere satisfy your perfect picture? Further, each of these goals must pass the SMAC test. As described in chapter 15, they must be specific, measurable, achievable, and compatible. Not only must each goal be achievable in itself, but it must also be compatible with all your other goals within the timeline you create. For example, a five-year goal of buying a Victorian home in Seattle may not be compatible with your other career and family goals over that same time span, and some trade-offs will be needed.

As you define your goals, break each one down into a series of smaller, correspondent *action steps*. In the example above, if owning a home is one goal, then saving money for a down payment will be one action step, and other steps might include getting a second job, investing five hundred dollars a month in a nonretirement account, and researching the housing market in Seattle.

You also need to calculate costs and establish a target completion date for each goal. Many goals, such as owning a home or sending kids to college, will cost money. How much can you realistically afford to pay for a home, how big of a mortgage do you want to carry, and what size down payment will you need? Other goals, such as "make partner at my firm by age thirty-five," may cost money initially (such as for training) and then *generate* money later. Estimate what each of your major goals will cost and determine when you plan to *start* and to *finish* paying for them. For shorter-term goals like buying a house in five years, it's relatively easy to research home prices, determine a reasonable down payment, set a target date, and set monthly savings goals (which we'll discuss in more detail in chapter 21). For longer-term goals, like paying for your infant child's future college education, the *date* will be easy to calculate, but costs must be guesstimated. You will need to research current costs at representative colleges, and then use a financial planning calculator (many are available online) to approximate what the future cost might be when your child is ready to enter the freshman class.

Although adequate retirement income should definitely be one of the named goals in your Vision, don't calculate the cost column for that particular goal until *after* reading chapter 24, "Begin Investing for Retirement."

Once you've listed the action steps and arrived at an approximate cost and target date for each goal, all the information you need to prioritize your goals and realistically evaluate your trade-offs will be consolidated onto one page in a simple, easy-to-understand format. Pretty nifty, huh? Getting from Here to There is definitely about making those trade-offs, so keep revising your goals, action steps, costs, and timeline till everything aligns. Few of us can have everything we wish for in our richest fantasies, but we *can* have the things that are most critical to our happiness, if we are willing to give up the things that are not.

Element 5: Set Your Goals and Action Steps

Goal setting is the final element of developing a Vision, and it's definitely the most labor intensive. In particular, the data gathering and calculations may seem a bit daunting. Stick with it, and take as many breaks as you need. If you have ten goals, knock out just one goal a day for ten days, spread it out over two weeks, or finish them all in one marathon sitting. Just remember that the hours you spend now will save you years of misery later *and* make you happier in the immediate future.

To start, open your notebook, sharpen your pencil, and draft a list of the personal goals that will help you realize your perfect picture.

Then, roll up your sleeves and get to work. Turn to the Financial Action Plan template in the appendix (page 257), and on a fresh page in your notebook, copy the four-column chart "Set Your Personal Goals and List Your Action Steps." First, plug each goal into the list, and then I suggest tackling the goals in the order of increasing difficulty. However, use whatever method works best for you. I liken this endeavor to completing a crossword puzzle: fill in the information you know first, and then add the rest of the data as it becomes available. For example, while retirement is an obvious goal, choosing a retirement date could require more consideration than you expect. As noted above, future college costs can be difficult to guesstimate, but you can still calculate a reasonable savings goal as an action step. Bottom line: be patient with yourself, trust the process, and breathe.

Once you've finished, fill in the chart in the Financial Action Plan template, or create a final version of this Step 1 chart in your notebook. Then give yourself a pat on the back. Congratulations! You have just completed the most important and the most difficult of the eight planning steps of your Financial Action Plan.

CHAPTER 21

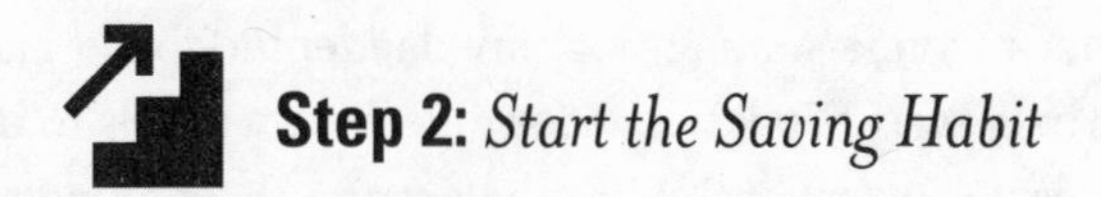

Step 2: *Start the Saving Habit*

Penny saved is a penny got.

— Henry Fielding

Now that you've identified the primary financial goals and approximate cost of your There, it's time to talk about *how* you will fund your Vision, which is Step 2 of making your Financial Action Plan.

The steps to growing money are not sexy or tricky or speculative. They don't require a degree in finance. Nor do they require constant hands-on management. They are simple and logical but not always easy to follow. They require only that we establish certain practices and habits of mind, then move on to whatever we find more interesting. The catch is: we must actually *observe* the practices.

Spend < Earn

The king of all money practices is to spend less than we earn *and* save whatever we don't spend. If we do only *one* smart thing in our money life, this is the one.

"Spend < Earn" is the first domino of wealth. In meditation, the fundamental practice is to sit. In *personal finance*, the fundamental practice is to *save*.

The absolute best thing we can do for our financial health and happiness is to start the habit of saving as early in life as possible. I was lucky enough to learn it as a child, and now I work hard to teach my children the habit. Few folks are so fortunate.

Whenever I earned a few extra dollars from doing a chore or got a paycheck from a summer job, my dad let me spend half and made me put half away. Today, I encourage my own kids to do the same. I don't care (too much!) what they spend their money on, as long as they're saving some. There are always cooler things to do with money than save, but it can quickly become a self-reinforcing habit if we let it. By the time I joined the workforce, saving was ingrained in me. Even though I hated forgoing fun, I liked the feeling of control over my life that saving gave me. I still do.

Your Balance Sheet

Managing personal finances is in many ways like running a small business. There are two financial statements every business possesses: the cash-flow statement and the balance sheet. The cash-flow statement tracks the money that comes in and goes out every month. The balance sheet is the net effect of that cash flow: our assets versus our liabilities — what we owe versus what we own.

If we spend more than we earn, our balance sheet will eventually go negative. In other words, we'll find ourselves in debt. We can play all the mental games we want with our savings versus our credit card accounts, but the simple fact is that a negative balance sheet is a negative balance sheet. We must get back into positive territory or we can't survive or thrive. And the only way we can return to the positive side is if our cash flow *in* is consistently greater than our cash flow *out*.

Our balance sheet needs to be strong enough to pay for the cost of our lifestyle while we're still working, plus some extra for the future. In the future, that same balance sheet will need to cover our living expenses *when we stop earning income*. Short of unexpectedly inheriting a massive windfall, the only way to reach that point is to start spending less — perhaps *much* less — than we earn *many years in advance*.

Ideally, there will come a day when we are able to live off the income generated by the difference between what we spent and what we made over the course of our career. If we always spend more than we make, that day never comes. This isn't as much about having more money as it is about having choices and freedom as we age.

Spending less than we earn is only part of the equation, though. We must also do something productive with the money we're not spending. That means putting our excess cash to work for us in a disciplined and dedicated way. We'll explore how to do that in more detail in the upcoming chapters.

Very Pleased to Meet Me

I wish every person could have a heart-to-heart conversation with his or her future self. In nearly every case, our future self would tell the present self: "Save more when you are young." A survey commissioned by Holiday Retirement, entitled "100 Years of Wisdom: The Perspective of Centenarians," queried the oldest members of their senior living communities about what made for a happy life. When asked what financial decisions they thought folks today would regret later in life, not saving enough and spending too much of what they earned were the top two responses.

We don't like to save during our younger years because the future seems abstract and distant, and we believe we're going to live forever. We're also at the low end of our earning capacity and have countless demands on our limited funds. Frankly, the trade-off just doesn't seem worth it when we're young. Why sacrifice fun, enjoyment, and status *now* for the sake of some imaginary old person?

Of course, our future self is *not* an imaginary person. That person is very real; he or she just hasn't manifested yet. And what our future self wants our younger self to do is to save like crazy today because every dollar we save now means much more freedom and enjoyment later. We can't imagine how much, but there is a very real tension between our present self and our future self. Although both of them want our spending concentrated on them, only our present self will be heard.

The reason saving early in life produces so much bounty later on is because — thanks to the wonder of compounding — saving early is far more effective than saving later.

Compound Interest

Albert Einstein probably never said, "Compound interest is the eighth wonder of the world." Yet compounding is a staggeringly powerful principle. Compounding means taking the returns our savings or investments generate and adding them back into the pile. This one small maneuver helps the pile continue to grow incrementally larger and earn increasingly higher returns over time.

For example, let's say we start with $1,000 and invest it in a portfolio that pays 8 percent annual returns. At the end of a year, we will have earned $80. We put that $80 back into the pile, so our total investment is now $1,080. We now invest that new total at 8 percent for another year. At the end of the second year, we will have earned $86 because the principal we invested ($1,080) in year two was greater than the original $1,000 in year one. If we plow our new $86 back into the pile, our total becomes $1,166, and at the end of year three, our earnings will be $93, and so on. Our money grows while we do nothing!

To guesstimate the potential impact compounding will have on your savings, you can use the "rule of seventy-two." This determines the approximate length of time it will take for money to double. This method is easy: you simply divide seventy-two by the return your money is earning. For example, if your money is earning 2 percent on average, then divide seventy-two by two, which equals thirty-six. That means it will take about thirty-six years for your money to double. Obviously, the rate of return makes all the difference. Let's say your money is earning 9 percent. Seventy-two divided by nine equals eight. Your money could double in only eight years.

The most powerful aspect of compounding, by far, is *time*. After about fifteen years, crazy growth kicks in. Money that is left to compound for thirty, forty, or fifty years begins to produce truly jaw-dropping results. So it's an exercise in patience. At the end of thirty years, even if we never add a penny to our original $1,000 investment, and so long as we continue to earn an 8 percent return, our total will be over $10,000. In forty years, our original $1,000 would be over $21,000; in fifty years, $47,000. Now imagine what happens if we keep adding more money to that total every year, *and* we are able to eke out a higher average rate of return over the life of the account. Although interest rates on bank savings accounts have been rock bottom in recent years, the global equity market has consistently delivered annualized returns in the neighborhood of 10 percent *over long periods of time* — but only to those who've practiced *faith*, *patience*, *and discipline* during the rough patches.

Compounding may not be a "miracle," but we must believe in it if we want our money to keep up with inflation and sustain our lifestyle into the future.

Time Is on Your Side

If they could, our future selves would remind us to think about compounding every time we spend money. For example, if our thirty-year-old self skipped one restaurant meal per week and saved that fifty dollars instead, we would save twenty-six hundred dollars every year. Compounded at a reasonable rate of return over time, this could easily amount to enough money to allow us to retire two or three *years* earlier than planned.

We can't just think in terms of what our savings *gain* us. We also have to consider what our expenditures *cost* us. *Over the long term*. A few thousand dollars spent on an unnecessary purchase when we're twenty-five might cost our retirement-age self a hundred thousand dollars or more due to lost compounding.

Take a car, for instance. Let's say we're thirty and we're considering springing for a luxury model that costs $25,000 more than a comparable midpriced car. That $25,000, invested at 8 percent and compounded annually, would be worth over $170,000 to our fifty-five-year-old self. That could mean early retirement, a two-year sabbatical to tour the world, or the funds to start a business. How much is a few years of luxury car-driving worth? I'm not saying never spend money on luxury goods. I'm just saying that we always need to factor compounding into our thinking to understand the true price we're paying for goods over our lifetime.

The earlier we start thinking about this stuff, the better. Every year that passes is a year of compounding we stand to lose. It also means the amount we need to save per month in order to reach our goals goes up.

Ranking Priorities

How can you save more and spend less? One way is to rank potential expenditures in terms of their importance. Rate them from 1 to 10. Cut out spending on the lower priorities — the things that mean less to *your unique version of happiness* — and save that money instead. You should take your whole life into account when you do this. Perhaps saving two hundred dollars a month for your kids' future education weighs in as more important than paying an extra two hundred dollars a month in mortgage payments for a house with a guest bedroom and hot tub. A mindful trade-off in the present moment allows your whole life to unfold more happily.

On that family trip to Greece I mentioned earlier, my wife and I fell in love with a painting in a local gallery. Price tag: three thousand dollars. We both decided to pass on the painting. Saving that three thousand dollars for our future freedom was a better investment for us. Of course, someone else might legitimately decide that a trip to Greece itself was an unnecessary luxury. That's fine. My wife and I made trade-offs for years — such as eating dinner at home six nights a week — so we could afford plane tickets to Europe for a family of four. Why? For me, it was in part so I could see the joy on my six-year-old daughter's face as she met and made friends with another girl just her age by communicating with hand signals and facial expressions because they didn't share the same language. The trade-offs each of us make will depend on what we value most. But we must also remember to give our future self a voice in our big financial decisions. We shouldn't bankrupt our tomorrow for the sake of the Mediterranean sun or forget that the world will still be there next year if we have to pay off a big medical bill this year.

How Much?

How much do you need to save? Unless you are saving for something with a fixed cost, saving a specific amount is not the goal. Rather, a better approach is to save a set percentage of your income every month. When I was still a kid, my dad said that I should save 10 percent of my salary when I joined the workforce. So I did. Even though I was paying off student loans and earning only eighteen thousand dollars a year, I saved my 10 percent. I didn't even know what I was saving for, but I saved it anyway.

When we're young, the biggest raise we're ever going to get is right out of college, when we get our first real job. That's when we stop living on ramen noodles and borrowing money and start *earning* an actual salary. The first day of a first job is the ideal time to begin saving. When we're earning so much more than we were before, we can put away 10 or 15 percent without even feeling the pinch. Though my dad told me to save 10 percent, I wish he had said 20 percent. Saving 20 percent is not that hard if we were previously earning next to nothing. Saving more will be *much* harder to pull off once we've gotten used to spending a certain amount per month, but if saving 20 percent becomes a habit right out of college, we could maintain the habit painlessly for a lifetime.

I now save 35 percent of my income, mainly because I want to send my children to college without student loans. I realize many people cannot save that much, but I am fortunate enough to earn a good income. I am also willing to fly coach, drive an older car, eat at home most of the time, and make other lifestyle trade-offs.

Even 10 percent is not a bad goal, provided we start young. Saving a set percentage guarantees that our savings remain proportionate to our income and lifestyle requirements. While a person earning seventy-five thousand dollars per year will save less actual currency than a person earning three hundred thousand dollars per year, they will both save the same amount *relative to their expenses.* Assuming each starts early enough, both should be able to maintain their current lifestyle upon retiring.

As an illustration of what saving just 10 percent can do, let's look at some fairly typical real-world numbers for an imaginary college graduate. Let's assume that our graduate's starting salary after earning a degree at age twenty-two is $40,000 and that our graduate's income increases by an average of 3 percent annually. Then let's assume that our graduate always saves 10 percent of her or his income *and* that our industrious graduate's investment portfolio grows by an average of 7 percent per year. If all those conditions are met, the results are nothing short of impressive:

- At age fifty-two, our graduate's annual income would be roughly $97,000 (with annual savings of about $9,700), and her or his portfolio value will be about $583,000.
- At age sixty-two, annual income would be roughly $130,000 (and annual savings about $13,000), and the portfolio value will be around $1,308,000.
- At the full retirement age of sixty-seven, our graduate's portfolio will be worth almost $2 million.
- And if that graduate saved 15 percent annually, *or* had a starting salary at age twenty-two that was 50 percent higher, then our graduate would have nearly $3 million at age sixty-seven.

It is amazing how simple it is to generate a comfortable level of wealth if we get into the saving habit right out of college. Even if we miss out on saving early in life, it is never too late to start. If we are fortunate enough to get a windfall through an inheritance or a stock-option payout, we can seize that opportunity to kick-start a new savings-driven mentality.

Autopilot

The other day I heard a media pundit say that some people may be saving too much. This is crazy talk. In all my twenty years as an adviser, I have never met one person who was saving too much. I do have some clients who are *over*saving *relative to the goals of their financial plan*, but they are doing so deliberately. They know that if they beat their goals, they can retire earlier, or travel more, or give more away, so they automatically max out their 401K contributions.

Anytime *you* can arrange for your savings to happen automatically, all the better. Most banks offer some form of automatic savings program. If you work for a company that offers a 401K plan, that's the best place to start. Not only is it an enforced habit, but the employer may also match your contributions.

Remember, however, that saving alone isn't enough to ensure a happy, financially secure future. The less you spend, the more freedom you buy!

Mindful Money Practice

Knowing how your finances add up is imperative if you want to create an effective savings plan. Even if you've never heard the terms *balance sheet* and *cash-flow statement* before, these two financial power tools are easy to learn and start using right now. Templates for both are in the appendix in Step 2 of "Your Financial Action Plan": "Your

Balance Sheet" (page 258) and "Your Monthly Cash-Flow Sheet" (page 259). As before, I suggest first creating rough drafts of each in your notebook. Once you've tracked down all the numbers, add them to the template or create a final version in your notebook.

To make a rudimentary balance sheet, draw a line in the center of a fresh sheet of paper. At the top of the left column, write the word "Assets." Below this, make a list of what you own, placing the value of each asset next to it in the column. Your assets may include your home, your car, the money in your 401K account or nonretirement investment account, your checking and savings account balances, and anything else of significant value, such as your business or your stamp collection. Utilitarian items like clothing and dishes can be left off the list. At the bottom, add up everything in the "Assets" column and write the total. This is the approximate financial worth of what you own.

At the top of the right column, write the word "Liabilities." Below this, list all your debts, placing the dollar value of each next to it in the column. Examples include the remaining balances on your student or car loans, your credit card debt, and the amount you still owe on your mortgage. At the bottom, add up everything in the "Liabilities" column and write the total. This is how much you owe.

To calculate your *total net worth*, subtract what you owe from what you own. If this is a positive amount, good start! If your total net worth is negative, adjust the goals of your financial plan to get yourself in positive territory. This total net worth is directly tied to your cash flow. When your cash flow is positive, your total net worth increases. When it's negative, the debt side of your balance sheet gets heavier, which weighs on your financial health *and* happiness.

Creating a cash-flow statement is similar. Draw a line in the middle of a page. Title the left column "Income," and list all the income you receive each month from work, Social Security, your business, investment dividends, and so on. At the bottom, add up the amounts and write the total. Title the right column "Expenses," and list all of your monthly expenses, such as rent or mortgage, food, gas, insurance payments, utilities, charitable donations, and so on. For annual expenses like property taxes, divide them by twelve. At the bottom of this column, add up those figures and write the total. Subtract your expenses from your income. If the difference is a negative number, start strategizing how to stop spending > earning today!

Finally, complete the third chart in Step 2, titled "Rank Your Goals and Establish Your Monthly Savings Plan" in the appendix (page 260) and copy this five-column chart on a fresh page in your notebook. The headings are: "Goal," "Total Cost $," "# Months (until Target Date)," "Monthly Cost $," and "Rank." First, list your goals from the Step 1 chart "Set Your Personal Goals and List Your Action Steps," then rank these goals by priority. However, now that you've looked carefully at your balance sheet and cash flows, you may want to add a few more goals to your monthly savings plan, such as allocating a certain amount of your income every month to whittle away at your credit card debt. Then, for each goal, list the total cost of that goal (from the Step 1 chart), calculate the number of months between now and the target completion date for that goal, and calculate how much you should save each month to reach that goal.

Once you're happy with your draft, enter all this information into the Financial Action Plan template in the appendix, or create a final chart in your notebook. As with your Vision, I recommend updating your balance sheet, cash-flow statement, and monthly savings plan at least annually, or whenever you have a major financial change in your life, such as an inheritance, a new job, or a new baby.

CHAPTER 22

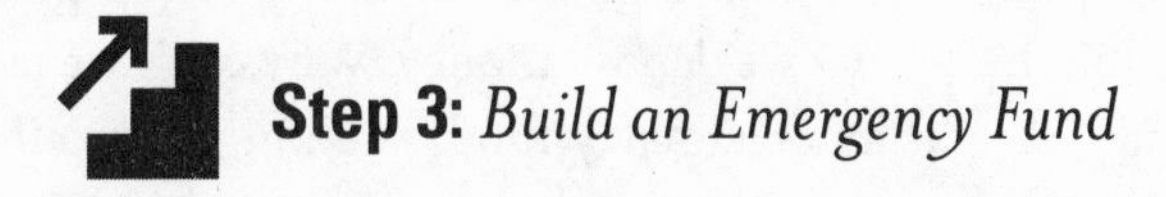

Step 3: *Build an Emergency Fund*

> Expect the best. Prepare for the worst. Capitalize on what comes.
>
> — Zig Ziglar

Once you've started the habit of saving, the first place to put those savings is into an emergency fund. Yes, cold, hard cash into a good old-fashioned savings account. Nothing can derail a financial plan more quickly than an unexpected emergency we are not prepared to handle, and there *will* come a time when a tree falls on our life, either literally or figuratively. When that happens, we'll need a ready supply of cash. *Bleep* happens, as every farmer knows. An emergency fund helps us clean up the *bleep* and stay on course.

The very fact that we have an emergency fund increases our peace of mind in the present, and it also allows us to withstand periods of volatility in our investment portfolio as we get closer to retirement. One of the main goals of financial planning is to reduce our stress about the future, so that we can be happier in the here and now. Distilled to its essence, financial planning is the art of insuring against what can go wrong in order to earn the luxury of investing for what can go right.

The emergency fund planning practice at the end of this chapter will guide you through this third essential step of your Financial Action Plan.

Why Cash?

The first question most clients ask me when I instruct them to fund an emergency savings account is "Why cash?" After all, at today's interest rates, a cash savings account starts losing ground against inflation the minute we deposit money. Why can't we use the equity in our home as an emergency fund, and put all of our excess cash into an investment portfolio, where it may generate healthy returns? Why tie up valuable money in a savings vehicle that pays essentially zero?

The reason is because cash is the only financial instrument that is completely dependable in a pinch. Ready cash can put a new roof on our house or tires on our car today, with no questions asked. Cash may not be the solution to all our problems, but the money in savings is readily available and the value of our account is not going to drop suddenly. The same cannot be said of our investment portfolios. Because of market volatility, our investment portfolio will go up and down. That's to be expected. The problem is, we never know when the dips will occur. While volatility is our friend when it comes to building a long-term portfolio, it's not our friend when it comes to covering emergencies or managing anxiety.

It is precisely the fact that cash *doesn't* fluctuate in value that makes it useful as an emergency resource. Yes, there is a lost-opportunity cost. Our money *could* be working harder, but the practical and psychological benefits are well worth that cost. Investment portfolios aside, our other assets are not as predictable as cash either. For example, relying on home equity to save the day can be problematic. Before the Great Recession in 2008, everyone considered home equity a dependable source of emergency funds. But in 2008, the banks stopped allowing even highly credit-worthy customers to pull money from their line of credit. Suddenly, that door closed.

I am a long-term optimist, but given the ever-present reality of turbulence in world markets and the economy, it just makes good sense to have a safety net. We can't know when our next temporary setback will occur, so we must plan for it to happen at any time. No one wants to be forced to dip into their investment portfolio when it's in decline. Cash is a stable buffer. It won't spike in value, but it won't collapse either.

The worst possible outcome of maintaining an emergency fund is that we never use it. And that's actually the *best* thing. The money we don't use now will be available to us in retirement, which is a tremendous benefit.

How Much Cash?

How much cash should you keep on hand for life's emergencies? Generally speaking, the older we get, the more cushion we need. Early in adulthood, our expenses are generally lower, we tend to have fewer financial responsibilities and dependents, and our risk is lower. Then life grows more complex. More people rely on us, our expenses go up, and we have a lot more at risk if our income nose-dives.

Young Adults

For individuals, couples, or families just starting out, three months of expenses is the minimum to keep aside. Remember, that needs to include *all* expenses. Not just for regular monthly bills like rent/mortgage, electricity, cable, and phone, but for out-of-pocket expenses like food, gas, and entertainment. Although it seems harder to save when we're young, as I mentioned earlier, the easiest time to start the savings habit is when we get our first full-time job.

We should grow our emergency fund slowly and deliberately. If we can only afford to add twenty dollars per paycheck or 10 percent of our salary each month, we should do that. But we should save a certain minimum amount to develop the habit. If and when we can do more, we should do more. The goal is to stay right at the edge of our comfort zone and never dip into savings unless it's a true emergency.

Middle Years

During the midpoint of our working life, from about thirty-five to fifty-five years old, our lifestyle costs are usually at their highest. We may be raising a family and/or investing in future obligations like retirement or college tuition. Meanwhile, there is the added risk of job loss. More companies are using downsizing as a way to maintain profitability, and those layoffs often happen at times when the market is dropping. Since we don't want to touch our investment portfolio when it's dipped in value, we need a bigger safety net in midlife: six to twelve months of expenses.

Nearing Retirement

During the final years of our working life, we should strive to have twelve to twenty-four months of expenses in our emergency fund, building up to two years by the day we retire. The years immediately before retirement pose the greatest risk to our long-term financial health. Financial advisers call this four- to five-year preretirement period the red zone. It is a critical time because much of our future income will likely come from our retirement investment portfolios, which are subject to unpredictable market swings. No one likes unpredictability, but we will need to invest if we hope to beat inflation.

If we're planning to retire in five years and our investments are doing well, we probably look forward to seeing a nice income stream from those assets. But the stock market historically takes a major dip every five years or so. This is not anything we can predict. It's just a possibility we can plan for. If the odds play out, there's a decent chance one of these dips will occur during our red zone. That's why we must build a buffer to protect us: an emergency cash reserve that is not subject to market fluctuations. Without it, a major market drop right before we retire could push our retirement date out a few years. Or worse. If we lose our job or total our car, we might need to pull money out of our investment account while it's down. Since we'll soon be out of the workforce, our portfolio may never fully recover, so we'll be forced to permanently lower our lifestyle.

Having an emergency reserve we can tap for living expenses buys valuable time for our investment portfolio to recover. This theory was tested during the market plunge of 2008. My clients who had ample cash reserves were able to refrain from touching their investments. As the market recovered, their portfolios bounced back and started making money again, allowing them to start drawing income again. Their portfolios are currently doing well enough to generate a surplus they can use to gradually replenish their cash reserves before the next inevitable market drop.

In Retirement

Ideally, once we retire, we should maintain *two years* of emergency savings for when (not *if*) the markets take a tumble, which is almost certain to happen multiple times over the course of our retirement. In fact, if we live thirty years in retirement, we may see at least a half-dozen periods where markets dip by 30 percent or more, based on historical averages.

If we mindfully saved two years of emergency expenses during our working years, that two-year emergency fund becomes an invaluable tool in our retirement.

What Is an Emergency?

When is it time to dip into the emergency fund? Only *you* can answer that. You may need to put a roof on your house or a transmission in your car. If you have a separate maintenance and repair fund to cover such eventualities, even better. The bottom line is that the emergency must be a true emergency *for you*: a large and unpredictable expense, not an unskillful desire, like a vacation you can't afford.

Perhaps the most common use for an emergency fund is a job loss. Many companies no longer give generous severance packages, leaving us to cover a job transition with no reliable source of income. Even just three months of cash can save us a lot of grief, provided we reduce our spending to subsistence levels. Once we spend our emergency funds on a *want*, that's when a need will arise.

Once we've set aside adequate cash reserves for emergencies, we can create a separate reserve fund to bankroll unexpected opportunities and foreseeable expenses. The more we budget for "predictable" emergencies, the better. Objects are impermanent by nature and they *will* break down. If we own a home, it will require a new roof every twenty years or so. Cars always need repairs, and property taxes come due twice a year. None of this should come as a surprise. We should build savings for these anticipated expenses into our monthly budget.

In the business world, it's common to reserve a percentage of profits to cover expenses like replacing the computers every few years, hiring new staff, marketing and advertising, and so on. A reserve fund is completely separate from an emergency fund. If you are planning to take a sabbatical to write a book, or your children are heading toward their college years, these are known expenses on the horizon. You should start saving now to cover them, not burn emergency cash to pay for an entirely expected expense.

The Beauty of the Buffer

The emergency fund is an especially sensitive issue because the more we need one — that is, the closer we are to the financial edge — the harder it is for us to save. Conversely, if we have a high income, and it is relatively easy for us to sock away money, the less critical building an emergency fund becomes.

For too many families today, job loss or a few weeks of illness for the main breadwinner can trigger a full-blown financial crisis. We must do everything we can to buffer ourselves from this situation. Having an emergency fund gives us the breathing room we need in tight spots. Once we start the savings habit, the slow but steady growth of our reserves inspires us to keep feeding that piggy bank.

The goal of an emergency fund is to put in cash and *leave it there.* Even if we never touch the money, we know it's there, which has a tremendous effect on our happiness and peace of mind. This small action affords us rare control over our fate.

Buddhists accept that there are many aspects of existence over which we have *no* control: death, aging, illness, decay, and loss. An emergency fund will not alter the impermanence of life. Nor will it stop *bleep* from happening. But it will make us equipped to deal with what comes our way. Better we have an emergency fund and not need it than need an emergency fund and not have it.

Mindful Money Practice

Step 3 of your Financial Action Plan is to calculate the target cash balance for your emergency fund, so that you can start saving for the unexpected now. As with the previous steps in your plan, I recommend making a trial run in your notebook before filling in the template in the appendix.

There are two data points you will need for this calculation:

- your total monthly expenses, and
- how many months of emergency savings you need or want to have.

First, consult the cash-flow statement you created in Step 2 of your Financial Action Plan and locate your total monthly expenses at the bottom of the "Expenses" column.

Next, multiply that monthly expense figure by the total number of months of emergency expenses you plan to save. Depending on your current phase of life, you can use the number of months I recommend in this chapter, which can range from three months to two years, or simply target a minimum benchmark of six months. In the appendix, “Step 3: Build an Emergency Fund” (page 261) includes a chart with these recommendations.

Then, assuming your monthly cash-flow statement shows a positive balance, decide how much per month you will devote to building up your emergency fund. Start saving that money in a cookie jar or bank account now.

As with the savings goals you established in Step 2 of your plan, divide your total emergency fund target amount by the dollar amount you plan to save each month to determine how long it will take to reach your goal. Or do the opposite: set your target amount and a target date to determine your monthly savings plan. For example, if your goal is to put twelve thousand dollars in an emergency fund within two years, you would plan to save five hundred dollars a month for twenty-four months. Even if you can only afford to allocate fifty dollars a month toward building your emergency fund, start saving now.

Once you’ve completed your draft calculation, document your goal in Step 3 of your Financial Action Plan template or finalize it in your notebook.

CHAPTER 23

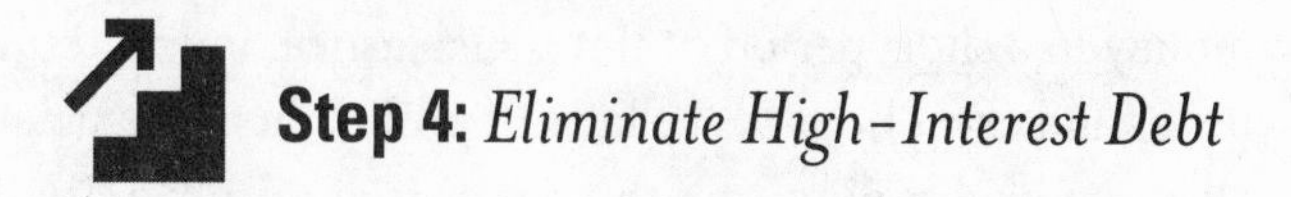

Step 4: *Eliminate High-Interest Debt*

The best thing money can buy is financial freedom.

— Rob Berger

As a quick review, so far you've completed Steps 1 through 3 of your Financial Action Plan. You have:

- developed your Vision,
- started the saving habit, and
- built an emergency fund.

The next step is to use the "extra" income you don't need for current living expenses, your savings plan, or your emergency fund to implement Step 4 of your Financial Action Plan: eliminating high-interest debt.

The *very* best thing you can do to increase your happiness dividend is to establish a concrete plan for paying off any high-interest credit cards and personal loans as soon as possible. These typically include 10, 15, 20, or even 29 percent compound interest charges, which is more than we can reasonably expect to ever earn through investments.

It's simple math. If we can reasonably expect our investment portfolio to make a 6 or 7 percent average return over the long term, but we're carrying large credit card balances at 10 percent interest or more, we're losing financial ground. On the other hand, low-interest debt (which can include many house and car loans) reverses this equation. When interest rates on debt are lower than 6 or 7 percent, we may make more money in the long run if we use our surplus cash flow for investing rather than for paying off cheaper debt more quickly.

While it's theoretically *possible* for an investment to double our money in a short period of time, such astronomical returns are pure flukes and exceptions to the laws of probability. Financial planning is all about probability. And there is a strong probability that a diversified portfolio won't earn us even 10 percent as a long-term average. If we're carrying debt at 10 percent interest or higher, it's wise to pay off that particular debt first before putting extra money into investing. There are a few notable exceptions to this rule, which we'll review later, but debt service needs to be at the top of our priority list.

Debt: The Bluebird of Unhappiness

Before we look at the financial aspects of dealing with debt, let's look at how debt relates to our overall happiness.

As *great* as it feels to be growing wealth for the future, it feels equally *bad* to be carrying major debt. A little personal debt is fine, and carrying a mortgage is generally better than carrying other debt. But a large amount of consumer debt relative to our income casts a pall on every other aspect of life. Debt is a major stressor that can keep our fight-or-flight response locked in the "on" position, increasing our chances of heart disease, sleep disturbance, and digestive conditions, among other things. Debt also carries a tremendous amount of shame, which may lead to self-defeating and self-destructive behaviors. Heavy debt also results in poor credit scores, which pollutes every aspect of our financial lives.

From a mindfulness point of view, one of the greatest drawbacks of debt is that it often goes hand in hand with denial. Since acknowledging debt is painful, we tend to push it to the back burner of consciousness. We refuse to deal with *what is*, and that denial takes an ongoing toll on our happiness.

As debilitating as debt can be, it is equally empowering to tackle it. For those who've once carried heavy debt, *freedom* from debt is the ninth pillar of happiness.

How Much and How Soon?

How energetically should we attack our high-interest debt? Should we dispose of all our debt before we invest *any* money in a retirement plan? There are no one-size-fits-all answers to these questions. The urgency of our need to eradicate debt increases with the size of our debt and the interest rate we're paying. One common pitfall to avoid is attacking our debt so aggressively that we sacrifice our emergency cash reserves. Without emergency reserves, we will be in double trouble if a crisis strikes. That's why paying off debt comes *after* creating an emergency fund.

But if our debt has a high interest rate — which I define as anywhere from 10 to 29 percent — we need to hit it as hard as we can as *soon* as we can. Once our emergency fund is in place, any excess money should be applied to our debt. If our credit is decent, we may be able to refinance our debt at a lower interest rate. Utilizing a low-interest balance transfer offer from a new credit card can also be a good option, provided we don't use the extra breathing room to take on more debt. Or worse, *increase* our spending. It's tempting to think, "Hey, now that my four-hundred-dollars-a-month payment is only a hundred dollars, I have three hundred dollars more to blow each month." Instead, we should keep our payments at four hundred dollars a month. This is an opportunity to pay off our debt faster, not buy a new wardrobe, kayak, or car.

The speed at which you'll want to pay off your debt comes down to your personal situation. For example, take someone who graduates college with six thousand dollars in credit card debt at a 20 percent interest rate. When that graduate gets his or her first good job, the person's income might jump significantly, perhaps from nine thousand dollars to forty-five thousand dollars or more. That person has just made a monumental leap in financial resources, and in this case, I'd suggest the following steps in this order:

1. Build the emergency fund.
2. Pay off the six thousand dollars in high-interest debt.
3. Then kick-start the miracle of compounding by opening a retirement account.

The person might choose to pursue all three steps at once, especially if his or her high-interest debt is relatively low compared to income. However, never skip debt payment.

The math suggests that paying off high-interest debt is the wisest use of our money, but it's exponentially more important the more debt we have and the higher the interest rate. There's a world of difference between a fifteen-thousand-dollar balance at 28 percent interest and a nine-hundred-dollar balance at 12 percent.

Nor is all debt "bad." Not only do home mortgages today carry low interest rates — so that the return we see on our investments will likely be higher than the cost of our mortgage debt — but there are often tax advantages to having a mortgage. If we invest in a 401K, and receive employer matching benefits, that might make a wiser investment for our extra money than paying down car loans, mortgages, and other low-interest debts.

It's Not All Numbers

Math isn't the only factor we need to consider. Psychology comes into play as well. Asset building is a powerful motivator. The psychological benefit of watching our retirement account grow often outweighs the purely mathematical advantages of paying off debt. It is exciting when the assets side of our balance sheet goes up. Seeing the debt side go down isn't quite as thrilling. The boost we get from increasing our assets can spur other mindful money behaviors that may benefit us even more than debt erasure — such as compounding.

It is crucial we start the compounding engine as soon as possible because time is literally of the essence. For the first fifteen years, we won't see much. Then the power of exponential returns shifts into high gear. Warren Buffett made 90 percent of his money after age sixty. Not because he suddenly got smarter, but thanks to compounding. Compound returns are the primary driver of financial freedom, so we should jump on the investment bandwagon today, even if it means living with some debt — unless that debt is completely unmanageable and carries crazy-high interest rates.

Striking the right balance is tough. While we can't ignore our high-interest-rate credit card balances, we don't want to postpone building our assets either. The maximum allocation I'd recommend is 50/50. We should commit at least half of any excess money to paying off more expensive debt before investing the remainder in our future. Of course, the larger our debts and higher the interest rates, the more important it is to pay them off quickly. Compounding may have to wait.

That River in Egypt

Many people are so ashamed of their debt that they hide it from themselves and others. If you are in an uncomfortable amount of debt, you need to come clean, both to yourself and to those who can help you. In chapter 19, I mentioned the need to examine our deep, dark financial fears and regrets in the clear light of day. Now's the time. Step out of denial. Accept the *what is*. Facing debt honestly and openly gives us the power to solve it and removes the terrible burden of secrecy, which kills both our health and our happiness. Admit the reality of your Here, whatever it is. Take a deep breath. Then move forward into the light. Be kind and patient with yourself as you take the difficult but rewarding steps to pay off your debt. Many have done this. You can, too.

Though it probably goes without saying, the primary step to paying off debt is to quit adding more debt. Do what you can to reduce or stop using your credit cards. Quit tapping your line of credit and convert yourself to an all-cash economy if necessary. If you have an overwhelming amount of high-interest debt relative to your income, consider seeking professional help, such as credit counseling or debt-relief programs. Or join Debtors Anonymous if you want an accountability partner. Even if you're drowning in debt, there *is* something you can do to turn the ship around.

Debt is inversely proportionate to our happiness. The greater our debt, the more it affects our enjoyment of life. But the greater the amount of debt we *conquer*, the greater our happiness dividend. Deal with debt ASAP and free up the capacity for more fruitful and skillful uses of your money.

Mindful Money Practice

There are two standard approaches to debt retirement. If you have more than one account with high-interest debt, some advisers favor paying off the smallest balances first. This is because totally knocking out one debt at a time provides a nice psychological boost. I prefer the tougher, more financially sound approach: throw as much money as possible at the debt with the highest interest rates first, while continuing to pay the minimum balance due on all other accounts, plus 100 percent of any charges and monthly interest accrued.

In the appendix, "Step 4: Eliminate High-Interest Debt" (page 261) provides a five-column chart for you to consolidate the key information about all your high-interest debts on a single page. Using this tool, you can prioritize and plan how you will eliminate that debt. As before, I recommend creating a draft of this chart in your notebook before finalizing your debt-reduction strategy, either in the Financial Action Plan template or on a separate page of your notebook.

In your draft chart, fill in the data for the first three columns first: "Debt," "$ Owed," and "Int(erest) Rate %." You'll need to gather all the data on each of your debts first before you can decide how you'll attack them. If you aren't sure what interest rate you're paying, call the customer-service department of the lender. Once you've compiled the essential information, consider the last two columns: "Monthly $" and "Order." Make a mindful decision about the order and pace you'll pay off your debt. Will it be higher interest rate or lower balances first? Decide what's right for you. In the "Order" column, assign a number to each debt, indicating the order in which you intend to pay them off.

Write your final plan in your Financial Action Plan template or in your notebook. Then begin diligently knocking out your debt a little (or a lot) every month. Don't forget to add those debt-reduction payments to your cash-flow statement in Step 2 of your Financial Action Plan, and remember to track your progress on your balance sheet once a year! Watching your total net worth climb slowly but surely out of the red zone and into the black will astronomically increase your happiness dividend.

CHAPTER 24

Step 5: *Begin Investing for Retirement*

> We must discipline ourselves to convert dreams into plans, and plans into goals, and goals into those small daily activities that will lead us, one sure step at a time, toward a better future.
>
> — Jim Rohn

Step 5 of your Financial Action Plan is the most challenging *and* rewarding: investing for retirement. Even for folks who love working, a comfortable retirement is the ultimate financial goal. We may each have our own definition of "comfortable," but we all need to take mindful steps toward it if we want to enjoy the secure old age we imagine. Social Security and/or the increasingly rare pension just won't be enough to sustain our standard of living, so we should begin investing for our retirement as soon as we've eliminated our high-interest debt. If you're already participating in a 401K at work, now's the time to start ramping up your contributions. If you work for yourself or a small company without benefits, establish an IRA account. Bottom line: sock away as much money as you can while you're still working for the day when those paychecks stop coming.

For most people, retirement is the single largest expense of their lifetime — and it is a *much* bigger concern for our generation than it was for our parents and grandparents, who could count on a pension. We must plan accordingly. If we don't save enough money, we can't retire *when* we wish or *how* we wish. It's that simple. Retirement planning is something many people get wrong. There are several factors they neglect to consider, as evidenced by the fact that people today earn more than their grandparents, but save far less. We need to reverse that trend.

What Is Retirement?

Up until a few generations ago, *retirement* didn't really exist. Most people toiled until they died or were incapacitated by illness or injury, at which point they were cared for by their extended families. Only in the twentieth century did the modern version of retirement — that is, a period of nonworking years in which one is still in relatively good health — become steadily more widespread. The advent of Social Security helped cement this notion of retirement into our collective consciousness.

A lot of folks think of retirement as the day you start collecting Social Security. That's when we imagine ourselves living life like our grandparents did after *they* retired: knitting, fishing, golfing, baking apple pies, volunteering, and rocking on the porch. But we're also living longer than our grandparents. Thirty years of putting greens and porch rocking is not financially viable for most folks these days, and few of us really want that, anyway. We desire a more active, productive, *engaged* retirement.

I think we need a new definition of retirement that fits our times. Our "fourth quarter" should be a period of maximum financial *and* personal freedom. We *may* decide to keep working in retirement, but we don't *need* to work in order to survive. We may want to take a part-time job, do some consulting, turn an avocation into a vocation, or work strictly on a volunteer basis. The choice should be ours, based on desire, not necessity.

Getting Kicked Out of the Driver's Seat

Unfortunately, no one has complete control of their destiny. If we are forced to stop working before we've saved enough for retirement, our lifestyle may be drastically and permanently reduced. This is a scary but very real possibility for many.

We may not be able to choose our retirement date. Today, the average age people stop working is actually sixty-two. That's because the employment landscape changes as we approach our sixties, and frequently one of three things happens:

1. We can't work anymore.
2. We don't want to work anymore.
3. They won't let us work anymore.

At age forty-five, we can't always imagine or anticipate the changes that will occur when we're sixty-five that may force us to retire sooner than we'd planned. One change we can't predict is declining health and energy. We may develop an illness that sidelines us or forces us to work fewer hours, or we may simply lack the drive, energy, or physical coordination we once had. Plus, the fact is, there often comes a point when the prospect of working no longer seems appealing. Even if we can still work, we lose our desire to do so.

Finally, of course, ageism in the workplace is real. Seniors are more likely to be passed over for jobs, raises, and promotions, and when layoffs happen, companies often cut older employees first. Older employees may not have the technical chops of younger colleagues, and they may not have the motivation or ability to master new skills. Conversely, senior employees at the absolute top of their game can find themselves priced out of the market. I see many brilliant people with fantastic résumés who are unable to find work in their fifties and sixties because no one can afford them. Start-up companies would rather hire a young MBA whose salary is easier on the bottom line, or someone willing to accept lower pay in exchange for potential equity in the company, that is, stock options.

Another hard reality is that leaving the workforce after age sixty is effectively an irreversible decision. We may never reclaim our former role once we've retired, so we shouldn't rush to the rocker until we're as prepared as possible.

The Big Trade-Off

The best strategy for protecting ourselves from being stranded with too little income is to start investing for retirement as early in life as possible. This means more than just establishing a regular savings plan. Determining what trade-offs we're willing to make is *the* most important factor in our financial success. We must remain ever mindful of that fact as we make our Financial Action Plan. Every financial decision we will ever make in our lives has a direct impact on the final pool of assets we will have at retirement. That final asset pool determines *when* we'll have the financial freedom to retire and what options we'll have once we do.

Our retirement fund is the "theater" where the effects of every single financial act in our life will ultimately play out. *Exponentially.* Thanks to the power of compounding, every dollar we've ever saved or *not* saved will, in retirement, be magnified by a factor of ten, twenty, fifty, or more. We must mindfully and consciously weigh the trade-offs we're making every time we choose to spend money to support our lifestyle — whether that's choosing our children's schools, the cars we drive, or the zip code we live in. The ongoing dialogue between our present self and future self must continue. All these choices will affect our retirement.

Simply put, every step we take in our financial lives is leading us toward the giant financial leap that is retirement. We must be careful to avoid waste along the way. Every dollar we throw away without realizing even a small happiness return is a dollar that could be harnessed toward a tremendous happiness return down the line.

Planning for a Long, Long Retirement

Retirement now lasts so long it amounts to a second career. Our enhanced longevity has made inflation *the* dominant issue to consider when planning for retirement. It doesn't matter how much *currency* we have in the bank; the real-world purchasing power of our *money* must keep pace with, and beat, inflation. I introduced this issue in chapter 9, but I want to explore it in more detail here.

According to Consumer Price Index data, over the past hundred years, the average annual inflation rate has been over 3.2 percent. That means that when we build our financial plan for retirement, we need to anticipate at least a 3.5 percent annual inflation rate. If we want to be superconservative, I suggest 4 percent. There is no guarantee that actual inflation rates won't be higher or lower, but 3 to 4 percent is a solid guesstimate in my opinion.

Similar to comparing the interest rates between our debt and our investments (which we did in chapter 23) to decide the most advantageous way to use our "extra" income, we need to ensure that our pool of retirement investments keeps pace with this annual inflation rate of 3 to 4 percent. If it doesn't, we're losing money. If our retirement investments earn less than 3 percent, they will fall behind and lose relative value no matter how soon in life we start saving.

However, inflation's *real* impact kicks in the day we retire. That's when we stop *building* our asset pool and begin drawing from it. Retirement ushers in a long period when the assets we've gathered must produce much, if not all, of our income. As we discussed in chapter 9, the average retirement age today is sixty-two, and one-fourth of today's sixty-five-year-olds will live to age ninety, according the Social Security Administration. No one knows how long they will live, but given those numbers, I think it's imperative we plan for another thirty years after retirement. Since life expectancy continues to rise, living for another forty years after retirement is a real possibility for some.

That's a long time to live without a monthly paycheck. Plus, as we plan for retirement, we need to determine how we'll replace our monthly paycheck *and* cover our ever-increasing expenses due to inflation.

We start by identifying our fixed-income sources, such as Social Security, spousal support, annual family gifts, and/or any pensions we expect to receive. The last item, a pension, has become much rarer, as companies today prefer to push the expense and responsibility of retirement onto their employees. Next, we take an honest look at our annual expenses. These expenses should include everything we currently spend money on and anything we plan to *continue* spending money on to preserve our lifestyle — from the water bill to our museum memberships to property taxes *and* restaurant lunches. Be realistic, as most folks underestimate how much they spend every year.

Then we need to give these numbers another hard look the year before we plan to retire. What is the difference between our fixed-income sources and our actual living expenses? That difference is the *gap* our retirement asset pool must help us fill. For example, imagine we receive a fixed income from Social Security of $32,000 during our first year of retirement, and our expenses are $56,000 that year. That makes our initial gap $24,000, so we will need to pull $24,000 from our retirement portfolio during year one of retirement.

Thanks to inflation, that gap will widen every subsequent year. That's why it's not enough to ensure our retirement investment account produces sufficient income in *year one*. That retirement portfolio needs to continue growing so it can provide sufficient income every year and keep up with the rising cost of living. If it doesn't, our buying power and lifestyle will steadily dwindle.

Rising costs are not the only reason the gap we need to fill gets larger each year. Inflation pretty much guarantees that our fixed income is worth relatively less every year as well. Some pensions and retirement investments have a built-in cost-of-living adjustment (COLA) that is pegged at a specific annual number, such as 2 percent. Others, including Social Security, are tied to a particular benchmark like the Consumer Price Index for Urban Wage Earners and Clerical Workers (CPI-W), which is determined annually by the Department of Labor's Bureau of Labor. Others have no COLA at all. Still, a COLA doesn't guarantee we can keep pace with inflation. If we *do* get a 2 percent increase every year, and inflation is 3 or 4 percent...

The chart below illustrates the effects of inflation on a hypothetical 1983 retiree during years five, ten, twenty, and thirty of retirement. I've included an imaginary pension with a fixed 2 percent COLA, Social Security income with the historical COLA for the specific time frame, and the gap that would need to be filled that year. Your sources of fixed income will vary from this example, but the *actual* inflation increase for each year is reflected in the last column.

	Cost of Living	Pension 2% COLA	Social Security	Gap	Annualized Increase
Year 1 (1983)	80,000	30,000	12,627	37,373	
Year 5 (1987)	95,020	33,122	14,799	47,099	4.73%
Year 10 (1992)	112,691	36,570	18,306	57,815	4.46%
Year 20 (2002)	144,498	44,578	23,417	76,503	3.65%
Year 30 (2012)	184,412	54,341	30,396	99,675	3.32%

What would be a $37,373 gap in the first year of retirement grows to $99,675 in year thirty. Mind the gap, as they say in the London Tube. Our portfolio must produce more income every year in retirement just to fill the hole, and the average growth rate of our asset pool must equal our withdrawals *plus* keep up with inflation.

For example, let's say that in order to keep up with inflation we set aside the first 3 to 4 percent of our annual returns and reinvest them back into our portfolio. At the same time, to meet our current income gap, we need to withdraw 4 to 5 percent out of our portfolio every year. That means our portfolio must generate 7 to 9 percent in average annual returns to maintain our buying power (or to keep us from spending our principal). I repeat: that's 7 to 9 percent just to buy *the very same stuff*!

At the start of retirement, our asset pool must also be so large that just 4 to 5 percent annual withdrawal will cover the gap amount we need (or the difference between our fixed income and our expenses). In the illustration above, our asset pool would need to be in the neighborhood of $850,000 on day one of retirement in order for it to earn enough to cover that year's $37,000 gap *plus* provide the additional $30,000 we need to reinvest back into our asset pool (so that our investments keep up with inflation). To earn that much, our asset pool would need to be heavily invested in stocks, which are the only investment vehicle that has historically produced 8 to 10 percent returns on average over time.

If our asset pool is not big enough or our rate of return is not high enough, we will have to dip into our principal every year to meet expenses. Every time we dip into our principal, it shrinks. As a result, it will produce less and less income, which means the gap will get bigger, and we will need to keep using more and more of the principal every year. This downward spiral leads to one place: a retirement account balance of zero.

Some retired folks genuinely *want* to spend all of their principal. Ideally, their very last nickel will leave their hand the day they die. But what if, as we victoriously clutch that final nickel on our deathbed, doctors find a miracle cure for what ails us? Presto! We live another eight years, but we're flat broke. Now what?

Finally, there's one more major consideration: The last few years of our life are often the most expensive — by orders of magnitude. Older folks often require more and increasingly costly medical care, so we must prepare for a huge and largely unpredictable expense bubble at the end.

Being able to look after ourselves is the primary reason we strive to build an asset base that grows with every passing year. But being able to look after others is a far more rewarding reason. Ideally, we'll retire with enough money to sustain a 4 percent withdrawal for living expenses plus that pesky 3.5 percent inflation rate. Even better, if our retirement investment portfolio increases annually by an average of 8 percent or more, our principal balance should keep going up, despite withdrawals and inflation. That means our money can keep doing good after we die. Why plan to spend every dime when we can steward that capital for the generations to come?

How Do We Get There?

As daunting as inflation is, we have two powerful weapons to combat it: time and compounding. If we're in our twenties when we start investing for retirement, we can make 10 percent our target savings goal. If we're older when we start, our goal should be much higher. The more we can save, the greater the odds that:

1. we won't run out of money,
2. we can retire earlier than we expected, and
3. we can leave a legacy to sustain who or what we care about most.

If freedom, security, and becoming a steward of capital (as we discussed in chapter 14) are important to you, save more.

Of course, financial experts toss around all sorts of numbers to quantify what they consider adequate retirement savings. Some pundits say that saving 10 percent is *more* than enough. Others say 30 percent is *nowhere near* enough. My personal savings goal is 35 percent of my annual income. Bottom line: the key to a secure future is to start saving and investing as *much* and as *soon* for retirement as you possibly can.

You should consider investing those monthly savings into a balanced (moderate) portfolio that contains a mix of 60 percent equities (stocks) and 40 percent fixed income (bonds) — or perhaps a 50/50 mix if you're more conservative or approaching retirement. In the appendix, at the end of the Financial Action Plan template, you'll find a sample of asset allocation models (see page 265). The simplest investment approach I know is to purchase mutual funds or exchange-traded funds (ETFs) that track major indexes like the S&P 500 or the Global Dow, although you can't invest directly in any index. For most folks, the easiest way to save for retirement is through an employer-sponsored 401K or self-directed IRA. If possible, arrange to have a set dollar amount automatically withdrawn from every paycheck.

For example, if someone's annual income is fifty thousand dollars, and they're targeting a 10 percent savings rate, they should transfer $417 to a retirement account monthly. Dollar-cost averaging the same amount into a retirement account every month is a gloriously simple, idiot-proof method of investing that requires almost no active management, but it can produce huge benefits.

If you're lucky enough to have a job that offers a 401K, especially one that matches your contributions, that is unquestionably the best place to start saving for retirement. A 401K allows you to save and grow your money without tax penalty until you begin withdrawing funds. If you don't get a 401K through your job, open an IRA savings account with a bank or through an investment adviser. There are also special 401Ks and retirement accounts for folks who are self-employed.

If your employer matches your 401K contributions up to a certain amount, strive to contribute at least as much as your employer will match. However, with or without an employer match, the real goal should be to contribute the maximum amount allowable every single year. Once you've maxed out your 401K contributions, keep saving more in an IRA and/or a taxable account.

The discipline of investing in our retirement accounts every month is much more important than the actual investments themselves. We can't control what those investments will do, but we *can* control our behavior. If we can live within our means, and start investing early and often, a secure, happy retirement can be ours.

Mindful Money Practice

For those who aren't math experts, and plenty of folks aren't, making retirement numbers add up is challenging.

Step 5 of your Financial Action Plan is to begin investing for retirement, but you'll need to do some math homework first. For previous plan steps, I asked you to create a rough draft in your notebook first. This time around, I recommend grabbing a sharp pencil with a clean eraser and proceeding immediately to Step 5 of the Financial Action Plan template in the appendix (see page 262). The template has step-by-step instructions for converting your current income gap into tomorrow's dollars, so that you can establish a monthly retirement investment plan to help you fill that hole. Some of the calculations on this planning worksheet require utilizing an online retirement calculator. Many are available on various financial websites, and you can also use the very simple retirement income calculator at www.happinessdividend.com/mindfulmoney.

You should allow at least an hour to work through these calculations, but as I've said before: this isn't rocket science. If you can do your own taxes, you can definitely complete this worksheet. Just go slowly, be patient with yourself, and fill in every box. The good news is that a few of the key data points will be very familiar to you from Step 2 of your Financial Action Plan. Although the level of detail required to complete the worksheet in Step 5 can be daunting, a happy, secure future is worth suffering through a bit of math.

CHAPTER 25

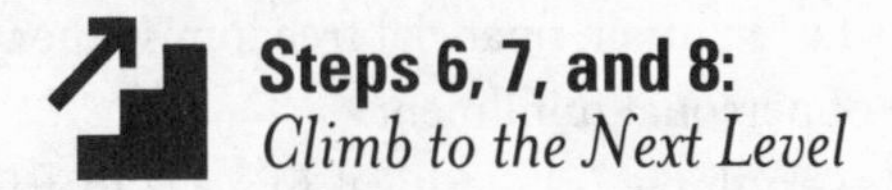

Steps 6, 7, and 8: *Climb to the Next Level*

> Sometimes it's the journey that teaches you a lot about your destination.
>
> — DRAKE

To put the finishing touches on your Financial Action Plan, there are three more steps you can take as time and your improved financial circumstances allow. As you can see, each one is an extension of previous steps you have already mastered:

- Step 6: Eliminate *low*-interest debt.
- Step 7: Increase your emergency fund.
- Step 8: Invest in a taxable nonretirement account.

These three steps separate the truly successful from the average bear. Not many folks are mindful, motivated, and committed enough to take their finances beyond subsistence levels. Even top wage earners often fail to follow the most fundamental money practices. They may have gotten their high-interest debt under control, but they don't necessarily have a healthy emergency fund *and* a growing retirement account that they dollar-cost average into every month. When we're doing well in the present, we can't imagine a day when our income will fall away, so it's a rare individual who masters the first five steps and progresses to these last three.

If you are already a "five-stepper," congratulations! By developing your Vision, making a habit of saving, building an emergency fund, eliminating high-interest debt, and investing regularly in a retirement account — all while making mindful trade-offs along the way — you're firmly on the path to a stable financial future. If you also take these *final* three steps, you will accelerate your success, reach your goals faster, attain financial freedom sooner, and achieve a higher degree of personal fulfillment.

Speed isn't everything. The critical thing is that we reach our goals by the time we reach our There. Still, by pushing ahead when we can, we will have more options to pursue our skillful desires and put our money where our meaning is.

Unlike the first five steps, these final three steps may not be necessary for everyone. They can be pursued in any order or even simultaneously, depending on your needs, preferences, and life situation.

Eliminate Low-Interest Debt

After establishing a retirement account, the next step is to get rid of debt entirely. Debt costs us money, so we are generally better off without it. Still, before we start throwing money at lenders, we should make sure we're getting the most bang for our buck. Paying off low-interest debt will certainly make us feel great. But if the interest rate on our debt is much lower than the potential for returns in our investment account, we might be better off investing. As discussed in chapter 23, if we are paying 3 percent annually to service a particular debt (like a mortgage), but our investment account can average over 8 percent returns, we make more money by investing. In this scenario, doing both might be optimal: use some of our excess income to pay down debt faster while putting the rest to work in a taxable investment account.

As a general rule, it's best to pay off any low-interest consumer debt first: furniture, computers, appliances, and anything that goes down in value over time. For most of us, that means everything but our house and car, with the possible exception of fine jewelry and collectibles. Student loans also fall into the category of things we should pay off *after* our consumer debt. Start with the highest-interest consumer debts and work your way down to the lowest ones.

Another general rule is to pay off collateralized debt last. Collateralized debt simply means that the purchased item is held "as collateral" by the lender. In other words, if we don't pay the debt, the lender will take the item away. Unless we have bad credit, these tend to be the lowest-rate loans we have. For many of us, the only collateralized loans we carry are for our primary residence and for cars — though Harleys, boats, vacation homes, and other big-ticket items fit this category, too. In most cases, pay off everything *but* cars and the primary residence first. Then tackle cars next, and the house last.

This approach goes against the grain for those who have been indoctrinated to pay the mortgage first, no matter what. Indeed, don't skip paying the *monthly* mortgage bill because that buys you a little of your house every month. But when using your excess cash flow to pay down *debt*, paying off the mortgage faster should be the last priority. That's because real estate typically increases in value. Even when it *does* go down, as happened during the 2008 recession, it historically recovers over time. A gradual increase in your home's value can offset much, if not all, of the interest rate you pay on your mortgage. Plus, don't forget potential tax breaks from home-related debt and property taxes.

Though it's better to be free of debt, it's not disastrous to retire while we still have a mortgage. This is becoming the inevitable reality for many people. Today, people are buying homes later in life, and banks are issuing longer-term mortgages. What truly matters is the type of mortgage we have: so long as we have a fixed-rate mortgage, we can reliably predict our mortgage payments and living expenses into the future, but a variable-rate mortgage can torpedo our retirement at any time.

Increase Your Emergency Fund

This next step is short and sweet. Along with paying down low-interest debt, we can plump up our emergency fund whenever we find some extra money. Having the recommended emergency savings for our current stage in life is a terrific start, but having a little extra never hurts. To the contrary, it can help tremendously.

The more we can increase our emergency cash fund, the better off we'll be in the long run. That said, the uses for our emergency savings will likely change as we approach and enter retirement. Once our parents pass away and our children are out of school, we will hopefully have fewer financial obligations to close family members. By the time we retire, our mortgage may be paid off, and we should have a hefty home repair fund to cover both unexpected plumbing disasters and general maintenance. Since we're already planning to leave the workforce, job loss is off the table as an emergency as well.

If we're in ship-financial-shape when we retire, our emergency fund can be a terrific buffer against market volatility. When (*not if*) the market goes down and our investment portfolio starts to sag, we can pull our gap living expenses from our emergency fund, leaving our portfolio to take advantage of the long-term growth opportunities that down markets offer. The larger our emergency fund when we retire, the more comfortable we'll be during market downswings, and the longer we'll be able to ride out market turbulence.

If we're financially fit but our health starts to fail, a healthy emergency fund can also help us fill in any gaps in our medical insurance and long-term care coverage, so that we can get the care we want and deserve in our old age. In fact, rather than qualifying for long-term care insurance when they are in their forties or fifties, many of my clients choose to build up their emergency fund before retirement, specifically so they can self-insure in the event they need or want care in later years.

Invest in a Taxable Nonretirement Account

For a variety of reasons, not everyone invests in a taxable nonretirement account. It's less important than the other seven steps, and taking care of those, along with monthly living expenses, may be all you can afford. Before doing this, I recommend making the maximum allowable contributions to a 401K or a traditional IRA. However, if you're already doing that, this is definitely worth considering.

This taxable account differs from the emergency fund in that it isn't meant to be a ready source of short-term capital. Savings goes in the bank, but you'll be *investing* this money. This investment account is meant for longer-term goals like placing a down payment on a house in five years or retiring more comfortably in twenty. Our planned use for these funds will determine the appropriate mix of equity funds versus fixed-income funds. As a rule, all investing involves risk, including the possible loss of principal. The sooner we anticipate using the funds, the lower percentage of equities we should consider. The right mix depends on your personal situation. As a reminder, in the appendix, the Financial Action Plan template has sample asset allocation models (see page 265).

As I say above, investing in a taxable nonretirement account to build your assets can be just as important and useful as becoming 100 percent debt-free. I think it's well worth the trade-off to carry *some* low-interest debt if it means you can rev up the compounding engine sooner rather than later. Asset building may be *the* best route out of poverty and into financial freedom. Once we establish a pool of compounding assets, we've immediately increased our chances of getting ahead in life. Otherwise, we will just tread water.

Over the long run as you build your assets, this also does much more for the bottom line on your balance sheet (per chapter 21) than quickly paying off modest debt, so long as investing produces a higher average return than the interest rate you're paying on your debt. Then, over time, compounding gradually ramps up to grow your asset base at ever-increasing rates. Don't completely ignore debt, but when you do the math, dollar-cost averaging into a taxable account often comes out ahead.

If compounding is the eighth wonder of the world, dollar-cost averaging is the ninth. When we automatically contribute a fixed amount every paycheck into a 401K or IRA, we dollar-cost average passively. Building a *taxable* account allows us to dollar-cost average far more deliberately, and without the contribution limits imposed on 401Ks and IRAs. We can add money at weekly, biweekly, monthly, or quarterly intervals, depending on our cash flow. We just need to add the *same dollar amount* every period, regardless of what the market is doing. When shares go up in cost, we'll buy fewer. When they go down, we'll buy more. Over time, the practice of dollar-cost averaging slowly drives the average cost of our shares down, so that when the price goes up, we earn better returns. Cool, huh?

Taxes and Fees

What's less cool? Taxes. I think it's essential to take a moment to consider a few of the primary tax implications for both tax-deferred and taxable nonretirement accounts, since the Tax Man will definitely cometh at some point, and so will the fee collectors.

Most of us understand that it costs money to make money. Before we start banking on our nonretirement account investment returns or begin withdrawing monthly income from our IRA, we must factor in the fees and taxes we must pay to various pipers for the privilege of reaping those rewards. The two primary costs associated with investment accounts are fees and taxes.

Potential fees include the following:

1. The investment companies that manage any exchange-traded funds (ETFs) or mutual funds in our retirement and taxable accounts charge often-sizable but invisible internal fees, which are known as the expense ratio.
2. The financial adviser who helps us select our investments (whatever those investments are) also charges a more transparent advisory fee, which typically comes out of our account every quarter or so.
3. The broker/dealer where our investment accounts are held may charge transaction fees, such as ticket charges

when we buy or sell an ETF or mutual fund, or an annual retirement account fee.

Taxes are levied in two primary situations:

1. The moment we withdraw money from tax-deferred retirement accounts, such as an IRA or 401K, we pay that deferred tax — and we also pay a penalty if we haven't yet reached the minimum age for distributions.
2. Whenever we receive capital gains, interest, and dividends from taxable accounts, we pay taxes, taxes, and still more taxes on that money.

Taxes often have the largest impact on our total investment returns. Here is a brief look at how they impact 401Ks, IRAs, Roth accounts, and taxable accounts.

401Ks and IRAs

Favorable tax treatment is the primary reason I suggest opening a *tax-deferred* retirement account first. The money we add to a 401K or traditional IRA is generally tax deductible the year we make the contribution, *and* we won't be taxed on that money until we start taking it out to fund our retirement, once we reach the minimum age for distributions — which is age 59.5 for most retirement accounts. At that point, the full distribution is usually taxed at our ordinary income tax rate. Both 401Ks and IRAs have limits on how much tax-deductible money we can add every year. If we have the choice, opening a 401K account is almost always the best option. A 401K generally allows for a *higher* annual contribution than traditional IRAs (plus your employer may offer matching benefits). A SEP IRA or solo 401K may be better options for the self-employed, but consult with a tax professional before making that determination.

Roth IRAs

The tax treatment of a Roth IRA contribution is the reverse of a traditional IRA. Rather than being a tax-deferred contribution, a contribution to a Roth IRA is taxed in the year it's made, but we get to avoid paying taxes when we withdraw the money in retirement, if the right conditions are met. At the same time, like a traditional IRA, we pay no capital gains taxes when we sell securities in a Roth IRA. Not everyone qualifies to open a Roth IRA. Certain maximum annual income criteria need to be met, and these criteria change every year. Roths can work particularly well for folks who expect to be in a higher tax bracket *after* they retire than they are today. If you're interested in opening one, consult a tax professional; don't rely on advice you read on the internet. However, even if you qualify for and want to open a Roth, I usually suggest waiting to do so until you've already contributed the maximum allowed to a 401K or a traditional IRA.

Taxable Accounts

As advertised, taxable accounts are subject to more tax consequences, namely capital gains taxes when we sell a security for more than we originally paid (the cost basis) or when we receive dividend or interest income. At the same time, nonretirement accounts usually have fewer restrictions and limitations than retirement accounts. This means we have more flexibility, both with how much we can add to our accounts and when we can withdraw our money without penalties. After you've utilized every *tax-deferred* (retirement) account option, begin dollar-cost averaging into a broadly diversified *taxable* account with the asset mix that works best for you.

Taxes are not something to be avoided at all costs. They are simply a fundamental *what is* we need to consider when making our financial planning and investing decisions. Having a mix of nontaxable retirement *and* taxable accounts gives us maximum optionality. We receive helpful tax breaks on our retirement contributions when we're younger. Once retirement arrives, we can have a lot more control over which tax bracket we're in, based on how much we withdraw from each of these sources. If our tax bracket is lower, we will pay less in taxes, perhaps significantly less than during our earlier, high-earning years.

When we take money out of a *taxable* investment account, any trades to free up cash are usually taxed at the lower *capital gains* rate. But when we withdraw money from a *nontaxable* retirement account, that withdrawal is taxed as *ordinary income*. Since the capital gains rate is almost always substantially lower than our ordinary income tax rate, we should strive to withdraw no more than the required minimum distribution (RMD) from our nontaxable account after we reach age 70.5. Having both taxable and nontaxable accounts allows us to moderate our tax costs. This is one area of our financial lives where a tax professional can prove invaluable.

You're in the Driver's Seat

In the appendix, the Financial Action Plan template has charts you can use to calculate and document Steps 6, 7, and 8 of your Financial Action Plan (see pages 264–65). These charts are similar to those used in Steps 3, 4, and 5, so turn to those chapters for instructions as needed.

If you've mastered these last three steps by the time you're fifty, relax and take a deep breath. You're well on your way to a secure retirement. Each time you eliminate some debt, increase your emergency fund, or invest more money in a taxable nonretirement account, you get a little closer to meeting *all* your big life goals — not just your retirement targets. You'll also have a lot more cushion to absorb those inevitable but unforeseeable mishaps.

If you remain focused on your compelling Vision, and adjust course when needed, you will get to your There. Even if you can only add a hundred dollars a month into a taxable account, be proud, but remain humble and calm. Now you can consider saving extra money for the skillful desires you always thought were out of reach: taking off six months to travel, volunteer, or write your novel. Or sock away even more money to build your legacy or buy more freedom.

In the end, the true benefit of financial planning is not financial.

And it's not just the security of knowing you're going to be all right. The emotional payoff is much bigger: your happiness dividend. Taking these eight steps will bring you ever closer to the life you choose to live.

Your financial plan *will* change as your life and goals evolve, but unless you specifically change some aspect of your plan, stick to it religiously.

Once your plan's done, celebrate yourself. A lot of folks spend more time planning their next birthday party than they do planning their financial future. By developing a thoughtful Vision and drafting a workable financial plan, you have done more to build a happy, fulfilling, and secure future than most people do in a lifetime.

Mindful Money Practice

This practice is 50 percent accountability review and 50 percent mindfulness motivation.

In your *Mindful Money* notebook, divide a fresh page into three columns labeled "Step," "Progress," and "Objective." In the left column, list the eight steps of your Financial Action Plan:

1. Develop Your Vision
2. Start the Saving Habit
3. Build an Emergency Fund
4. Eliminate High-Interest Debt
5. Begin Investing for Retirement
6. Eliminate Low-Interest Debt
7. Increase Your Emergency Fund
8. Invest in a Taxable Nonretirement Account

Remember to leave yourself enough space between each one for notes. In the middle column, briefly summarize the progress you've made on each step, no matter how slight. You can even count reading the corresponding chapter in *Mindful Money*. In the right column, write a simple objective for each step, including a realistic target date for completing that objective. Identify baby steps that will give you a sense of accomplishment rather than naming huge leaps that may be hard to complete.

Before closing your notebook, set a firm date for revisiting your progress on these eight steps of your Financial Action Plan.

CHAPTER 26

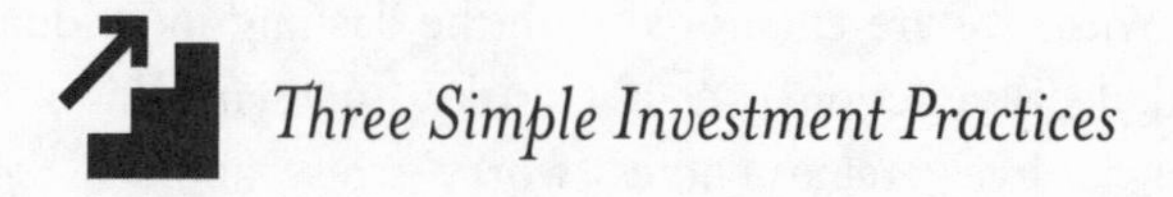

Three Simple Investment Practices

'Tis the gift to be simple, 'tis the gift to be free.

— Joseph Brackett

We've already accomplished quite a lot on our *Mindful Money* journey. Together we've done the following:

1. Debunked your big illusions.
2. Identified your true sources of happiness.
3. Considered your values, purpose, mission, and life vision in relation to those sources of happiness.
4. Considered the trade-offs you're willing to make to achieve your heart's deepest desires.
5. Made a Financial Action Plan to take you from Here to There.

In this chapter, we focus on implementing that Financial Action Plan by establishing a simple, disciplined, easy-to-follow investment program. The *Mindful Money* approach to investing is based on a practical philosophy that allows us to invest with stillness and confidence, instead of desperately pursuing the ever-changing *investment du jour*. This philosophy boils down to just one basic precept: Give up the unlikely possibility of making a windfall in exchange for the priceless blessing of never getting blown away. Stop chasing the hot stock, the hot trend, the hot guru. Trust that the growth of the world equity markets and the law of averages will continue their gradual upward trajectory, as they always have in the past.

In chapter 7, I mention the Taoist concept of *wu wei*, which can be translated loosely as "doing by *not* doing." *Wu wei* holds that sometimes the most powerful action is to take no action at all. In the West, we are enamored with the dashing individual who takes bold, decisive action, even if it's risky. But trying this in our personal financial lives creates endless worry, stress, and self-recrimination, not to mention financial failure.

Simplify, simplify, simplify. Financial simplicity supports day-to-day happiness, and it actually *works*. The straightforward financial planning practices I've described thus far have proven their efficacy decade after decade, era after era. If you patiently put these practices to work for you, you'll discover they are far more reliable in the long run than following any hot trend or guru.

Now let's turn our attention from planning to *investing*. Taking a more mindful investment approach requires us to make peace with the idea that someone somewhere will always beat our returns. In any given season, there will be friends, foes, and financial figures who make huge windfalls, and we will be tempted to follow in their investment footsteps. But if you gamble big, you can also lose big, and the odds are that those folks will lose bets as often (or more often) than they win. Meanwhile, if we patiently follow the path of *wu wei*, we can expect steady growth in our accounts over time.

Now let's explore three simple investment practices that require very little conscious action. Like *wu wei*, they can deliver impressive results, but only if we follow them consistently. These practices are asset allocation, diversification, and rebalancing.

Asset Allocation

Asset allocation is the strategy of dividing an investment account into three primary asset classes, which include:

1. equity assets like stocks, equity exchange-traded funds (ETFs), and equity mutual funds;
2. fixed-income assets like government, corporate, and municipal bonds or bond funds; and
3. cash or cash equivalents, such as treasury bills, money market funds, and bank CDs.

How we choose to allocate funds to these three asset classes will be based on our individual needs and goals *and* our ability to tolerate volatility.

The key to successful asset allocation is to recognize that each of the three primary asset classes pays a different average rate of return, based on its particular level of volatility:

1. Equity assets like stocks tend to pay the highest rate of return over extended periods, but they are also the most volatile.
2. Fixed-income assets like bonds tend to pay lower returns than stocks and are often less volatile.
3. Cash doesn't pay much of a return, but it provides liquidity when we need ready funds, and it reduces volatility in an investment account, since its face value is relatively stable.

Generally speaking, the more stable and predictable the asset class, the less it pays the investor long-term. The more volatile an asset, the higher the long-term potential payout. There are no guarantees, but return, in essence, is compensation for volatility.

Let's look at each of the three asset classes a bit more closely:

Stocks, or equities, represent shares in a company. When we own a share of stock, we own part of a company and are entitled to some of that company's assets. Because a stock is tied to a single company's fortunes, stocks are the most volatile asset class. One particular company might struggle, or even go bankrupt; we *can* lose all of our money on a stock. Owing to this volatility and risk, stocks *must* pay the premium return on average. As a result, there's a relatively high payoff when a company succeeds. There's no guarantee of a return from any particular stock, or from the stock market in general. But over time, the historical tendency is for stocks to go up faster, and more, than other asset classes.

Bonds are less volatile. A bond is effectively a loan we make to an entity such as a government or corporation. The loan is paid back at a set interest rate on a set schedule. Hence, the term *fixed-income*. Bonds tend to be more stable than stocks. In the case of corporate bonds, the company usually has certain legal responsibilities to its bondholders that exceed its responsibility to stockholders. The fundamental trade-off with bonds is lower expected returns in exchange for lower volatility and risk. Volatility aside, fixed-income investments are problematic in a rising-cost world, so relying exclusively on bonds is rarely a good long-term plan. Perhaps the best reason to have bonds in a portfolio is to mitigate stock volatility.

Cash is the least volatile of the three asset classes. Although it can technically lose all of its value, that's highly unlikely. If it did, that would mean the entire nation's economy had gone to hell, and we would all be growing our own food and wearing buffalo hides. Cash is liquid, accessible, and all but 100 percent reliable. It doesn't go up, but it doesn't go down either. Cash's stability makes it a vital part of the mix.

Make Decisions Based on Financial Goals

The long-term success of an investment portfolio depends more on asset allocation than the success of any particular investment in the account. How we allocate our assets may be the most important financial decision we make.

What percentage of your account should you commit to each asset class? To reduce a complex conversation down to a simple answer: it depends.

When you developed your Vision in Step 1 of your Financial Action Plan, you established a set of goals to accomplish over time, which I call your Route; if successfully executed, these goals will get you from Here to There. I asked you to put a price tag on those goals. To make appropriate, effective decisions with asset allocation, you need to refer to the cost and timeline for accomplishing your goals. Asset allocation is normally based on how aggressively your money needs to work for you. That asset allocation will be based on two major variables: your ability to tolerate volatility and your savings ability.

To sum up, we set our asset allocation based on the return we'll need to get (knowing there are no guarantees), given the savings we already have, in order to reach the goals we have established.

This sometimes requires hard trade-offs. For example, we may do the math and realize that the amount we're able to save, combined with the returns we hope to generate from our investment portfolio, will not get us to the goals we have in mind. At that point, we must ask ourselves three hard questions:

1. Can I save more? Are there more trade-offs to make that would cut down on expenses or increase income?
2. Can I tolerate more volatility in my investment accounts? If my asset allocation is conservative, can I shift more of the portfolio into stocks and stomach the ups and downs?
3. Can I reduce my goals and expectations? Perhaps I need to modify certain goals in my financial plan, or extend the timeline, if more savings are impossible and more volatility isn't tolerable.

If we make *no* adjustments, the most likely result is that our plan won't succeed.

However, if you do the math and realize that a relatively conservative portfolio (say, 40 percent equities and 60 percent fixed income) will give you the return you need to meet your goals, then I suggest sticking with that asset allocation. Be happy! Why take on more volatility than necessary?

Bottom line: we need to choose an asset allocation designed to generate the long-term returns we need to reach our financial goals.

Diversification

Diversification is the heart of the "don't get blown away" philosophy. It is the disciplined practice of choosing a variety of investments *within* each asset class. I understand how tempting it can be to pump more money into investments that are performing well and to avoid or sell investments that are doing poorly. This is a very human instinct. But like many *other* human instincts, it is unreliable. Diversification is the tool that keeps us from foolishly putting all our eggs in the wrong basket. It is our honest admission that we can't outguess the market, so we're not even going to try. Instead of guessing which stocks will outperform the others, we invest in *our inability to guess*.

Diversification means that we try to own as much variety as we can within each asset class. For example, we try to own both big and small companies. Growth stocks and dividend stocks. Companies in Europe and the United States, as well as in China and the emerging markets. We also want to own companies in various industries and sectors of the economy, both high-tech and low-tech, new players and old favorites. Within the fixed-income asset class, we want high-yield bond funds, some conservative bond funds, and maybe a CD. Why? Because we *can't* guess what's going to be hot or cold next. So we need to buy a diversity so that at least some of our assets will have a chance of doing well, regardless of what the others are doing.

Rebalancing

Rebalancing is the tool that regularly aligns our asset allocation and diversification. Over time, our portfolio gets out of balance because certain assets do well and others do less well. This means more money winds up in the vehicles that are producing high returns, and less ends up in those that are producing lower returns. Rebalancing periodically readjusts our portfolio to the original percentages we established to reach our long-term goals.

We rebalance *among* asset classes and *within* asset classes. In other words, we rebalance the overall mix of equities and fixed income, but we also rebalance the individual equity or fixed-income investments in our account.

For example, if our asset allocation model calls for a 60/40 mix of equity and fixed income, but equities have done so well that we're now at 70/30, we should sell 10 percent of the equities and buy 10 percent more fixed income. Or maybe our diversification strategy calls for a mix of 25 percent international equities and 35 percent US equities, but international equities have outperformed, so our account has drifted to 30/30. We will need to sell some international and buy some US equities to return our portfolio to balance.

By rebalancing at specific intervals, such as quarterly or annually, we automatically sell the outperformers and buy the underperformers — which is exactly what we want to do. Since price is inversely proportional to value, we must make a practice of buying low and selling high if we want to realize value. Rebalancing makes this practice routine and automatic.

Finally, there is a tendency for both unnatural highs and unnatural lows in the markets to snap back to the average over time. This process is known as reversion to the mean. By rebalancing periodically, no matter what's happening in the markets, we create a system that is immune to human foibles, short-term fads, and investor fears or fantasies that drive irrational market swings.

In the end, there is one downside to diligently practicing asset allocation, diversification, and rebalancing: you are never going to knock the investment ball out of the park. However, over the long haul, through zigs, zags, and multiple market cycles, you will end up faring better than most. So give up the greed. Give up the fear. Give up the urgency. Opt instead for a mindful, measured approach to money.

CONCLUSION
A Wider View

> Success is getting what you want; happiness is wanting what you get.
>
> — Dale Carnegie

There are two types of truth: conventional truth and ultimate truth. *Conventional* truth is limited to the everyday facts of life as viewed from our imperfect human perspective: the sky is blue, grass is green, and what goes up must come down. *Ultimate* truth is Truth with a capital *T*. It contains the deepest truths in the universe, beyond the limits of our senses and logic. Conventional truth holds that we are all separate beings. The ultimate truth is that all beings are dependent on one another.

Most of us spend the vast majority of our lives dealing with conventional truth. It's big and in our face constantly. But we also need to step back from time to time and view our lives from the perspective of a higher reality. When a tsunami strikes halfway around the globe and we are moved to offer our support, it becomes clear that we are not at all separate from the people and animals directly affected by the tragedy. In a very real sense, we truly *are* one and the same.

Ultimate truth gives us a wider lens. Once we see the big picture, it's easier to endure the slings and arrows life doles out and put the small stuff in perspective.

The financial world is full of perfectly valid conventional truths: If the Federal Reserve raises interest rates, home purchasing *is* affected. A foreign policy decision in China *can* cause certain stock prices to tumble. A drought in the Midwest *does* affect food prices. These statements are all true, conventionally speaking.

You can choose to spend your entire financial life focused on these conventional truths, as many people do. And you wouldn't be wrong — conventionally speaking. But you *will* inherit the conventional set of anxieties and nervous reflexes that are the product of fortune's daily ebb and flow.

As an alternative, you can choose to go with a bigger, more universal truth: the human race and the world economy will continue to advance. Period. That is the only truth you need to accept to make all the practices in this book work.

"I hold this truth to be self-evident," to paraphrase the Declaration of Independence. Our fellow citizens of the world will continue to outgrow their old stuff and replace it with new. They will continue to work their way up to the middle class and better their lots in life. They will continue to have transportation needs and brush their teeth and use phones and computers. All of us on the planet will keep trying to solve problems and make our own little corner of the world a bit better, which will lead to ongoing innovation and improvement. Why would this ever stop?

People question whether it is possible to have continued growth in the future. What evidence is there to suggest any other possibility? Yes, our planetary resources are limited, but that just inspires us to create more renewable resources and use them more intelligently. Yes, the population may stop growing someday, but that just means more and more people will move into the middle class, and standards of living for everyone will continue to rise — if not for eternity, then for many, many generations to come. Yes, setbacks and crises will occur. Industries will rise and fall. But I believe growth will win out, as it always has. If that is true, then every practice I've outlined in this book *has* to work.

Of course, on a day-to-day basis, none of us knows what's going to happen next. Conventional truth will continue to shift. Change is the only constant. But *it's the very constant you can invest in*. Knowing that the individual pieces will always be in flux, you can stop watching them like a hawk, step back, and focus on the big picture.

It's okay to stop, take a deep breath, and be still. You *can* take your mind off money matters and focus on more important things. Not because money is unclean or unworthy of your attention, but because money doesn't *require* very much of your attention. Why not focus on your friends, your family, your passions, your life, and your happiness instead?

When you take the minimal money steps required for financial success, you free up the forces of growth to do their thing. And they will. After all, a gardener doesn't *make* vegetables grow. All a gardener needs to do is create the conditions that allow growth to happen, then step back and watch the bounty flow. In much the same way, all you really need to do with your money is follow a few simple steps that create the conditions for growth to occur, and then get out of the way and *allow* wealth and happiness to happen.

APPENDIX
Your Financial Action Plan

Step 1: Develop Your Vision

Identify Your Personal Values (See instructions on page 181.)	
VALUE	RANK

State Your Meaningful Purpose (See instructions on page 182.)

Picture Your Perfect Life

(See instructions on page 184.)

Develop Your Professional Mission Statement

(See instructions on page 186.)

Set Your Personal Goals and List Your Action Steps
(See instructions on page 188.)

GOAL	LIST ACTION STEPS	$ COST	TARGET DATE

Step 2: Start the Saving Habit

Your Balance Sheet (See instructions on page 199.)			
ASSETS*	$	LIABILITIES**	$
TOTAL ASSETS	$	TOTAL LIABILITIES	$
TOTAL NET WORTH (TOTAL ASSETS – TOTAL LIABILITIES) =			$

* Examples: IRA, 401K, home value, savings account, etc.

** Examples: credit card #1, credit card #2, mortgage balance, etc.

MINDFUL MONEY REMINDER: If your total net worth is a negative number, implement steps 3 and 4 of your Financial Action Plan today!

Your Monthly Cash-Flow Sheet
(See instructions on page 199.)

INCOME*	$	EXPENSES**	$
TOTAL INCOME	$	TOTAL EXPENSES	$

* Examples: job #1, job #2, pension, rental income, Social Security, etc.

** Examples: mortgage, rent, food, property taxes, savings, etc.

MINDFUL MONEY REMINDER: If your total income is less than your total expenses, you must increase your income and/or reduce expenses!

Rank Your Goals and Establish Your Monthly Savings Plan
(See instructions on page 201.)

GOAL	TOTAL COST $	# MONTHS	MONTHLY COST $*	RANK

* Monthly $ savings should = Total Cost $ / # Months to target date

MINDFUL MONEY REMINDER: Remember to add the monthly savings goals to the expenses column of the cash-flow sheet in Step 2.

Step 3: Build an Emergency Fund

Set Your Emergency Savings Target*
(See instructions on page 209.)

PHASE OF LIFE	MONTHLY EXPENSES $ FROM CASH-FLOW SHEET	TARGET # MONTHS	EMERGENCY $ SAVINGS TARGET
Young adult (18–35): 3 months of expenses	$		$
Midlife (35–55): 6–12 months of expenses	$		$
Nearing Retirement (55–65): 12–24 months of expenses	$		$
Retirement and Beyond (65+): 24 months of expenses	$		$

* Monthly Expenses $ from Cash-Flow Sheet x Target # Months = Emergency $ Savings Target

MINDFUL MONEY REMINDER: Remember to add to your monthly savings plan.

Step 4: Eliminate High-Interest Debt

Rank Your Debts and Set Monthly Payoff Plan
(See instructions on page 216.)

DEBT	$ OWED	INT. RATE %	MONTHLY $	ORDER

MINDFUL MONEY REMINDER: Remember to add the monthly debt-reduction payments to the expenses column in the cash-flow sheet in Step 2.

Step 5: Begin Investing for Retirement (See page 228.)

List your expected annual fixed income resources at retirement:

$	Social Security
$	Pension
$	Other (alimony, part-time job, etc.)
$	Total expected annual fixed income

Quantify your annual income gap in today's dollars:

________	–	________	=	________
Current annual living expenses [Use Monthly Expenses in Cash-Flow Sheet x 12]		Total expected annual fixed income		Annual income gap in today's dollars

Estimate the minimum retirement assets you'd need in today's dollars to generate adequate annual income to cover your gap:

________	÷	0.04	=	________
Annual income gap in today's dollars		Use 0.04 to ESTIMATE 4% retirement withdrawal rate (ACTUAL RATE MAY VARY).		Total assets you'd need in today's dollars to cover annual income gap

Gather the information you need to plan annual income gap savings:

	Your current age*
	Your target retirement age
$	Your current total retirement assets
$	Total retirement assets needed in today's dollars to cover annual income gap (see above)

Calculate the total retirement assets you may need in tomorrow's dollars to generate adequate annual income to cover your gap:**

$	Total assets you'd need in tomorrow's dollars to cover annual income gap

Begin investing this much (or more!) every month in a 401K, IRA, or other qualified retirement account.†

$

* For couples, use the age of the younger partner.

** See www.happinessdividend.com/mindfulmoney for a toolbox containing simple annual income gap savings calculator and enter the data from previous step.

† From the annual income gap savings calculator. Need help determining the best type of retirement account for you? Consult with an investment adviser, CPA, or your employer's HR department, or log on to www.happinessdividend.com/mindfulmoney.

MINDFUL MONEY REMINDER: Remember to add the monthly retirement savings goal to the expenses column of the cash-flow sheet and savings goals in Step 2.

Step 6: Eliminate Low-Interest Debt*

Rank Your Debts and Set Monthly Payoff Plan
(See instructions on page 232.)

DEBT	$ OWED	INT. RATE %	MONTHLY $	ORDER

* Increase payments as soon as high-interest debt is eliminated!

MINDFUL MONEY REMINDER: Remember to add the monthly debt-reduction payments to the expenses column of the cash-flow sheet in Step 2.

Step 7: Increase Your Emergency Fund

Boost Your Emergency Savings Target*
(See instructions on page 234.)

PHASE OF LIFE	MONTHLY EXPENSES $ FROM CASH-FLOW SHEET	TARGET # MONTHS	EMERGENCY $ SAVINGS TARGET
Young adult (18–35): 6–12 months of expenses	$		$
Midlife (35–55): 12–24 months of expenses	$		$
Nearing Retirement (55–65): 24+ months of expenses	$		$
Retirement and Beyond (65+): 24+ months of expenses	$		$

* Monthly Expenses $ from Cash-Flow Sheet x Target # Months = Emergency $ Savings Target

Step 8: Invest in a Taxable Nonretirement Account*

What Are Your Investment Goals?
(See instructions on page 234.)

GOAL**	$ AMOUNT	FREQUENCY†	RISK TARGET‡

* Dollar-cost average the same amount at regular intervals (see instructions on page 235).

** Be specific: Buy a house in five years, more retirement savings, etc.

† Examples: monthly, every paycheck, annually, etc.

‡ Example: preservation, conservative, balanced, growth (see asset allocation discussion on page 244 and sample models on page 265).

MINDFUL MONEY REMINDER: Need help deciding the appropriate risk target/investment mix for your goals? Not sure how to select mutual funds or ETFs for your portfolio? Consult with an investment adviser or log on to www.happinessdividend.com/mindfulmoney.

Sample Asset Allocation Models by Risk Target*

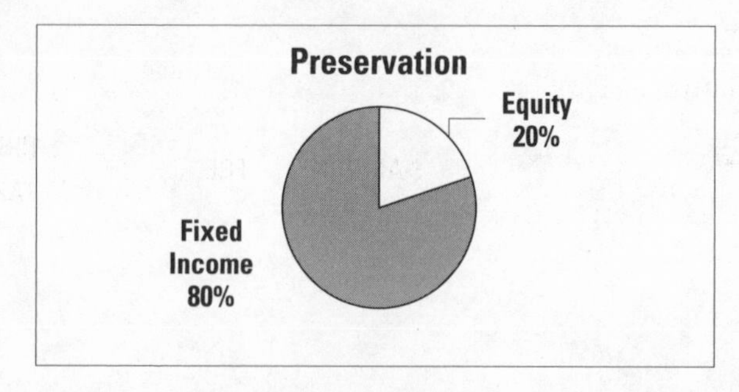

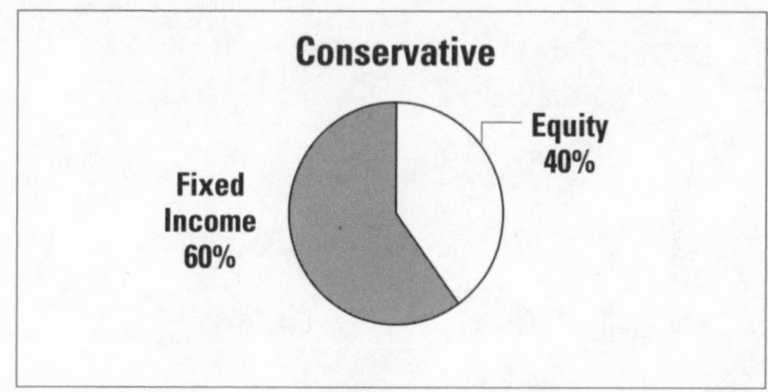

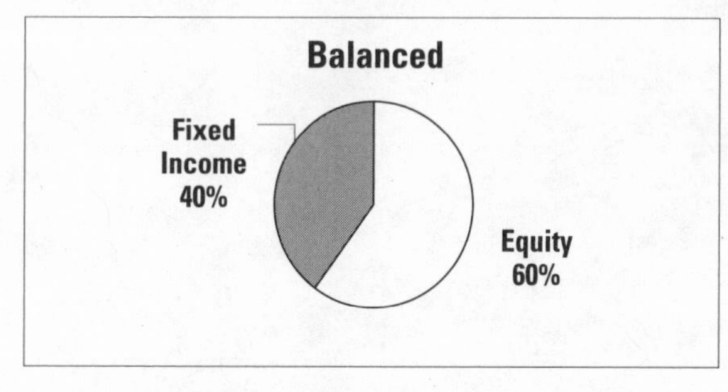

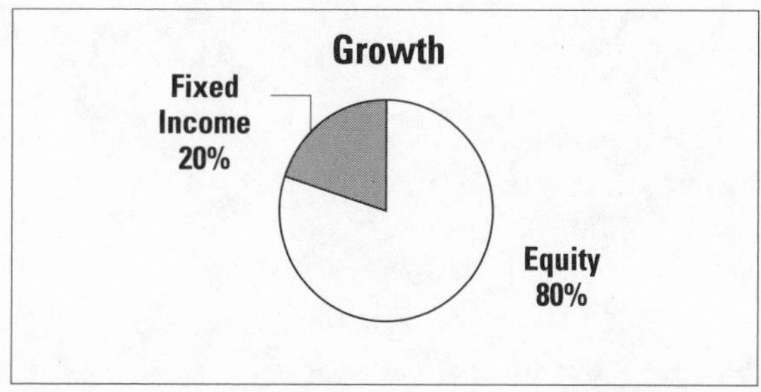

* For illustration only. Your actual risk and returns will vary. All investing involves risk, including possible loss of principal.

ACKNOWLEDGMENTS

I would be nothing today without terrific parents. Thank you for building the solid foundation I know will support me and my own family all the days of our lives. Mom, thanks for teaching me to be practical. Dad, thanks for encouraging me to dream. David, thanks for being my brother and the unassuming rock I've always been able to count on. Another big thank you to my mom's family, the Olsens, for showing me that anything is possible. And to my dad's family, the DeYoes, for proving that you can survive and even smile through nearly any hardship. And, always and forever, thank you to my wife, Kate, for her love, friendship, and devotion to our two beautiful children. You inspire me every day to become the best husband, father, and man I can be. Eli and Annie, thanks for being the best kids a dad could hope for and pointing out all the things I don't yet know. I'm honored, humbled, and amazed as I watch each of you endeavoring greatness in your own unique way.

Thank you to my team for their hard work, expertise, tireless dedication to clients, and commitment to making DeYoe Wealth Management a truly great place to work. Nancy Wright Cooper, I am constantly impressed by your professionalism, stubbornness, and incredible loyalty. Your unflagging support and editorial skills have proved invaluable. Thank you to John Madden, the original "solid citizen of the real world," for launching our planning department and keeping it central to the client experience; to Naomi Evans for picking up the financial planning baton and leading our next generation of advisers; to David Glotzer for your sage advice and erudition; and to Kristen Breyer Castleman for making sure all of us are where we need to be, when we need to be there, with everything we need to do the job right. And Kevin Sean Halle? You may be long gone, but I haven't forgotten that you were at my side when this all began.

Thanks to my agent, Ted Weinstein, for believing that *Mindful Money* could be a book before I believed it myself, and to my editors at New World Library, Georgia Hughes, Jeff Campbell, and Kristen Cashman, for making my dream of bringing the *Mindful Money* approach to a wider audience a reality. And to Adam Rogers, Greg Opitz and the Peak Advisors Alliance, Scott Jacobs, Vlad Tsyn, and the countless friends, confidants, clients, and fellow investment professionals who let me bend their ear or gave me a piece of their mind, thank you for your time, generosity, and guidance.

Most importantly, thanks to Albert Azadian, Chris Williams, Dave and Judy DeYoe, Edgar Gallardo, Gail Craine, Jim Aron and Paulette Erickson, John and Karen DeYoe, and Nancy Allison Carter, the folks who trusted me on day one of the journey, and to all the clients who've joined me along the way. I can point you in the right direction and help you unlock the door, but nothing I have to offer will ever be as effective as the conscious, deliberate steps you take for yourself.

SOURCES

Chapter 4. Illusion 3: Money Gurus Have a "Secret Sauce"

Page 37, *Plenty of studies have confirmed the randomness factor:* One of my recent favorite studies is Aye M. Soe, "Does Past Performance Matter? The Persistence Scorecard," *S&P Dow Jones Indices*, January 2016, https://us.spindices.com/documents/spiva/persistence-scorecard-january-2016.pdf.

Chapter 6. Illusion 5: Volatility = Risk

Page 51, *In my favorite financial dictionary, Investopedia.com,* volatility *is defined:* See http://www.investopedia.com/terms/v/volatility.asp.

Chapter 7. Illusion 6: Market Timing & Stock Selection Are the Keys to Success

Page 61, *In his oft-cited paper, "Efficient Capital Markets":* Eugene Fama, "Efficient Capital Markets: A Review of Theory and Empirical Work," *Journal of Finance* 25, no. 2 (May 1970), doi: 10.2307/2325486, http://www.jstor.org/stable/2325486?origin=JSTOR-pdf&seq=1#page_scan_tab_contents.

Chapter 8. Illusion 7: Investing = Speculating or Speculating = Investing

Page 69, *According to 2014 data from the Center for Research in Security Prices:* "Time & Risk" chart, Center for Research in Security Prices, University of Chicago's Booth School of Business, accessed on September 9, 2016, http://www.crsp.com/files/investments_illustrated/BP_h_2015_crsp_us-en.pdf.

Chapter 9. Illusion 8: There's Plenty of Time to Plan for Retirement

Page 76, *Current data published by the Social Security Administration:* "Calculators: Life Expectancy," US Social Security Administration, accessed on September 9, 2016, https://www.ssa.gov/planners/lifeexpectancy.html.

Page 76, *At the same time, according to a 2014 Gallup report:* Rebecca Riffkin, "Average U.S. Retirement Age Rises to 62," Gallup.com, April 28, 2014, http://www.gallup.com/poll/168707/average-retirement-age-rises.aspx.

Page 78, *To put it in perspective: In January 1985, the average cost of a half-gallon of ice cream:* "Average Retail Food and Energy Prices, U.S. City Average and Northeast Region," US Bureau of Labor Statistics, accessed on September 9, 2016, http://www.bls.gov/regions/mid-atlantic/data/averageretailfoodandenergyprices_usandnortheast_table.htm.

Chapter 10. Happiness Is Not a Mystery

Page 90, *In their oft-cited 2010 paper "High Income Improves Evaluation of Life":* Daniel Kahneman and Angus Deaton, "High Income Improves Evaluation of Life but Not Emotional Well-Being," *Proceedings of the National Academy of Sciences* 107, no. 38 (September 21, 2010), doi: 10.1073/pnas.1011492107, http://www.pnas.org/content/107/38/16489.

Chapter 11. Happiness Pillar 1: Health

Page 96, *According to Vasilios D. Kosteas of Cleveland State University:* Vasilios D. Kosteas, "The Effect of Exercise on Earnings: Evidence from the NLSY," *Journal of Labor Research* 33, no. 2 (June 2012), doi: 10.1007/s12122-011-9129-2, http://link.springer.com/article/10.1007/s12122-011-9129-2.

Chapter 12. Happiness Pillar 2: Engagement

Page 103, *Anyone who has ever seen the Bureau of Labor Statistics chart:* "Employment Projections," US Bureau of Labor Statistics, accessed on September 9, 2016, http://www.bls.gov/emp/ep_chart_001.htm.

Page 105, *One counterintuitive finding in happiness studies, such as Paulina Pchelin:* Paulina Pchelin and Ryan T. Howell, "The Hidden Cost of Value-Seeking: People Do Not Accurately Forecast the Economic Benefits of

Experiential Purchases," *Journal of Positive Psychology* 9, no. 4 (2014), doi: 10.1080/17439760.2014.898316, http://www.tandfonline.com/doi/abs/10.1080/17439760.2014.898316?journalCode=rpos20.

Chapter 13. Happiness Pillar 3: Relationships

Page 109, *Still, in their 2010 paper "Social Relationships and Health":* Debra Umberson and Jennifer Karas Montez, "Social Relationships and Health: A Flashpoint for Health Policy," *Journal of Health and Social Behavior* 51, no. 1 (November 2010), doi: 10.1177/0022146510383501, http://hsb.sagepub.com/content/51/1_suppl/S54.long.

Page 110, *In his book* Vital Friends: The People You Can't Afford to Live Without: Tom Rath, *Vital Friends: The People You Can't Afford to Live Without* (New York: Gallup Press, 2006).

Page 111, *And yet, according to Matthew Brashears in his 2011 report "Small Networks":* Matthew Brashears, "Small Networks and High Isolation?: A Reexamination of American Discussion Networks," *Social Networks* 33, no. 4 (October 2011), doi: 10.1016/j.sconet.2011.10.003, www.sciencedirect.com/science/article/pii/S0378873311000566.

Page 113, *In a 2013 paper, John F. Helliwell and Haifang Huang examined:* John F. Heliwell and Haifang Huang, "Comparing the Happiness Effects of Real and On-Line Friends," *PLoS ONE* 8, no. 9 (September 3, 2013), doi: 10.1371/journal.pone.0072754, http://journals.plos.org/plosone/article?id=10.1371/journal.pone.0072754.

Chapter 15. Happiness Pillar 5: Accountability

Page 133, *His three core principles*: Nick Murray, Behavioral Strategies conference, October 9, 2015, New York Marriott Marquis, New York, NY.

Chapter 16. Happiness Pillar 6: Generosity

Page 138, *In one experiment (published in 2008 as "Spending Money on Others":* Elizabeth W. Dunn, Lara B. Aknin, and Michael I. Norton, "Spending Money on Others Promotes Happiness," *Science* 319, no. 5870 (March 2008), doi: 10.1126/science.1150952, http://science.sciencemag.org/content/319/5870/1687?sid=8d59e134-ee6d-4103-9f24-4e79561e4d52.

Page 139, *Witnessing even the smallest act of generosity may inspire observers to commit:* James Fowler and Nicholas Christakis, "Social Contagion Theory: Examining Dynamic Social Networks and Human Behavior," *Statistics in Medicine* 32, no. 4 (February 2013), 556–77, doi: 10.1002/sim.5408, http://onlinelibrary.wiley.com/doi/10.1002/sim.5408/abstract.

Page 140, *According to a 1999 study "Volunteerism and Mortality":* Doug Oman, Kay McMahon, and Carl E. Thoresen, "Volunteerism and Mortality among the Community-Dwelling Elderly," *Journal of Health Psychology* 4, no. 3 (May 1999), doi: 10.1177/135910539900400301, http://hpq.sagepub.com/content/4/3/301.short.

Page 141, *We effectively* make *the recipient deserving in our minds:* Jon Jecker and David Landy, "Liking a Person as a Function of Doing Him a Favour," *Human Relations* 22, no. 4 (August 1969), doi: 10.1177/001872676902200407.

Chapter 17. Happiness Pillar 7: Optimism

Page 147, *Medical journalist Dr. Michael Mosley has suggested just the opposite:* Michael Mosley, "The Truth about Personality," episode 17, *Horizon*, BBC (2013), http://www.bbc.co.uk/programmes/b036ypxw.

Page 147, *In a 2009 research study of nearly a hundred thousand women:* Hilary A. Tindle, et al., "Optimism, Cynical Hostility, and Incident Coronary Heart Disease and Mortality in the Women's Health Initiative," *Circulation* 120, no. 8 (August 25, 2009), doi: 10.1161/circulationaha.108.827642, http://www.ncbi.nlm.nih.gov/pubmed/19667234.

Page 148, *In 2013, Shane Lopez of the University of Kansas and his colleagues:* Matthew Gallagher, Shane Lopez, and Sarah Pressman, "Optimism Is Universal: Exploring the Presence and Benefits of Optimism in a Representative Sample of the World," *Journal of Personality* 81, no. 5 (October 2013), doi: 10.1111/jopy.12026, http://onlinelibrary.wiley.com/doi/10.1111/jopy.12026/abstract.

Page 151, *For a truly masterful discussion of this topic, I recommend reading David Foster Wallace's:* David Foster Wallace, "This Is Water," commencement address, Kenyon College (2005), http://bulletin.kenyon.edu/x4280.html.

Chapter 18. Happiness Pillar 8: Gratitude

Page 155, *In a 2003 research study, Robert A. Emmons of the University of California:* Robert A. Emmons and Michael E. McCullough, "Counting Blessings Versus Burdens: An Experimental Investigation of Gratitude and Subjective Well-Being in Daily Life," *Journal of Personality and Social Psychology* 84, no. 2 (February 2003), doi: 10.1037/0022-3514.84.2.377, http://www.ncbi.nlm.nih.gov/pubmed/12585811.

Page 156, *Gratitude can have a significant impact on our financial behavior:* David DeSteno, Ye Li, Leah Dickens, and Jennifer S. Lerner, "Gratitude: A Tool for Reducing Economic Impatience," *Psychological Science* (April 23, 2014), doi:

10.1177/0956797614529979, http://pss.sagepub.com/content/early/2014/04/22/0956797614529979.

Chapter 21. Step 2: Start the Saving Habit

Page 193, *A survey commissioned by Holiday Retirement, entitled "100 Years of Wisdom":* Holiday Retirement, "100 Years of Wisdom: The Perspective of Centenarians," August 2014, http://media.holidaytouch.com/~/media/documents/100yearsofwisdom.pdf.

Chapter 24. Step 5: Begin Investing for Retirement

Page 222, *According to Consumer Price Index data, over the past hundred years:* Tim McMahon, "Long Term U.S. Inflation," InflationData.com, April 1, 2014, accessed on September 9, 2016, http://inflationdata.com/Inflation/Inflation_Rate/Long_Term_Inflation.asp.

INDEX

ABOUT THE AUTHOR

Jonathan K. DeYoe is a California-based financial adviser and a longtime Buddhist. During his twenty years as a financial adviser, he has managed investments at Morgan Stanley, UBS Paine Webber, and Salomon Smith Barney. In 2001 he founded his own wealth management firm, DeYoe Wealth Management. Today he manages nearly $250 million for over two hundred families and foundations in the United States and overseas. In his spare time, Jonathan speaks publicly about personal finance and contributes opinion pieces to publications such as *Business Insider*, *Huffington Post*, *Yahoo! Finance*, *SF Business Times*, *The Wall Street Journal*, *MarketWatch*, *The Motley Fool*, and *The Christian Science Monitor*. Jonathan lives in Berkeley with his wife and two children. His blog can be found at www.happinessdividend.com, and you can follow him on Twitter @HappinessDiv.

NEW WORLD LIBRARY is dedicated to publishing books and other media that inspire and challenge us to improve the quality of our lives and the world.

We are a socially and environmentally aware company. We recognize that we have an ethical responsibility to our customers, our staff members, and our planet.

We serve our customers by creating the finest publications possible on personal growth, creativity, spirituality, wellness, and other areas of emerging importance. We serve New World Library employees with generous benefits, significant profit sharing, and constant encouragement to pursue their most expansive dreams.

As a member of the Green Press Initiative, we print an increasing number of books with soy-based ink on 100 percent postconsumer-waste recycled paper. Also, we power our offices with solar energy and contribute to non-profit organizations working to make the world a better place for us all.

Our products are available in bookstores everywhere.

www.newworldlibrary.com

At NewWorldLibrary.com you can download our catalog,
subscribe to our e-newsletter, read our blog,
and link to authors' websites, videos, and podcasts.

Find us on Facebook, follow us on Twitter, and watch us on YouTube.

Send your questions and comments our way!
You make it possible for us to do what we love to do.

Phone: 415-884-2100 or 800-972-6657
Catalog requests: Ext. 10 | Orders: Ext. 10 | Fax: 415-884-2199
escort@newworldlibrary.com

14 Pamaron Way, Novato, CA 94949